HALLYU WOOD
한류우드

THE ULTIMATE GUIDE TO KOREAN CINEMA

BASTIAN MEIRESONNE

BLACK DOG
& LEVENTHAL
PUBLISHERS
NEW YORK

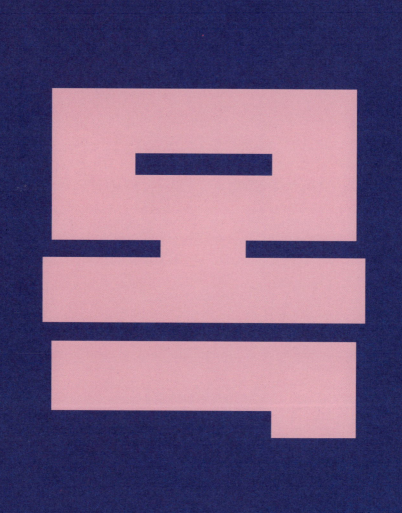

CONTENTS

Previous page spread: *The Handmaiden*
(Park Chan-wook, 2016).

INTRODUCTION

THE VISIBLE AND THE INVISIBLE:
THE SINGULARITIES OF KOREAN CINEMA

"Once you overcome the one-inch-tall barrier of subtitles, you will be introduced to so many more amazing films."

These words, spoken by Bong Joon-ho during his acceptance speech at the Golden Globes on January 6, 2020, for the Best Foreign Language Film award for *Parasite* (2019), obviously apply to films from all over the world, including Korean films. At the time of writing, *The Roundup* (Lee Sang-yong, 2022), *Decision to Leave* (Park Chan-wook, 2022), *Lucky Strike* (Kim Yong-hoon, 2020), and *Parasite* (Bong Joon-ho, 2019) are among the latest Korean films to have been released around the world. These successes follow those of the last 20 years: *Painted Fire* (Im Kwon-taek, 2002), *Spring, Summer, Fall, Winter . . . and Spring* (Kim Ki-duk, 2003), *Old Boy* (Park Chan-wook, 2003), *The Host* (Bong Joon-ho, 2006), *The Chaser* (Na Hong-jin, 2008), *I Saw the Devil* (Kim Jee-woon, 2010), *Poetry* (Lee Chang-dong, 2010), *Snowpiercer* (Bong Joon-ho, 2013), *The Handmaiden* (Park Chan-wook, 2016), *Train to Busan* (Yeon Sang-ho, 2016), and *Burning* (Lee Chang-dong, 2018).

At the same time, during these first two decades of the twenty-first century, other successful films released directly on DVD, VOD, and streaming platforms are proof of the extraordinary richness and diversity of Korean cinema. However, these titles represent only a tiny fraction of the century-old corpus of over 8,000 films.

Previous page spread:
Parasite (Bong Joon-ho, 2019).

Memories of Murder (Bong Joon-ho, 2003).

A FIRST IMPRESSION

The title of the book, *Hallyuwood*, is likely to displease film buffs and fans of Korean cinema, who will say that the term is "wrong," or at least a "poor choice"! The exact definition of the term *hallyu*, associated with Korea, refers to the worldwide spread of global Korean pop culture since the late 1990s, which therefore covers not only films, but also k-pop (music), k-dramas (TV series), and any other product linked to its culture.

As for the *wood* suffix, it could also be perceived as "inappropriate" because of the big difference between Korean cinema and the Hollywood film industry.

This is all true.

Hallyuwood is in fact a wink to both "misleading false (first) impressions" and introducing the content of the book. The word *hallyu* should be taken in its literal translation of "wave" and not in the sense popularized on a global scale over the last two decades alone. The "hallyu phenomenon" evokes a (global) flood of Korean cultural products, whereas a *wave* is a natural phenomenon, with only the crest visible to the naked eye, but we should not forget the invisible part, below the surface, of the overall movements that give birth to it and are its driving force. The book *Hallyuwood* thus deals with the visible part of Korean cinema, as well as its submerged aspect, exploring its origins and its extraordinary basic elements.

As far as the *wood* suffix is concerned, it is indeed reductive, but only in the sense of reducing the many past and present foreign influences on Korean cinema to the Hollywood film industry alone. "Foreign influences" should be understood in the sense of "inspiration," because one of the main characteristics of Korean cinema is that it has skillfully blended all its cultural influences in the construction of its own artistic identity, as confirmed by its recent successes.

Korean cinema is often reduced to the successes of the last two decades. *Hallyuwood* invites you to take another look at Korean cinema by exploring its submerged side, to discover its origins and the reasons for its current popularity. And, in homage to director Bong Joon-ho: "Once you overcome the one-inch-tall barrier of subtitles, you will be introduced to so many more amazing films."

This introduction therefore examines the different "cultural inspirations" and some of the extraordinary idiosyncrasies of Korean cinema. The following chapters offer a series of historical summaries that present the specific trends, genres, and themes of the various periods, from the beginnings of Korean cinema to the 2020s. The book can therefore be read chronologically or by picking and choosing according to your own interests.

A CINEMA SUBJECT TO INFLUENCES

Korea's geographical location in Asia makes it a veritable cultural cross-roads, which explains the foreign influences that have been present throughout its history. Initially populated by communities from the Altai Mountains and central Asia, the country was invaded on several occasions by the Mongols, the Chinese, and the Japanese, leading to numerous cultural exchanges between the different peoples.

Despite the annexation of Korea by Japan and the difficult 35-year period of occupation from 1910 onward, Korean cinema emerged in 1903 with the screening of Pathé short documentaries, followed by Japanese, European, and American films. The release of *Fight for Justice* (Kim Do-san) on October 27, 1919, marked the official debut of Korean cinema; this short film was a *kino drama,* combining the plot of a *shinpa* play (Japanese "new school" melodrama) with the popular American serials of the time for an adventure full of twists and turns in the heart of Seoul. Korean cinema is therefore inspired both by its own cultural history and by the combined influences of the United States, Europe, and above all Japan, which was obviously a major reference during the birth of cinema under occupation.

Burning
(Lee Chang-dong, 2018).

JAPANESE INFLUENCE

At the beginning of the twentieth century, the Japanese film industry was one of the most advanced in the world, and many Korean filmmakers were trained in Japanese schools and studios. This influence persisted even after the end of the Japanese occupation in 1945. Although all imports of Japanese cultural products were strictly forbidden until 1998, directors in the immediate post-war period continued to apply the cinematic language they had learned during their formative years. In the 1950s and 1960s, Korean filmmakers who traveled to Japan or attended international festivals were inspired by the world-renowned Japanese productions of the time. The numerous articles on film releases published in Japanese film magazines smuggled into Korea encouraged some filmmakers to produce unofficial remakes without even having seen the original films.

In 1960, a relaxation of the law allowed the publication of Japanese literature in Korea, sparking a craze for literary adaptations, both official and unofficial, and giving rise to the youth film genre, inspired by the Japanese *taiyozoku* (tribe of the sun) movement, which defines works featuring idle young people in contemporary Japanese society. In the 1970s, Korean gangster films were inspired by their *Yakuza* (Japanese) equivalents from the same period, while Japanese children's cartoons broadcast on Korean television triggered a wave of animated films imitating their storylines.

AMERICAN INFLUENCE

Early Korean cinema was also strongly influenced by the American film industry. While the famous serials of the 1910s inspired the very first Korean film, *Fight for Justice* (1919), the short and medium-length Hollywood films of the 1920s and 1930s starring Douglas Fairbanks and Errol Flynn served as a model for the first Korean action films. After Korea's liberation in 1945, the massive import of American productions had a profound effect on Korean cinema, leading in particular to the emergence of modern melodramas and big-budget historical dramas. The 1960s saw the rise of anti-communist action and espionage films inspired by the *James Bond* franchise, while Hollywood battle-of-the-sexes films were at the root of Korean comedy in the 1960s and 1990s. And more recently, American blockbusters spawned the first Korean blockbusters of the 2000s.

WORLD INFLUENCE

Korean cinema also draws its inspiration from France, Italy, and Hong Kong. It borrowed from the French New Wave, which gave rise to the literary films of the 1960s and the two successive Korean New Waves of the early and mid-1990s. Spaghetti Westerns gave rise to the Manchu action films (or so-called kimchi Westerns) of the 1970s. Finally, Hong Kong cinema inspired a major wave of Korean martial arts films in the 1970s and gangster films in the 1990s.

Lady Vengeance
(Park Chan-wook, 2005).

서문

A UNIQUE VOICE

As early as the 1920s, the first Korean filmmakers were wondering how to create a "Korean cinema for Koreans," raising the question of their own identity. At the same time, the first film collective, the Korean Artist Proletarian Federation (KAPF), questioned the primary function of the cinematographic tool by making a series of sociorealist films in the 1930s, with the aim of awakening class consciousness.

Numerous films of various genres produced after 1945 attest to a constant desire to tell the national story. The modern Korean melodramas of the 1950s, although inspired by the Hollywood model, were distinguished by their desire to transcribe the tragedies of their own country, the consequences of the various periods of Korean history, and more particularly those of the Japanese occupation and the division from the Korean War. Above all, this cinematic movement brought with it the specifically Korean sub-genre of the family drama, questioning the place of the father in Confucian patriarchal society, which was in the throes of change at the time.

The desire to tell a national story also manifested itself in more popular genres, such as "Korean Westerns," which transposed the world of the American West to the desert landscapes of Manchuria and recounted the resistance struggles during the Japanese occupation. The first domestic blockbusters of the late 1990s and early 2000s adopted the tight scriptwriting and dynamic direction typical of Hollywood to tell the story of national historical tragedies.

In 1970, the director Ha Gil-jong co-founded the Era of Image collective, a group aiming to "break down the walls of authoritarianism" and promote a cinema that moved away from the stereotypical representations often imposed under the military regime, with the government censoring cinema to project the image of a happy Korea, both to Koreans and to the rest of the world.

The short phases of democratic transition at the beginning of the 1960s and in the 1980s gave rise to some of the masterpieces of Korean cinema, such as *The Housemaid* (Kim Ki-young, 1960) and *Aimless Bullet* (Yu Hyun-mok, 1961), followed by *Good Windy Day* (Lee Chang-ho, 1980) and *People of the Slum* (Bae Chang-ho, 1982), with more realistic representations of the Korean society of their times.

Korean cinema's desire to find its own identity persisted in the 1980s, in the face of globalization and the resurgence of international trade. In 1984, under pressure from the United States, the Cinema Act was amended to encourage the import of foreign films, which had previously been limited to a third of local production since the 1960s. This gave a generation of students and film buffs access to a multitude of films from all over the world. The boom in the video market has also

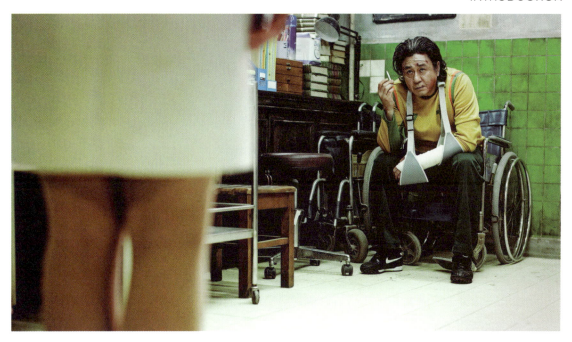

I Saw the Devil
(Kim Jee-woon, 2010).

made it possible to record programs broadcast on television, to analyze in detail certain sequences of cinema classics.

At the end of the 1980s, students like Kim Jee-woon, Park Chan-wook, and Bong Joon-ho were part of the pop culture generation, marked by globalization and easy access to world popular culture. These future filmmakers were not content to simply draw from universal film genres, but, following in the footsteps of their predecessors, blended them with their own culture to create globally recognizable works, with that extra "Korean touch."

With the abolition of censorship in 1998, Korean cinema was finally able to express itself freely and embark on a period of revival and world-wide recognition.

KOREAN CINEMA: LOCAL COLOR

What better example than *Parasite* to celebrate, in 2019, the culmination of the centenary evolution of Korean cinema? It is by no means its only representative—Korean cinema is far too rich and diverse for *Parasite* to claim that title on its own—but it is a worthy heir to the Korean cinema of the past, drawing its influences from the absolute masterpiece, *The Housemaid* (Kim Ki-young, 1960), and it also perfectly sums up Korea's remarkable ability to look to foreign influences to create a unique artistic path.

The finest proof of *Parasite*'s success in reaching audiences the world over is undoubtedly its incredible festival track record: It is the first Korean film to win the Palme d'Or at the Cannes Film Festival in 2019, and the first to win four Oscars—for Best Picture, Best International Film, Best Director, and Best Original Screenplay—thus equaling the record held since 1954 by Walt Disney for the number of statuettes won by a single person! It is also the first foreign film to win the Screen

Actors Guild Award for Best Distribution and the first Korean feature film to win the Golden Globe. Finally, it is the biggest success for a foreign film at the American box office since *Crouching Tiger, Hidden Dragon* (Ang Lee, 2000), taking $53 million in the United States and Canada, with a worldwide total of over $263 million.

The universal scope of *Parasite*'s subject matter means that audiences all over the world can identify with the story of an underprivileged Korean family who live in a dark basement flat and who, little by little, infiltrate the life of a wealthy family living in a magnificent villa perched high above the city by becoming their servants. Under the guise of pure entertainment, *Parasite* clearly tackles the universal theme of class struggle; but above all it tells the story of "hell Joseon," or the story of contemporary Korean society, where ultracapitalism is widening the socioeconomic divide between classes and generations.

Hell Joseon ("Korean hell") is a Korean neologism that was popularized in 2015 via social networks before becoming part of everyday language. It describes the living conditions currently considered disastrous throughout the country, evoking the name of the former kingdom of Joseon (1392–1910), characterized by the rule of a small elite over a population subjected to hereditary poverty. The term is therefore a form of hyperbole, comparing the era of the Joseon dynasty to that of present-day Korea, where modern capitalists would maintain a large part of the population in a highly regulated system based on a certain form of exploitation. Bong Joon-ho succeeds in channeling global film genres to tell a story that is fundamentally national but that speaks to everyone.

KOREAN CINEMA: EMOTIONS

Korean culture is characterized by a unique set of feelings that can sometimes be difficult for the uninitiated to grasp. These emotions obviously exist in other cultures too, but they are generally grouped together under generic terms such as "happiness," "sadness," or "anger," whereas Koreans pay much more attention to them and describe them in a more nuanced way.

Han is undoubtedly the most well-known emotion worldwide and certainly the most prominent in Korean cinema in recent decades. It can be roughly translated as a deep feeling of melancholy stemming from the difficulty of living. In Korea, it is thought to have arisen from a succession of difficult historical experiences, from multiple invasions, through the period of Japanese occupation from 1910 to 1945, to the division of the country in 1948 and the Korean War from 1950 to 1953.

The Korean term *han* is a relatively new word, which is sometimes perceived as offensive or negative by some Koreans. It has its origins in the Chinese word *hen,* which expresses a set of negative feelings such as hatred, regret, or resentment. In 1907, during the Japanese occupation before annexation, the Japanese philosopher Soetsu Yanagi created the Korean derivative *han* to describe the particularity of Korean ceramics as a reflection of the art of channeling the people's negative emotions. Since then, the term *han* has become part of the everyday Korean language, to express a feeling of deep melancholy.

Hwabyeong is derived from the han sentiment and literally means "illness of anger" or "fire." It is characterized by an accumulation of frustrations and repressed anger. When a person suffering from this illness

Bong Joon-ho, director of *Parasite* (2019).

Previous page spread:
Poetry (Lee Chang-dong, 2010).

is faced with a stressful situation, he or she may experience a sudden outburst of anger, which can sometimes lead to violent behavior.

Han and hwabyeong emotions were depicted in the earliest Korean films, particularly in the nationalist productions of the 1920s and 1930s. In *Arirang* (Na Un-gyu, 1926), a former militant activist tortured in prison goes mad and physically assaults a pro-Japanese Korean collaborator. In *The Ownerless Ferry Boat* (Lee Gyu-hwan, 1932), a man who has lost everything under the occupation attempts to destroy the construction of a railway bridge that threatens to deprive him of his new job as a lock keeper.

The final reaction (no spoiler intended) of the father in *Parasite* can therefore be explained (rather than justified) by this typically Korean emotion. Other hwabyeong scenes can be found in many Korean gangster and revenge films, the most famous of which is certainly *Old Boy* (Park Chan-wook, 2003), although non-Korean viewers do not necessarily associate it with this Korean emotion.

Other specific feelings permeate Korean cinema. *Kibun* is a benevolent attitude, aimed at ensuring the comfort and well-being of the person with whom you are speaking, while avoiding blaming them directly, especially in public. It explains the respect and gentleness in the relationships between the characters in certain films, including family dramas. *Nunchi,* on the other hand, is an intuitive perceptive ability that allows you to immediately grasp the atmosphere of a place or situation. A character's lack of nunchi is often the source of funny situations in Korean comedies.

The Korean term *jeong* describes a feeling of deep and unconditional attachment to a person and is often used in melodramas and romantic stories. It is also used in gangster films, with the betrayal of this feeling. On the other hand, the concept of *gwonseonjinga* is inspired by Confucian ideals of poetic justice, which advocate the idea of a "reward" for good deeds, while bad deeds inevitably have negative repercussions for oneself, one's family, and those around one. This concept is often present in Korean horror, gangster, and revenge films.

The various emotions and feelings in Korean cinema therefore serve to reinforce the moral values of the stories. Although not necessarily instinctive for many viewers, particularly in the West, these emotions tend to appeal to the subconscious and elicit an "invisible" empathy for the characters and situations.

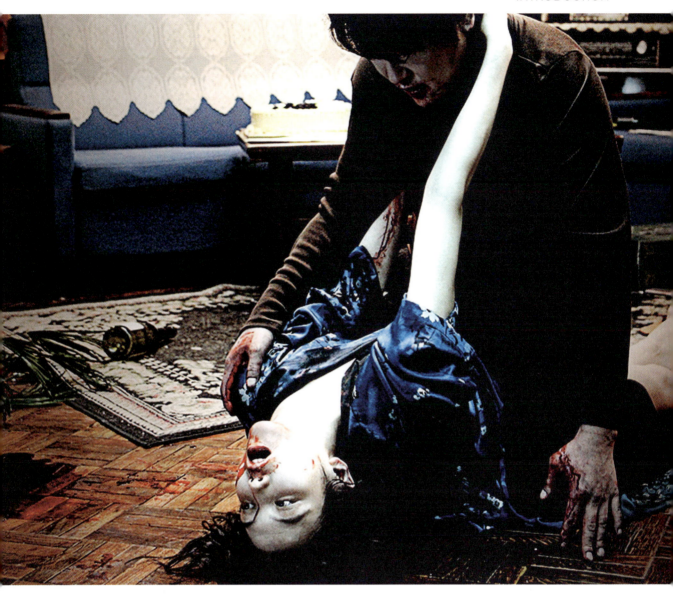

A GLOBAL PATH

The success of Korean cinema over the last 20 years is also closely linked to Korea's tremendous success in disseminating and promoting its culture on a global scale.

Korean cinema was little known worldwide before the 2000s, largely because of the Japanese occupation, which hampered its development, but also because of periods of military rule and the country's retreat from the outside world, which did not favor exports. The country's increasing openness to the wider world in the 1990s contributed greatly to the revival of Korean cinema and its worldwide representation.

The creation of the Busan International Film Festival in 1996 enabled the first Korean productions to be selected and rewarded at prestigious international festivals. And the creation of units dedicated

Thirst (Park Chan-wook, 2009).

Snowpiercer
(Bong Joon-ho, 2013).

to international sales within the major production companies also encouraged the export of feature films.

A series of new political support and promotion measures in the second half of the 1990s gave rise to the hallyu phenomenon, the widespread distribution of Korean cultural products. This movement had its first impact in China, before spreading throughout Asia and the rest of the world. The first successes were the k-dramas, high-quality Korean television series that were less expensive to produce.

They adopted American narrative structures while featuring stories deeply rooted in Asian culture and Confucianism. They were initially distinguished by the absence of explicit scenes of sex and violence, placing greater emphasis on moral values. This factor appealed to regions such as the Middle East, where these series are less subject to censorship than their American and Western counterparts.

Although experts predicted a rapid end to the hallyu phenomenon, the sustained export of Korean cultural products, such as k-pop (music), cinema, fashion, and cuisine, as well as products from other industries, such as televisions, mobile phones, and cars, has enabled Korea to enjoy continued international success over the last 20 years.

Finally, the revival of Korean cinema is also closely linked to the advent of the digital age. The emergence of websites, blogs, discussion forums, and then social networks has given Korean cinema unprecedented visibility. The rapid development of these technologies has facilitated access to Korean films and series, first through illegal downloads in the 2010s, then gradually via VOD sites and, more recently, streaming platforms.

The Covid-19 pandemic in the early 2020s may have interrupted theatrical screenings, but it did not affect the hallyu wave. Successive periods of containment simply shifted mass audiences' interest from the big screen to the small screen, with the repeated success of series such as *Squid Game* (9 episodes, Hwang Dong-hyuk, 2021) and *All of Us Are Dead* (12 episodes, Lee Jae-kyoo, 2022). The global film industry may currently be undergoing a profound reshuffle, following the change in audience behavior since the pandemic, but Korea is demonstrating an incredible ability to adapt to new digital techniques to intelligently perpetuate the prosperity of its cinema.

READING NOTES

Some readers may probably wonder why a particular film, star, or theme is not mentioned in this book. I would very much like to spare readers the slightest frustration, but this is obviously an impossible mission.

Given that many prints have disappeared for various reasons over the decades, it is simply impossible to compile an exhaustive list of the more than 8,000 feature films produced since the first Korean film in 1919. In addition, it is of course impossible to review all the films—even those that are still available—or to list all the professionals in the Korean film industry or to cover every conceivable theme.

It is also likely that I have unfairly left out people or subjects, or omitted names and titles due to my own limitations of knowledge: even after years of research, viewing, and reading, I am still learning, understanding, and rediscovering things on a daily basis. This is a good thing, because it is the best proof of the incredible richness of Korean culture and cinema.

This book has therefore been designed to serve as an introduction to the fascinating history of Korean cinema. There are still many aspects to explore and variations to consider—and I look forward to reading future books on this subject.

A NOTE ON KOREAN NAMES

The use of different systems throughout history, each based on a different logic, makes the transcription of Korean names into the Latin alphabet extremely complicated. Contrary to popular belief, Korean characters are not ideograms, but syllables made up of consonants and vowels. The romanization system most commonly used in the twentieth century is the McCune-Reischauer system, but this is an imperfect system as it does not enable certain important distinctions to be marked.

In 2000, the South Korean government tried to solve the problem by adopting a new system, which unfortunately contributed even more to the confusion. As a result, Korean names can be spelled in different ways, depending on the author and the era. "Chang Yoon-hyun" and "Jang Yun-hyeon," for example, are, despite appearances, one and the same name in Korean, but spelled according to the old and new systems, respectively.

The names in this book have therefore been romanized, as far as possible, according to the official transcriptions; if not, by using the most common script or by proposing a transcription based on South Korea's official revised romanization system for less well-known people

and for older personalities. I cannot guarantee the absence of errors and typos, despite endless proofreading sessions, but at least all the names cited should be standardized.

Actor Song Kang-ho won the Best Actor prize at the 75th Cannes Film Festival for his role in *Broker* by Japanese director Kore-eda.

A NOTE ON FILM TITLES

Film titles appear in their official English translation on the IMDb digital database (which may sometimes seem strange). Some titles that have never had an official translation are provided in the literal translation of their Korean names recorded in the Korean KMDb database.

A NOTE ON ENTRY NUMBERS

I have taken care to include the key figures for the biggest hits of each period to assess the importance of their films. Before the 1980s, any film with an audience of more than 100,000 was considered a success, and this threshold rose to 1 million in the second half of the 1990s. Following the extraordinary public response to the revival of Korean cinema in the 2000s, the new standard for success is 10 million viewers, which is still around one in five Koreans.

However, figures prior to 2000 are approximate, as only audience figures in Seoul were considered, before the inclusion of those from the rest of the country in 1998. Despite this, I have taken care to verify the reported successes by referring to articles from their respective periods.

서문

FURTHER INFORMATION

Decision to Leave
(Park Chan-wook, 2022).

Following page spread:
*Spring, Summer, Fall, Winter . . .
and Spring* (Kim Ki-duk, 2003).

If you would like to see more of the titles mentioned on these pages, the free and legal YouTube channel of the Korean Film Archive offers over 100 Korean films from before 2000. The catalog is updated regularly, and most of the feature films are subtitled in English: https://www.youtube.com/koreanfilm.

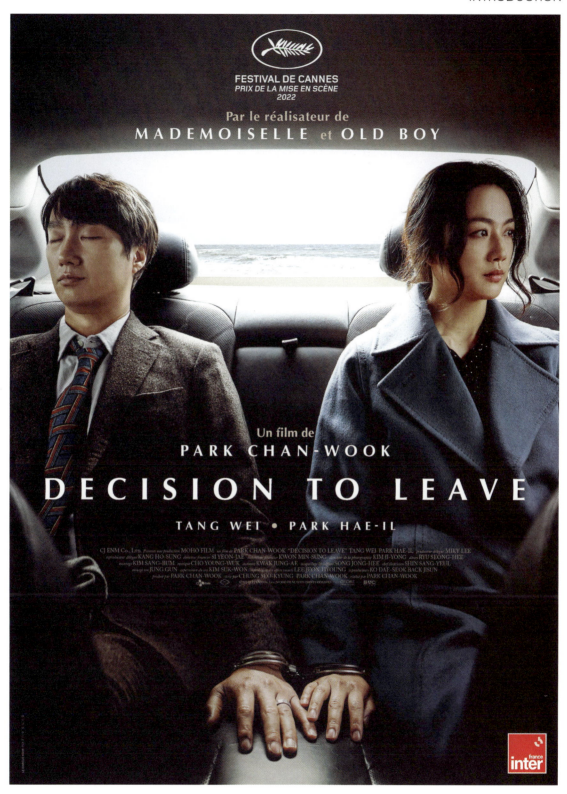

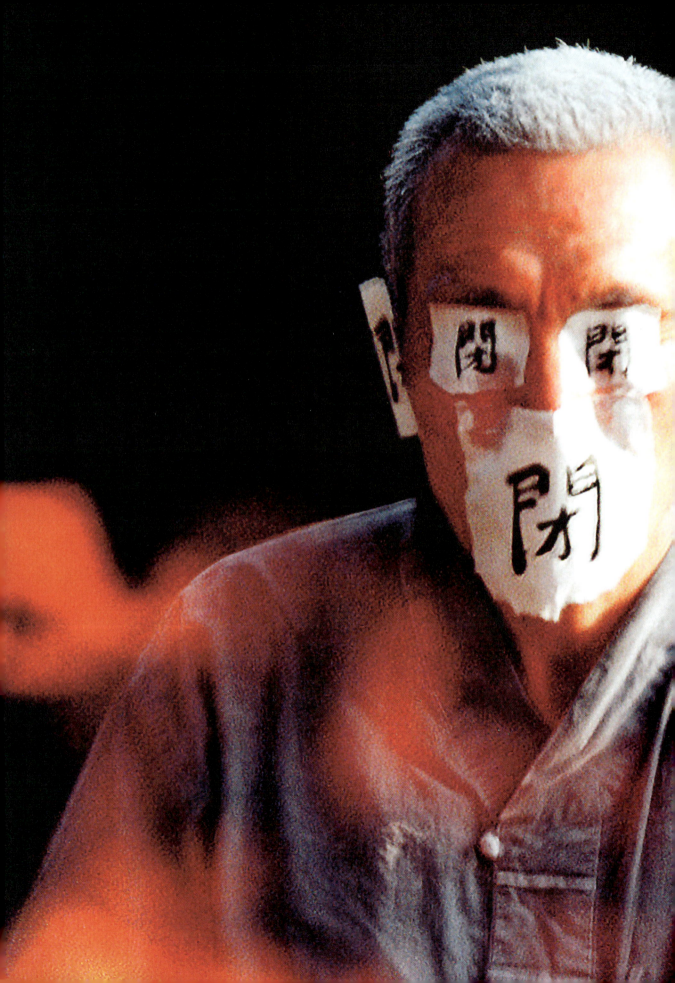

기원

1903
1919

1903–1919

THE ORIGINS OF KOREAN CINEMA

Korean cinema has its roots in the Western technologies that were introduced to Korea, as they were to the rest of the world, through international imports. As early as the second half of the nineteenth century, optical devices such as the stereoscope made it possible to view photographs in 3D, while magic lanterns, the forerunners of future slide cameras, projected images painted on glass plates through a lens.

Cinema arrived in Korea with the official visit of Ambassador Min Young-hwan, who attended a film projection at the coronation of Tsar Nicholas II in Saint Petersburg in 1896. Impressed, he informed King Gojong of this discovery on his return. In 1899, the American documentary filmmaker Elias Burton Holmes demonstrated the Kinora at the royal court. This device, in the form of a small box, enabled 600 photographic prints printed on paper to be viewed through a lampshade. Holmes is also known for having taken the first photographs in Korea, filming scenes of daily life, such as men practicing archery or *gisaeng* (Korean courtesans) dancing.

While there is no certainty as to the precise date of the first film screenings in Korea, several oral and written accounts indicate that private screenings took place as early as the end of the nineteenth century in basic huts, organized for wealthy Japanese businessmen in various districts of Seoul. This hypothesis is plausible, given that the first films by the Lumière brothers began to circulate internationally at the same time and that Korea's openness to the world and the presence of Japanese enthusiasts for new technologies probably encouraged the import of cinematographic equipment into the country.

In 1903, screenings were held in a warehouse of the power station now known as the Korea Electric Power Corporation, located in the Dongdaemun district. The power station was built in 1887 with a view to introducing public lighting to Seoul and enabling the first tramway to be introduced in 1898. Originally intended simply to entertain employees, the company eventually decided to open the screenings to the general public, in the light of their success. It also took the opportunity to promote its tramway line, which had been poorly accepted by a local population reluctant to embrace technological progress. Admission was initially charged in exchange for a coin or proof of a used tram ticket; later, the company entered into a partnership with a tobacco brand to allow spectators to exchange an empty packet of cigarettes for a ticket.

The first programs featured documentary films lasting just a few minutes, which fascinated audiences as they discovered peoples, landscapes, objects, and cultures from all over the world. The cinema operators introduced concerts, songs, and dances, extending their appeal to the general public. This is because Korea did not have a network of dedicated theatres, concert halls, or opera houses, since the performing arts had historically been performed outdoors, in accordance with Confucian tradition, making it possible to accommodate a mix of spectators while maintaining a respectful distance.

Some people were hostile to this new technology, and the city's only theatre, the

Hyeobryulsa (in what is now the Jongno-gu district, renamed Wongaksa before it was demolished), paid the price: the management, sensing the commercial potential of film screenings, installed a projector to compete with the Korea Electric Power Corporation; but the initiative was quickly banned under pressure from religious associations, which denounced the promiscuity between men and women, the presence of gisaeng and the discovery of foreign cultures. According to them, such elements risked perverting the spectators' minds.

In 1905, the Korea Electric Power Corporation decided to transform its warehouse into a real performance venue, the Dongdaemun Moving Pictures Venue, with the aim of offering a better welcome to the public. In 1907, Alfred Martin, a French businessman and owner of a private mansion, organized private screenings for the royal family, before opening them up to the general public with the unstoppable advertising slogan: "Programme seen and approved by the King." Temporary screening rooms were sometimes set up in conference halls or public squares to show educational films. The Korean Doctors Study Group regularly took over school playgrounds to raise awareness of sanitary conditions, and Christian associations organized screenings of the first feature-length films of a religious nature, such as the Italian *Quo vadis* (Enrico Guazzoni, 1913), to discuss episodes from the Bible.

These early venues, often set up in basic huts exposed to the vagaries of the weather, very cold in winter and too hot in summer, reeked of sweat, cigarette smoke, and even urine, with unsanitary toilets located on one side of the screen. Frequent power cuts regularly interrupted screenings. The audience was unruly, spitting and throwing rubbish on the floor, booing or cheering the films and the *byeonsa* (film narrators). The darkness of the premises was conducive to prostitution, theft, and trafficking of all kinds. The wealthy classes considered these sheds to be places of debauchery and perversion.

After the Japanese annexation in 1910, there was a proliferation of theatres and cinemas, with establishments for the Japanese in districts south of the Cheonggyecheon canal reserved for Japanese expatriates, and those for Koreans in the northern districts. In 1910, a Japanese entrepreneur used the great American cinemas of the time as a model to create "the most beautiful cinema in the world," the Gyeongseong Supreme Entertainment Theater (renamed Umi-gwan in 1915).

With 600 seats on the ground floor and tatami mats upstairs for the wealthier classes, it could accommodate up to 2,000 spectators. There were hostesses at reception, an orchestra in the auditorium, and a projectionist trained in Japan. This cinema was soon rivaled by a new cinema complex, the Daejeonggwan, with a 1,200-seat auditorium, a smoking room, a tearoom, a shop, public baths, and even a heated gym, which programmed Japanese plays and broadcast comedies and melodramas.

Previous page: Cover of the serial novel
Zigomar by Léon Sazie.

According to Confucian tradition, women (over the age of 11) entered last and were separated from men, either by wooden partitions or by being seated on the other side of the room, or even upstairs. Although cinemas were officially open to all, establishments located in Japanese neighborhoods often reserved the worst seats for Korean spectators, or even refused them entry altogether. Moreover, the *benshis* (Japanese-language film narrators) discouraged many Koreans from attending the screenings.

From 1912 onward, *serials* (episodic series) gained a loyal following, due to their plot twists and turns, which always ended with an open ending to encourage viewers to return. Among the most popular series were *Zigomar* (4 episodes, Victorin Jasset, 1911–1913; plus 10 unofficial Japanese sequels produced in 1911–1912), *Stuart Webbs* (47 episodes, Joe May, 1913–1930), *The Broken Coin* (22 episodes, Francis Ford, 1915), and *Les Vampires* [*The Vampires*] (10 episodes, Louis Feuillade, 1915); these programs offered 2 new episodes twice a week.

During the 1910s, serials were so successful that they turned programming upside down, favoring films over animations. For the first time, cinema admissions exceeded those for traditional shows. American films supplanted European productions, which were in sharp decline after World War I. The screening of feature films remained limited due to the complexity of the stories and the difficulty of translation, despite the increasing presence of byeonsa. Some exhibitors cut feature films into several parts, like serials, to increase the number of screenings and build audience loyalty.

In 1914, Umi-gwan signed an exclusive contract with Universal Studios, renowned for their serials, and became the most popular cinema in Seoul. This unprecedented partnership inspired other cinemas to seek similar deals with the studios. Japanese distributors, such as Nikkatsu, Tenkatsu, and Shochiku, preferred to work with more partners to gain a better understanding of the emerging Korean market. They signed contracts either per film or "per month," providing not only films but also projection equipment, a projectionist, a technician, a supervisor, and a Japanese film narrator to ensure that screenings ran smoothly. From 1916 onward, this strategy enabled them to take control of the most profitable cinemas in Seoul and extend their network to other cities, such as Daegu (1922), Pyongyang (1923), Incheon, and Mokpo (both in 1926).

By 1916, Seoul had around 15 cinemas, the smaller ones showing popular titles at reduced rates for less-affluent audiences every few weeks. This contributed to a significant increase in the number of cinema-goers and encouraged some entrepreneurs to invest in the first local film productions.

American documentary filmmaker Elias Burton Holmes (1870–1958) demonstrated the Kinora camera at the Royal Court in 1899 and is considered the first filmmaker to shoot footage of daily life in Korea at the beginning of the twentieth century.

THE SMOOTH-TALKING BYEONSA

When the first silent films were released, Korean audiences did not necessarily have the necessary codes to understand images and shots that were too far removed from their own culture. Likewise, they were, for the most part, unable to understand foreign-language intertitles. Although it is difficult to trace the precise origins of the byeonsa—the narrators who accompany the screenings—their appearance seems to have coincided with the first screenings, in 1903, and played an essential role in the beginnings of Korean cinema.

The Korean byeonsa of the twentieth century is the Korean variation of the Japanese benshi, a narrator who commented on *kabuki* (traditional dramatic Japanese theatre) and *bunraku* (literary puppet theatre) shows in Japan from the seventeenth century onward. With the arrival of cinema in Korea in the 1900s, the byeonsa was initially tasked with translating the intertitles and explaining certain parts of the film. And with the arrival of the first feature films, they also assumed the task of dubbing the actors and creating the soundscape, using their voices, their bodies, or various objects to accompany the orchestra playing in the cinema. At each reel change, the byeonsa entertained the audience with animations, comic interludes or additional explanations of what had just been shown.

In Korea, the byeonsa was often placed to the left of the screen and used a megaphone or, later, a microphone to be heard. At the time of the first hand-cranked projectors, he communicated with the projectionist, located at the back of the room, by means of a cord connected to a bell, which enabled him to adjust the speed of the film according to his own narrative rhythm.

View of Seoul and Myeong-dong Cathedral in the early 1900s.

One strike meant acceleration, while two indicated a request to decelerate.

The byeonsa became increasingly famous over the years, with their names displayed in capital letters on the front of cinemas, even above those of the film's stars. They entered the cinema to the sound of a brass band and the cheers of the crowd. They were admired not only for their talent as performers, but also for their ability to read, their mastery of foreign languages, and their knowledge of distant cultures, which was rare among cinema-goers at the time. Their every move was closely followed by the press, which could celebrate their performances or condemn any indiscretions. One of the most infamous examples is that of Seo Sang-ho, who regularly made the headlines for his many love affairs and drinking sprees. His death from an opium overdose in 1938 was widely covered by the press.

The byeonsa specialized according to cinema and film genre to divide up the work more evenly. Lee Byoung-joo was known for dubbing action films, Seong Dong-ho for romantic comedies, and Seo Sang-ho for melodramas. During screenings, it was not uncommon for a commentator to completely reimagine the original story, thus encouraging the audience to return several times to see the same film. Some byeonsa also used the screenings as a political platform, such as So Sang-pil, who was arrested for comparing the famous scene of the Jews' revolt against the Romans in the American film *Ben-Hur* (Fred Niblo, 1925) to the situation of Koreans under the Japanese occupation. Seong Dong-ho, meanwhile, contributed to the reputation of the legendary film *Arirang* (Na Un-gyu, 1926) with his politically committed speeches.

These excesses did not escape the attention of the authorities, who from 1910 required the presence of a Japanese official at every screening, ostensibly to ensure the safety of spectators from the numerous pickpockets. But, in reality, it was to keep an eye on the commentators. From 1912, any attempt to incite public unrest was punishable by imprisonment. In 1922, a compulsory license was introduced for byeonsa, who needed to pass an examination to obtain the license to practice their profession. Candidates were judged on their appearance, elocution, and the content of their speeches. In 1926, byeonsa were even obliged to submit the text of their future performances to a Japanese censorship committee for approval.

The byeonsa played an essential role in the beginnings of Korean cinema. In fact, the script for the very first Korean film, *Fight for Justice* (1919), was co-written by the director Kim Do-san and the star narrator of the time, Kim Deok-gyeong, who was responsible for the order of the scenes and the rhythm to be adopted to enable the future byeonsa to perform perfectly. Some of them even became actors, such as Kim Choon-gwang in *The Story of Chun-hyang* (Koshu Hayakawa, 1923). Their popularity ensured an even larger audience, and spectators were fascinated to see them on stage doubling their own screen roles.

The byeonsa profession declined with the arrival of talking pictures in the early 1930s. Many of them became radio presenters, theatre actors, or comedians. The profession did not disappear, however, as film subtitles still required translation during the early years of talking pictures. Similarly, silent films continued to be produced and shown in Korea until the 1950s, due to the high cost of sound recording on film shoots and the fact that cinemas were lagging behind in terms of sound systems. Although the profession of the byeonsa finally disappeared in the first half of the 1950s, it is still occasionally practiced at rare screenings of classics from the silent era.

In addition to a few sound recordings preserved in the Korean Film Archive, there is still a restored copy of *Independence Night* (Choi In-kyu, 1948), a silent film in which all the characters were dubbed in post-production by a single commentator in a monotone voice. *A Public Prosecutor and a Teacher* (Yun Dae-ryong, 1948), on the other hand, is a real treat for the ears, with Shin Chul, the star byeonsa at the time, seemingly literally possessed by the characters and describing each scene in great detail to emotionally involve the viewer.

Im Kwon-taek, one of the greatest Korean directors of all time, paid a vibrant tribute to the art of the byeonsa in his historical epic *The General's Son* (1990): at the fourteenth minute of the film, the narrator's character solemnly takes his place at a lectern placed at the side of the screen, to the cheers of the enthusiastic crowd. The screening begins with a strongly committed commentary from the byeonsa: "Times are rough as the bone-chilling winds from Siberia blow with no mercy for the starving people of Korea. The winter is cold, and the people are hungry. Life is hard for the people of Korea." The two officials sitting at the back of the room, responsible for keeping an eye on the proceedings, were far from appreciative of these remarks critical of the Japanese occupiers, and tension mounted with each new retort from the joker. The police were about to intervene to stop the session when a scene of on-screen dialogue defused the situation.

Children on the ramparts of Seoul, Dongdaemun district, 1904.

THE BIRTH OF KINO DRAMA

Korean cinema was officially born on October 27, 1919, with the release of Kim Do-san's *Fight for Justice*, although this date remains controversial. In fact, the film was not a real feature film, but a kino drama, a show combining theatre and the projection of filmed scenes. The film was a great success, with over 100,000 spectators at the time of its release, encouraging the production of similar shows and the launch of future Korean feature films.

The development of Korean cinema is closely linked to the proliferation of screening venues in Seoul, in particular dedicated theatres during the 1910s. The performing arts were very popular in Japan, where ritual dances led to three major trends from the fourteenth century onward: *noh* (elegant and poetic lyrical drama), *bunraku* (literary puppet theatre), and *kabuki* (dramatic performance). During the Meiji era (1868–1912), *shingeki* (Western-style experimental theatre) and shinpa (new school melodrama) broke with classical theatre to introduce more modern forms.

These latter theatrical movements were very popular with Japanese audiences in the early twentieth century and were exported to occupied Korea. After the annexation of Korea in 1910, the number of Japanese residents in Seoul rose considerably, from 88 in 1885 to 34,468. To satisfy the entertainment needs of these expatriates, the authorities created a vast network of theatres, with a varied program, mainly of shinpa plays, which blended elements of traditional Japanese theatre with Western influences, reinventing the form and content by introducing, among other things, stage lighting to enliven the stories and capture the audience's attention.

Young Korean directors were impressed by this trend and incorporated it into their own culture of *pansori* (sung storytelling). Kim Do-san was a leading theatre personality at the time, seeking to push back the boundaries of the stage, as demonstrated by his creation of an electric machine to simulate thunderstorms in his play *Remaining Spirit*. In 1918, he was fascinated by *The Wife of the Captain,* performed as part of the Hwanggeum-gwan theatre's second anniversary celebrations. This play is a *rensageki* ("chain theatre" or combined shows), a show combining theatre and filmed scenes, which had its moment of glory in Japan between 1910 and 1916 and which enabled the transition from theatre to cinema at that time.

Kim Do-san wanted to re-adapt the plot of the original play, the story of a young man who must thwart the diabolical plans of his stepmother, who wants to get her hands on the family inheritance. To add dynamism to his show, he incorporates elements borrowed from the serials fashionable in Korea, such as *Les Vampires* (Louis Feuillade, 1915) and *The Broken Coin* (Francis Ford, 1915). Kim Do-san worked with a byeonsa to draw up an initial version of the script and give rhythm to the narrators' contributions.

He then presented the project to Park Sung-pil, director of the Dansungsa theatre, describing it as a kino drama, the Korean equivalent of the Japanese rensageki, which combines theatrical elements with filmed sequences.

Park Sung-pil agreed to invest 5,000 won (a handsome sum for the time) to make a series of action sequences lasting around 40 minutes in iconic locations in and around Seoul, such as Yeongneung (King Sejong's tomb), Jangchungdan Park, and Geumcheon Bridge. Upon its release, *Fight for Justice* was a huge public success with over 100,000 spectators and received rave reviews, such as that from *The Korea Daily News,* which wrote: "This film is not only spectacular, but also aesthetically magnificent with scenes comparable to those in Western productions." Several decades later, in 1962, the Korean authorities officially validated the release date of *Fight for Justice*, October 27, 1919, as the "official birth of Korean cinema."

The profits enabled Park Sung-pil to expand Dansungsa and produce Kim Do-san's next kino dramas, *This Friendship* (1919), *A Detective's Great Pain* (1919), and *The Chivalrous Robber* (1920). He also financed the projects of other famous directors, such as Lee Ki-se's *A Truly Good Friend* and *Eternal Love of Su-il and Sun-ae* in 1920. *Eternal Love of Su-il and Sun-ae* was a milestone because it cast the first female actress in the history of Korean cinema, Ma Ho-jeong, at a time when female roles in theatre had been the exclusive preserve of men. Lee Ki-se also directed another kino drama, for the rival Umi-gwan cinema, *A Truly Good Friend* (1920), which marked the debut of the first cinematographer and future pioneer of Korean (sound) cinema, Lee Phil-woo.

Despite waning public interest in kino drama after the first Korean feature films were made in 1923–1924, the Dansungsa continued to finance other shows throughout the 1920s and 1930s, including adaptations of *Cyrano de Bergerac* and *The Count of Monte Cristo*

as *Shinerano* and *Amgurwang* (both 1932), directed by the star of the age, Na Un-gyu (*Arirang*, 1926). Another curiosity was the production, between 1925 and 1927, of several kino dramas by the Gisaeng Association, in which all the roles, male and female, were played exclusively by courtesans.

Some of the pioneers of the golden age of kino dramas met with tragic fates. While Lee Ki-se, tired of theatre and cinema, chose to return to journalism, Im Seong-gu, director of *Students Day* (also known as *The Fidelity to a Student's Principle*) (1920), died of an illness at the age of 34. The great Kim Do-san died in a car accident during the filming of *The Border* (1923). Kino drama gradually disappeared during the 1930s, before making a fleeting resurgence between 1945 and 1953, when cinemas ran out of feature films during the difficult post-war period in Korea.

Les Vampires (1915) was one of the most popular serials of the 1910s.

초기

1919
1945

초기

1919–1945
THE BEGINNINGS OF KOREAN CINEMA

The year 1919 was marked not only by the date of October 27, the official day of the birth of Korean cinema, with the release of Kim Do-san's *Fight for Justice*, but also by that of March 1 and Samiljeol, the first major popular uprising in favor of independence since Korea's annexation by Japan in 1910. This protest movement was triggered by the death of Gojong, the last king of the Joseon dynasty, on January 21, 1919, rumored to have been caused by poisoning.

On that day, 33 resistance fighters decided to organize a reading in a restaurant of the Declaration of Independence of the Republic of Korea, a symbolic decree drawn up following the speech made by US President Woodrow Wilson (1913–1921) at the Paris Peace Conference on January 20, 1919, which presented "the right of self-determination." to the peoples of the world.

Against all expectations, the small group of resistance fighters was joined by thousands of students and citizens, leading to the intervention of Japanese forces. The situation degenerated, resulting in 7,000 deaths, over 15,000 injured, and 45,000 arrests, including those of Na Un-gyu, Kim Tae-jin, and Yun Bong-chun, future directors of the golden age of Korean cinema in the 1920s. Over the following months, the demonstration led to hundreds of other rallies across Korea and around the world, mobilizing more than 2 million people in all.

The scale of the movement led to a certain relaxation of Japanese repression, with the introduction of a cultural policy known as *bunka seiji*, between 1919 and 1926: three daily newspapers, new magazines, and radio stations were allowed to broadcast Korean news in the Korean language. Literature was reborn with the advent of the *shinmunhak* (new literature) movement, and the publication of poems and novels in *hangeul* (Korean alphabet), which served as a source of inspiration for Korean films from the second half of the 1920s to the 1960s.

Korean cinema benefited from this period of relative freedom before the return of stricter censorship from 1926. The success of *Fight for Justice* (Kim Do-san, 1919) led to the production of around 20 other kino dramas and 250 short and medium-length "educational" films designed to raise public awareness of Korean-Japanese intercultural relations, hygiene measures, and other "good behavior" to be adopted during the occupation.

These films led to the production of a second symbolic work from the early days of Korean cinema, *The Vow Made Below the Moon* (Yun Baek-nam, 1923).[1] The fact that it is now considered to be "the first fiction film in the history of Korean cinema" is at least as controversial as the designation of *Fight for Justice*, a kino drama, as the beginning of Korean cinema: This production is in fact a 33-minute "educational" medium-length film, financed by the Japanese occupiers to raise public awareness of the benefits of saving money. Its posthumous fame is linked above all to its author, Yun Baek-nam, one of the most important filmmakers of his generation.

The story tells of the misfortunes of a young couple, the fiancé spending all their meager funds on gambling during a drunken evening. Fortunately, the young man's father ensures a happy ending, paying off the debts with money from his savings account. The medium-length film was screened in April 1923 at the Gyeong-seong Hotel in front of a select audience of journalists and guests, who praised the film for its technical quality and the remarkable performance of the actors.

The first feature film in the history of Korean cinema was *The Story of Chun-hyang*, directed by Japanese director Koshu Hayakawa in 1923. This film was a huge success, with over 150,000 tickets sold, triggering a wave of adaptations of pansori and traditional tales known to the public, including the very first all-Korean production, *The Story of Jang-hwa and Hong-ryeon* (Kim Yeong-hwan, 1924). The other leading genre of the period was shinpa melodrama, derived from the Japanese theatrical movement of the same name and popular in Korea from the 1910s onward.

Despite the courageous attempts of Korean cinema pioneers such as Lee Gu-yeong, Lee Gyeong-son, Lee Phil-woo, and Yun Baek-nam to diversify genres and attract audiences, the beginnings of Korean cinema remained precarious. Local cinema struggled to develop under Japanese control. An example of these harsh conditions can be found in the feature-length fiction film *Spring on the Korean Peninsula* (Lee Byung-il, 1941), which realistically depicts the difficulties of filming under Japanese occupation.

Na Un-gyu was the first Korean to capture the imagination of the masses. His film *Arirang* (1926) became a symbol of resistance under the Japanese occupation and laid the foundations for the first golden age of Korean cinema, between 1926 and 1937, when the other masterpiece of the period, *The Ownerless Ferry Boat* (Lee Gyu-hwan, 1932) was released. The genres diversified, with melodramas, action, horror, and educational films that borrowed as much from American as from Japanese cinema. The film collective KAPF (Korean Artist Proletarian Federation) questioned the primary function of cinema by producing a series of sociorealist productions advocating political education for the underprivileged classes.

The development of Korean national cinema prompted the Japanese to further tighten censorship. In 1922, a "regulation of entertainment films and their distribution outlets" required byeonsa to pass an examination before they could practice their profession. In 1926, the introduction of "regulation of films and their censorship" to monitor the content of works broadcast prompted approximately 20 film industry professionals, including some of the

Previous page spread: *Eternal Love of Su-il and Sun-ae* (1926), adapted from a popular novel by Japanese writer Koyo Ozaki, was one of the first major public successes in Korean cinema.

most renowned directors, to go into exile to try their luck in China. For instance, Jeong Gi-tak filmed *Firework* (1928) and *Exit Path* (1933) and Lee Gyeong-son made *The Yangtze River* (1930) and *Goodbye, Shanghai!* (1934) in China.

The false-flag sabotage of their railway at Mukden in 1931 gave the Japanese the pretext to invade Manchuria and pursue their expansionist policy in China. It was also an opportunity for the Japanese forces to impose a series of new censorship measures in occupied Korea. The showing of foreign films was subsequently restricted by a third in 1934, then again in 1938, before being banned altogether following the attack on Pearl Harbor in 1941.

A new generation of Korean filmmakers trained in Japan then attempted to revive the film industry and make up for the lack of foreign productions by making feature-length films intended both for the Korean market and for wider Asian distribution, including *The Street Cleaner* (Bang Han-jun, 1935), *Wanderer* (Lee Gyu-hwan, 1937), and *Tuition* (Choi In-kyu and Bang Han-jun, 1940). October 4, 1935, was another important date in the history of Korean cinema, with the release of the very first talking film, *The Story of Chun-hyang* (Lee Myeong-u). With over 150,000 spectators, it paved the way for other productions, such as *Sweet Dream* (Yang Ju-nam, 1936), *Arirang 3* (Na Un-gyu, 1936), and *The Story of Shim-cheong* (Ahn Seok-yeong, 1937); however, due to the high cost of sound recording equipment and the lack of adequate equipment in cinemas, most films continued to be made in silent form.

In 1937, the Japanese stepped up their policy, banning the use of the Korean language in schools, the media, and the cinema, and then requiring surnames to be changed to Japanese. In 1941, the entire Korean film industry was placed under the sole government institution, Choson Film Distribution, and filmmakers were only allowed to produce propaganda films to encourage Koreans to enlist in the army. Old cop-

ies of film were destroyed to recover the nitrate, which was useful for making munitions for use in World War II. The occupation of Korea ended with the Japanese surrender on August 15, 1945, ushering in a new era for Korean cinema.

1. In the 2000s, some historians questioned the date and title of Korean cinema's first feature film. They claimed to have found press articles referring to *The Border* (Kim Do-san, 1923), a film that was initially intended as a kino drama before becoming a feature film, and which was even shown in cinemas before being banned by the occupying forces. However, the lack of tangible evidence has invalidated this hypothesis.

Previous page spread: The Seoul Capitol, a Japanese colonial administration building built in 1926, is a symbol of Japan's historical oppression of Korea.

Bird in Cage (1926) is a landmark film of the 1920s that introduced a "modern woman" who dictates the conditions of love to two very different men, one of whom is played by Na Un-gyu.

ADAPTATIONS OF PANSORI

The success of the educational film *The Vow Made Below the Moon* (Yun Baek-nam, 1923) marked the second beginning of Korean cinema. The first feature-length films were often inspired by traditional folk arts such as pansori or classical literature, to attract audiences and try to mask the technical shortcomings of the nascent cinema. Reflecting the richness of Korean culture, these films are a source of pride for Koreans: they are the symbol of a country in the midst of a transition from its traditional past to its modern future.

Pansori emerged during the flourishing cultural period of eighteenth-century Korea. It accompanied shamanic ceremonies in public squares before becoming an art form in its own right in the nineteenth century. It declined somewhat under the Japanese occupation, before virtually disappearing when the best singers moved to North Korea following the division of the country in 1948. After a timid revival under Park Chung-hee's regime in the 1970s, pansori was revived with the success of *Seopyeonje / The Pansori Singer* and *Chunhyang / The Song of the Faithful Chunhyang* (Im Kwon-taek, 1993 and 2000). As pansori is an oral tradition, there are now only five surviving stories, which were listed as an Intangible Cultural Heritage of humanity by UNESCO in 2008.

The Story of Chun-hyang (Koshu Hayakawa, 1923) is the first film adaptation of the most famous pansori, from which it takes its name. The story takes place in Namwon, in the northern province of Jeolla, where the courtesan Chun-hyang has an affair with Mong-ryong, the son of the magistrate, which is forbidden on account of her lower class. She is captured and forced to become the concubine of a corrupt official. She owes her salvation only to the intervention of Mong-ryong, now a secret royal inspector, who manages to save her.

The first feature film in the history of Korean

cinema, it was directed by wealthy businessman Koshu Hayakawa (real name Manjiro Hayakawa), manager of the Hwanggum and Choson cinemas. He gave the lead role to the star byeonsa of the time, Kim Choon-gwang (1900–1949), whose fame and the added value of dubbing his own role on stage ensured a huge success, with over 150,000 spectators, despite the film being said to be of mediocre technical quality.

The 15 or so versions that followed this first adaptation also reflected the different stages in the evolution of Korean cinema: Lee Myeong-u's version (1935) was the first talking film; Lee Gyu-hwan's version (1955), which attracted over 180,000 spectators, marked the revival of Korean cinema in the 1950s. Finally, Yun Yong-gyu's film

(1959), which won the Best Photography prize in Moscow, made it one of the first Korean films to win an award at a festival abroad.

In 1961, *Chun-hyang* was at the center of one of the first major confrontations between two leading figures in the film industry: Shin Sang-ok, the director-producer, undertook an expensive Technicolor adaptation with his wife, Choi Eun-hee, in the title role; his great rival at the time, the filmmaker Hong Seong-ki, followed suit by announcing his own version with his wife, Kim Ji-mi, as the lead actress. In principle, a law prohibited the simultaneous filming of two competing projects, but as Jo Yong-jin, the person responsible for overseeing such matters at the time, was also the co-producer of Hong

Seong-ki's version, the joint production of the two films was "tolerated."

This event also symbolized the rivalry between two currents in Korean cinema: Hong Seong-ki was the embodiment of the traditional cinema of the 1950s, and Shin Sang-ok the figure of the revival. Shin Sang-ok won the battle by a wide margin, achieving the biggest box office success of the period, with over 380,000 tickets sold, and becoming the most important filmmaker of the golden age of Korean cinema in the 1960s, while his rival, Hong Seong-ki, ended his career.

This pansori once again became the subject of controversial adaptations with the arrival of 70mm film in the 1960s: To create some controversy, Kim Soo-yong falsely claimed that his 1968 version was the first in this format, whereas in fact Lee Seong-gu's 1971 version was the first. But the best-known adaptation to date is Im Kwon-taek's *Chunhyang* (*The Song of the Faithful Wife Chunhyang*), the first Korean film to be presented in official competition at the Cannes Festival in 2000.

Following the triumph of *The Story of Chun-hyang*, Koshu Hayakawa produced an adaptation of another famous pansori, *Nolbu and Heungbu* (1925), performed once again, but also directed by byeonsa Kim Choon-gwang. Based on a children's folk tale, it tells the story of two brothers, the greedy Nolbu and the wise Heungbu. After the death of their father, Nolbu inherits all the wealth and lives lavishly, leaving his brother penniless. One day, Heungbu saves a crane, which gives him a reward of magic seeds that grow money. Nolbu deliberately injures and then nurses back to health another bird in an attempt to share the same fortune, but of course ends up ruined by his own greed.

The Story of Chun-hyang (1935), the second adaptation of the most famous pansori, was the first talking film in Korean cinema. It was a huge success.

Director Kim Soo-yong claimed that
The Story of Chun-hyan (1968) was the
first Korean feature shot on 70mm film.
His claim was false, but it attracted the
theatre crowds nonetheless.

The film was a failure, but this did not prevent other, more successful versions from being made: Lee Gyeong-son's version (1950) attracted over 100,000 spectators; Kim Hwa-rang's parody Skinny and Fatty (1959) with the title comic duo, and Gang Tae-ung's first Korean puppet animation (1967).

The film The Story of Shim Cheong (Lee Gyeong-son, 1925) is based on the third—and more tragic—pansori, which tells the story of Shim-cheong, a goddess who assumes the guise of a young girl raised by a blind old man. In the story, she is sacrificed to the gods and thrown into the sea because she is unable to provide for her family. Saved by a goddess, she becomes queen of the seas and is reunited with her father, who has regained his sight. This film inspired six new adaptations, including Lee Hyung-pyo's charming version (1962) with striking special effects using simple mirrors, and the North Korean version directed by Shin Sang-ok (1985). Shin, who had been kidnapped on orders of Supreme Leader Kim Jong-il and taken to North Korea to raise their standards of cinema, escaped in 1986.

Directors and producers in the early days of the Korean film industry sought to captivate their audiences by drawing inspiration not only from pansori, but also from traditional folk tales. Following the success of The Story of Chun-hyang, the managers of the Dansungsa cinema adapted the traditional horror tale The Story of Jang-hwa and Hong-ryeon (Kim Yeong-hwan, 1924), the very first all-Korean production, starring Lee Phil-woo, the future creator of talking pictures, as lighting director. The story is about twin sisters who have apparently died by suicide, but actually have been killed by their "wicked stepmother"; they come back to haunt their murderer to take revenge. This first Korean horror film was not a great success, unlike later adaptations from 1936, 1956, 1962, and 1972, as well as A Tale of Two Sisters (Kim Jee-woon, 2003) and its American remake The Uninvited (Charles and Thomas Guard, 2009).

The Legend of Hong Gildong (attributed to Heo Gyun, circa 1608–1613) is one of the most important works of classical Korean literature. This story of a thief who takes from the rich to redistribute wealth to the poor is reminiscent of the Western Robin Hood. Its adaptation as a diptych, The Story of Hong Gil-dong (Kim So-bong and Lee Myeong-u, 1935–1936) laid the foundations for many future historical, martial arts, and animated films, including the very first Korean cartoon, A Story of Hong Gil-dong (Shin Dong-hun, 1967).

The Story of Shim Cheong (1925) is the adaptation of the third—and most tragic—of the five surviving pansori. It also marks one of the first major appearances of Na Un-gyu, in the role of the father.

THE SHINPA MELODRAMAS

While the first Korean productions were largely inspired by pansori and traditional literature, they were also influenced by the shinpa movement, which imbued the Korean films of the following decades with its melancholy.

Shinpa originated in Japan in the 1880s. The young intellectuals behind this movement sought to modernize theatre, breaking with the traditions of bunraku (literary puppet theatre) and kabuki (dramatic performance) to create a more modern form. They mixed the melodramatic stories of kabuki with more Western influences. They shortened the length of the plays by eliminating the musical and choreographic interludes, they renewed the traditional costumes and make-up, and their stage-only lighting better captivated the audience, plunged as it now was in darkness.

Shinpa plays were exported to Korea in the early 1910s, inspiring a young generation of Korean directors, some of whom went on to become filmmakers. The first film in the history of Korean cinema, *Fight for Justice* (Kim Do-san, 1919)—a kino drama—was inspired by a shinpa play, *The Wife of the Captain*. It was to serve as a model for the storylines of future feature films.

Shinpa films are, broadly speaking, popular melodramas focusing on the misfortunes of their main characters, torn between a past and present world. Women are systematically portrayed as victims of their social condition. The first shinpa films featured gisaengs who suffered from the restrictions of their lower class and social prejudice. Over the decades, these dramas focused more on wives, mothers, or young women, who sacrifice their own happiness for that of their family or husband.

In 1924, Japanese directors Koshu Hayakawa and Kanjo Takasa made their first two shinpa melodramas based on unpublished scripts, *The Sorrowful Song* and *The Sorrowful Song of the Sea*. The first tells the classic story of the impossible love between a gisaeng and a young man from an upper-class family. It inaugurates a long series of dramas featuring grieving courtesans. The second tells the story of a thwarted love affair between two people who end up discovering that they are brother and sister.

Lee Gu-yeong achieved great success with *The Twin Jade Pavilion* (1925), adapted from a popular soap opera, published daily in a newspaper. The radio broadcast of a song specially written to accompany the release ensured the film's success, with over 100,000 tickets sold. *Eternal Love of Su-il and Sun-ae* (Lee Gyeong-son, 1926) was adapted from the novel that gave it its title, by Koyo Ozaki, one of the three Japanese writers behind the shinpa literary movement. Already successfully transposed as a kino drama (1920) by Lee Ki-se, its film version became another triumph, with over 100,000 spectators. Ultimately, shinpa melodramas accounted for almost three-quarters of the total of 153 films produced between 1923 and 1945.

The arrival of numerous theatre artists to support the rebirth of Korean cinema after the Korean War (1950–1953) renewed the genre. Jeon Ok, a famous film and theatre actress, was a key figure in this revival. Although she appeared in several feature films by director Na Un-gyu, such as *Farewell* (1927) and *Ok-nyeo* (1928), she is best known for her theatrical roles as a sacrificial working-class woman. In 1958, she starred in three adaptations of shinpa plays written by herself and directed by the young beginner Ha Han-soo: *Snowy Night*, *Tears of Mokpo*, and *Lullaby*. Their success earned her the nickname Queen of Tears.

At the same time, another actress, Lee Kyoung-hee, became the "Second Queen of Tears," appearing in *A Mother's Love* (Yang Ju-nam, 1958) and *Brother and Sister* (Hong Il-myung, 1958), a great success with over 100,000 spectators. She went on to specialize in leading roles in contemporary melodramas. The arrival of a new generation of more modern directors, such as Yu Hyun-mok, Shin Sang-ok, and Kim Ki-young, also marked the end of the golden age of shinpa melodrama. The genre is now considered old-fashioned in a post-war Korean society that is in the throes of change.

However, the shinpa melodrama enjoyed an unexpected revival in the late 1960s with the surprise success of *Love Me Once Again* (Jung So-young, 1968), which sold over 390,000 tickets. The story follows Hye-young, who unknowingly has an affair with a married man, Shin-ho. She only discovers the truth when she becomes pregnant. She runs away and settles in a secluded coastal village. Eight years later, unable to provide for her son, she sends him to join his father so that he can have a better life. The man is faced with the dilemma of having to choose between his family and his illegitimate child.

Love Me Once Again conforms to the usual codes of shinpa melodrama by depicting the dilemma of two characters, which is resolved by the sacrifice of the female character for the happiness of her former lover; but unlike traditional films, it is set in a middle-class family typical of the period, is distinguished by the refined acting of its leads and takes a novel final twist.

The film became an instant classic, with three sequels between 1969 and 1971 and two successful remakes in 1980 and 2001. It also triggered a new wave of shinpa productions, which swept through the cinema during the dark period of the 1970s, when for some, tears in the cinema were as much an outlet for their repressed emotions as the violence in martial arts films or the eroticism of hostess films for others.

The shinpa craze continued into the 1980s, a decade marked by the production of poor-quality erotic films. The remake *Love Me Once Again* (Byun Jang-ho, 1980) triumphed with 364,000 spectators, ranking as the fifth best-selling film of the decade and leading to other films in the genre, including the popular trilogy *The One I Love* (Jang Il-ho, 1981–1984) and *My Rose Mellow* (Park Cheol-su, 1988).

After a certain decline in the 1990s, the genre was revived again in the early 2000s with a series of romantic shinpa melodramas aimed at young teenagers, including *Obsessed* (Kim Dae-woo, 2014) and *Salut d'Amour* (Kang Je-gyu, 2015).

Often scorned for having its origins in a genre imported by the Japanese occupiers, shinpa melodrama is nonetheless one of the oldest and most symbolic genres in the history of Korean cinema.

ARIRANG
THE CINEMA OF NA UN-GYU

While *Fight for Justice* (Kim Do-san, 1919) and *The Vow Made Below the Moon* (Yun Baek-nam, 1923) are said to be the origins of Korean cinema, *Arirang* (1926) is considered its founding stone. This film is inextricably linked with the legendary screenwriter, director, editor, and producer Na Un-gyu, who also acted in 27 feature films, 15 of which he directed himself.

Born on October 27, 1902, in Hoeryong, in what was to become North Korea, he was fascinated by shinpa theatre from an early age. Hav-

ing taken part in the uprising of March 1, 1919, against the Japanese occupiers, Na left to join the Korean resistance in Manchuria. During his return to Seoul, he was imprisoned from 1921 to 1923 and never fully recovered from the ill-treatment he suffered. After a stint in a theatre company in his hometown, Na Un-gyu joined the new production company Joseon Kinema Corporation in Busan to play supporting roles. He starred in the adaptation of *The Story of Shim Cheong* (Lee Gyeong-son, 1925), a pansori, and went on to co-write, co-direct, and star in the film *Bird in Cage* (Lee Gyu-seol, 1926).

The success of *Bird in Cage*, with over 100,000 spectators, enabled him to make his first feature film, *Arirang* (1926). The film tells the story (partly autobiographical) of a student driven mad by the torture he suffered in prison after taking part in the March 1, 1919, movement. He violently assaults a pro-Japanese Korean

---

A rare photograph of the crew on the set of *Arirang* (1926). The feature film, now lost, is considered one of the most important films in Korean cinema history and is a symbol of Korean resistance under Japanese occupation.

who tries to rape his sister. Finally recovering his senses after the attack, he is taken away by the police, watched helplessly by the other villagers. The film miraculously escaped censorship, because no Japanese played the villain and because the attack could be explained by the hero's "mental disorder."

Audiences were under no illusions, however, about the metaphorical significance of the story, which denounces the harsh conditions of Koreans under Japanese occupation, of a man driven mad by torture in prison, whose repressed anger is expressed in a final outburst of violence in the face of supreme injustice. The film was a triumph, selling over 150,000 tickets. It provided an excellent platform for the byeonsa, who peppered their speeches with political allusions when they managed to escape the vigilance of the officials present in the cinema, and it became an outlet for the public, who sang the patriotic song "Arirang"[1] in chorus at the end of each screening.

Arirang led to a wave of national films in the 1920s, but also caused a minor revolution in the film industry: until then, producers had mainly adapted existing, popular subjects to attract the crowds. *Arirang*'s original screenplay proved that a good story could also have an appeal for audiences. As a result, many of the films that followed offered new plots set in contemporary Korea.

Na Un-gyu, who had become a symbol of anti-Japanese resistance, dug deeper with his next film, *Soldier of Fortune* (1926)—the plot of which recalls his own years as a resistance fighter in Manchuria—with the story of a Russian-Korean soldier who returns to a devastated (unnamed) country where greed and covetousness reign. His melodrama *Goldfish* (1927), about a married man and good family man who ends up dying by suicide in prison after falling victim to the schemes of his Japanese employers, is a metaphor for the Japanese occupier as a direct threat to the Korean family unit. *Arirang 2*

(Lee Gu-yeong, 1930) and *Arirang 3* (Na Un-gyu, 1936) repeat the story as new anti-Japanese indictments.

Na Un-gyu's films did not escape censorship. The filmmaker was forced to remove certain key words from the poster of *Arirang* (1926) on the grounds of "disturbing public order." *Field Mouse* (1927) was the first case of direct Japanese intervention in the history of Korean cinema, with the outright banning of the film the day after its release. The Japanese would not tolerate the fact that the main character was a vigilante-brigand who prevented an arranged marriage between a young woman and a rich Japanese businessman. The film was released in a truncated version with a different ending.

The blockbuster involving several thousand extras—*Across Tuman River* (1928) recounted the exile of Koreans, disappointed with their life under Japanese occupation, to Manchuria; en route, they were attacked by both the Japanese army and Chinese bandits. The feature film was released under the modified title *In Search of Love* so as not to encourage viewers to attempt to "cross the Tuman River" to Manchuria, considered to be the cradle of the Korean resistance.

In addition to his patriotic films, from 1927 Na Un-gyu also tried to "make Korean films for Koreans," through his own production company, Na Un-gyu Productions. *Ok-nyeo* (1928), a triangular relationship between two brothers in love with the same woman, offered a realistic portrait of the lower social classes. *Town Across the River* (1935) denounced the social inequalities between town and country by recounting the misfortunes of a young farmer trying to make his fortune in Seoul.

The first film star, Na Un-gyu (left), directed the blockbuster *Across Tuman River* (1928) under Japanese occupation. The movie fell victim to censorship.

These two films were flops and led to the bankruptcy of Na Un-gyu's production company after only two years in business. In 1931, he incurred the wrath of public opinion by joining the Wonsanman studio, founded by the Japanese actor Mitsuru Toyama, to star in the propagandist production *A Husband Goes to the Border Garrison* (Do Jeon-jang, 1931), which encouraged Koreans to enlist in the Japanese army, and in *The Grief of Geumgan* (Na Un-gyu, 1931), in which he had a love affair with a Japanese woman.

Although Na Un-gyu re-established his image somewhat by appearing in the other flagship title of the golden age of Korean nationalist cinema, *The Ownerless Ferry Boat* (Lee Gyu-hwan, 1932), he never again achieved the success of his early work in a film industry increasingly controlled by the Japanese. Stricken with tuberculosis, he died shortly after the release of his last film, *Oh Mong-nyeo* (1937).

Arirang is now mythical because of its popularity at the time of its release, its impact on the film industry, and its disappearance. All copies are said to have disappeared, although they are still being actively sought by associations solely dedicated to this quest. Several remakes have been made over the decades: Lee Kang-cheon's 1954 version was one of the first anti-communist films, transposing the original plot from the period of occupation to the height of the Korean War, with North Korean soldiers taking the place of the Japanese. Kim So-dong's 1957 version was a faithful adaptation made to mark the twentieth anniversary of Na Un-gyu's death, with appearances by actors from the original trilogy, such as Sin Il-seon, Yim Woon-hak, and Yun Bong-chun.

In 2003, veteran director Lee Doo-yong directed a new version to mark the centenary of Na Un-gyu's birth. The filmmaker, uncomfortable with the idea of a "simple remake," created an experimental black-and-white feature film (apart from the end) in 18 frames per second,

accompanied by a soundtrack provided by a byeonsa, as a tribute to the origins of Korean cinema rather than to the film itself. This is the first feature film in the history of Korean cinema to be released simultaneously in South Korea and North Korea. Na Un-gyu was born in North Korea and is also famous there.

1. "Arirang" is a folk song that originated ten centuries ago in Jeongseon. Hummed alone or in a group during daily chores, its relatively simple tune lends itself easily to the improvisation of new lyrics to suit different situations. There are currently more than 50 versions in South and North Korea, and over 6,000 variations depending on the dialect and region. Long considered a "folk song" by the aristocracy, it became a symbol of resistance under the Japanese occupation. The version recorded for the 1926 film *Arirang*, at the height of the golden age of the gramophone, is now the "reference" version. Since 2012, the song has been included on UNESCO's Representative List of the Intangible Cultural Heritage of Humanity.

The Big Grave (1931), depicting the massacre of 5,000 Koreans by Japanese armed forces in the 1920s, miraculously got past censors but was a commercial failure.

AN INITIAL GOLDEN AGE: NATIONALIST FILMS

Korean cinema had a difficult start in the 1920s, with a fragile film industry. Producers lacked experience, technicians were insufficiently trained, infrastructures were non-existent, and filming equipment was scarce. Films were limited to a single cinema in the major cities, before a limited number of prints were circulated in certain local cinemas and in the provinces, making it difficult to achieve a return on investment.

The success of the adaptation of the famous pansori *The Story of Chun-hyang* (1923), directed by the Japanese filmmaker Koshu Hayakawa, caused a stir among Korean artists, who deplored the fact that the occupying power had appropriated a symbol of their culture. Park Sung-pil, producer of the "first film in the history of Korean cinema," *Fight for Justice* (Kim Do-san, 1919), and manager of the only Korean-owned cinema in Seoul, the Dansungsa, decided to finance the first feature film made entirely by a Korean team, *The Story of Jang-hwa and Hong-ryeon* (Kim Yeong-hwan, 1924), which became a success, with over 100,000 spectators.

In 1923, Yun Baek-nam (real name Yun Gyo-jung), director of the first fiction film, *The Vow Made Below the Moon* (1923), tried to bring together Korean professionals to create a national film industry. He encouraged them to make Korean films for Koreans, with the aim of releasing a feature film every three months to build audience loyalty.

Yun Baek-nam set an example by producing another adaptation of a pansori by Lee Gyeong-son, *The Story of Shim Cheong* (1925). The latter followed with *The Pioneer* (1925), a transposition of a novel by Lee Kwang-soo from the contemporary *shimunhak* (new literature) literary movement, and *The Captain of Bandits* (1926), a production that mixed martial arts with Japanese samurai and American action films in an attempt to appeal to a wide audience. Lee Phil-woo joined the movement by producing and directing the first transposition of a *man-wha* (Korean comic strip), *Fool* (1926).

These films were all flops, running up against the divide between audiences in the different cinemas, with Koreans refusing to watch Japanese-inspired subjects and Japanese viewers showing absolutely no interest in works based on "local" culture. Only American productions attracted all audiences, accounting for more than three-quarters of total admissions. Lee Gu-yeong and Lee Gyeong-son therefore set about making *The Twin Jade Pavilion* (1925) for Korean audiences and *Eternal Love of Su-il and Sun-ae* (1926) for Japanese audiences. These films were indeed successful but provoked the anger of their colleagues in the Korean film industry for daring to draw their subject matter from a typically Japanese genre rather than seeking to create a "distinct local cinema."

The success of *Arirang* (Na Un-gyu, 1926) launched what would eventually be dubbed the first golden age of Korean cinema, with 80 feature films shot between 1926 and 1937 out of a total of 153 made between 1923 and 1945. A new generation of filmmakers set about producing a series of sociorealist films that reflected the society of the time, making "Korean films for Koreans." Kim Tae-jin directed *An Ox Without Horn* (1927) and *Be a Winner, Sun-i* (1930), both meticulously depicting the difficulties of life in the countryside under Japanese occupation.

Yun Bong-chun's first film, *The Robber* (1930), depicted a young Korean forced to steal from his own parents to avoid starving to death, followed by *The Big Grave* (1931), a reconstruction of the historical episode of the massacre of 5,000 Koreans by the Japanese armed forces in Manchuria in the early 1920s. Both films were flops.

Hwang Un directed the ambitious docudrama *The Pitiful People* (1932) with over 1,500 extras. This adaptation of a true story—a man sinks into madness after being unfairly dismissed from a fertilizer factory—denounced the difficult conditions of Korean workers under the Japanese occupation. Unfortunately, the film was heavily censored by the authorities.

The period also saw the emergence of the first film collective in the history of Korean cinema, the KAPF (Korean Artist Proletarian Federation), which questioned the primary function of cinema. Its members denounced the films of Na Un-gyu and other Korean filmmakers as mere entertainment intended solely for the cultural elite. In their view, cinema should, on the contrary, reflect society and serve to create class consciousness.

The KAPF began by showing "educational" films in remote rural areas to "educate" workers and peasants. Its members went on to make a handful of sociorealist films, including *The Dark Road* (Gang Ho, 1929), a portrait of farmers ruined by Japanese reforms; *Underground Village* (Gang Ho, 1930), which depicts the help given by city dwellers to workers to set up a trade union; and *Fire Wheel* (Kim Yu-yeong, 1931), which tells the story of a former activist who, after his release from prison, organizes a factory strike with his friends to denounce the difficult working conditions of the time.

These films, which have unfortunately disappeared, are said to have been of mediocre quality due to the lack of technical equipment and filmmakers' know-how. Released only during tours organized in remote villages, they offered no real return on investment. Censorship seriously curtailed most of these films, and

even banned them, as in the case of *Fire Wheel*. The Japanese colonial government eventually arrested several members for "disturbing the peace," leading to the dissolution of the collective in the early 1930s. Some members agreed to make propaganda films as a way of "repenting," while others joined North Korea after the division of the country in 1948.

Among the national films that followed in the footsteps of *Arirang*, *The Ownerless Ferry Boat* (Lee Gyu-hwan, 1932) became another symbol of resistance from this period. The story follows a father (Na Un-gyu) who raises his daughter alone and loses all his fortune in Seoul, the occupied capital. He leaves to rebuild his life in the countryside by becoming a boatman. When the Japanese build a bridge that threatens to put him out of work again, he loses his mind and tries to destroy it. He is hit by a train, while his daughter dies in a house fire. The film resonated with audiences just as much as *Arirang* had a few years earlier, but this time the Japanese quickly banned it from being shown

to prevent any public disturbance. The film was re-released in a fundamentally truncated version and with a happy ending.

During the 1930s, increasingly strict censorship finally got the better of nationalist films. Enthusiasm for local productions did not wane, however, particularly following the huge success of the first talking film, *The Story of Chunhyang* (Lee Myeong-u, 1935), promoted by one of the pioneers of Korean cinema: Lee Philwoo. The director, editor, and cinematographer was so fascinated by the broadcast of the first American talking film in Korea, *Paramount on Parade* (Collective, 1930), that he left to study sound recording techniques in China and Japan

---

Previous page spread: *Sweet Dream* (Yang Ju-nam, 1936).

Crossroads of Youth (1934) was intended to be the first talking film in Korean cinema but was eventually released as a silent movie due to the poor quality of the sound recordings.

between 1930 and 1933. *The Story of Chun-hyang*, directed by his brother Lee Myeong-u, was therefore the fruit of his knowledge acquired abroad. The film's success led to other talkies, such as *Sweet Dream* (Yang Ju-nam, 1936), *Arirang 3* (Na Un-gyu, 1936), and *The Story of Shim-cheong* (Ahn Seok-yeong, 1937).

The tightening of censorship in 1937 marked the definitive end of the first golden age of Korean cinema. A new generation of Japanese-trained directors decided to work more closely with the occupying power in an attempt to find other ways of consolidating the Korean film industry.

Wanderer (1937), the first official co-production with Japan's Shinko Kinema studios, was celebrated for its exceptional technical quality but also criticized for its stereotypical portrayal of Koreans.

FILMS OF LOCAL COLOR

The second half of the 1930s saw the gradual decline of nationalist film production. Although the Japanese occupiers never attempted to take complete control of the Korean film industry, their influence was palpable. With the exception of the Dansungsa cinema, all the cinemas were owned either by wealthy Japanese businessmen or by one of the three major Japanese studios of the time. In addition, most Korean films, including those by Na Un-gyu, were financed by Japanese investors, and actors and actresses from Japan began to infiltrate the film industry using Korean screen names.

The new directors of the second half of the 1930s were all born under Japanese occupation. Most of these filmmakers had been trained in Japan and sought to use their knowledge to develop the national film industry. They were looking for new sources of funding to improve the technical quality of their productions and new means of distribution to increase the return on their profits.

Bang Han-jun (*The Street Cleaner*, 1935) and Park Gi-chae (*Spring Wind*, 1935; *Heartlessness*, 1939) were the first Korean directors to team up with businessmen based in Japan rather than Korea. Although their films were technically remarkable, thanks to their higher budgets and the participation of Japanese-trained technicians, their distribution remained limited to the Korean market.

A second group of directors decided to team up with the three major Japanese studios of the time, Toho, Shochiku, and Shinko Kinema. The latter co-produced *Wanderer* (Lee Gyu-hwan, 1937), providing funds, a trained technical team, and its studios for shooting all the indoor scenes. Although this film was one of the first to be released in both a Japanese and a Korean cinema in Seoul, as well as in another cinema in Japan, it was a failure.

Subsequent co-productions, such as *Mil-

itary Train (Seo Gwang-je, 1938), produced by Toho, and *Fisherman's Fire* (An Cheol-yeong, 1938), supported by Shochiku, had a wider initial release, but this was limited to cinemas only in the neighborhoods of *zanichis* (Korean residents in Japan). These films were quickly dubbed "films of local color" (or "films of the Korean colony" or "films of the peninsula") because their stories were shot in Korea but based on the shinpa melodrama model to encourage their export. Faced with critics at the time, who complained that these productions portrayed Koreans in a stereotyped, even degrading way, the directors justified themselves by arguing that they were trying to make their country better known abroad.

With *Tuition* (1940) and *Homeless Angel* (1941), Choi In-kyu was the first director to entrust the writing of his films to Japanese scriptwriters and to include famous Japanese actors in the cast; this time, it enabled him to benefit from wider distribution, in a network of dedicated art-house cinemas in Japan. Unfortunately, these films were coldly received by Japanese audiences, who considered the vision of the Korean population in disadvantaged neighborhoods "too dark" and the tone of these productions "too melancholy."

Jeon Chang-keun took a different path: After studying cinema in China, he worked with Korean filmmakers in exile in Shanghai, and as an actor appeared in *The Patriotic Spirit* (Jeong Gi-tak, 1930) and *Yangtze River* (Lee Gyeong-son, 1931). On his return to Korea, at the start of the Second Sino-Japanese War (1937–1945), he directed the blockbuster *Miles Away from Happiness* (1941) for the Manchukuo Film Association, Asia's largest studio, specially created by the Japanese occupiers to produce educational and industrial propaganda films in Manchuria.

Miles Away from Happiness took two years to shoot and involved over 3,000 extras to tell the story of a Korean community living happily in exile in Manchuria. Jeon Chang-keun, later known for his nationalist and patriotic productions, certainly shot a pure work of propaganda, but only with the avowed aim of improving technical standards and trying to experiment with new distribution networks under the Japanese occupation to raise the profile of Korean cinema.

The Japanese government finally took control of the Korean film industry on January 1, 1940. Of the 30 films produced between 1940 and 1945, 21 were intended to support the war effort. Among the first genre films, *Garden of Victory* (Bang Han-jun, 1940) and *Volunteer* (Ahn Seok-yeong, 1941) promoted the Japanese policy of "one people united by blood," i.e., the assimilation of Koreans into the Japanese Empire.

The first official propaganda blockbuster, *Portrait of Youth* (1943), was directed by Japanese cinema veteran Shiro Toyoda. Despite having a considerable budget to finance, among other things, an impressive skiing sequence

in the Japanese mountains, the film was supplanted at the box office by another propaganda film with a much more modest budget, *Straits of Chosun* (Park Gi-chae, 1943). The failure of *Portrait of Youth* prompted Japanese producers to entrust the production of this type of film exclusively to Korean filmmakers so they could better target their audience.

Portrait of Youth, Straits of Chosun, followed by *Dear Soldier* (Bang Han-jun, 1944) and *Children of the Sun* (Choi In-kyu, 1944) all share the story of young men who are very "enthusiastic" about joining the Japanese army. These films were compulsory viewing for all Koreans of fighting age. The feature film *Our War* (Shin Kyeong-gyun, 1945) went even further, openly encouraging the conscription of the entire Korean population to support the total war effort.

Choi In-kyu's *Sons of the Sky* and *Love and Pledge* encouraged Koreans to become kamikaze pilots to sacrifice themselves for their "dear Japanese Motherland." These films were released a few weeks before August 15, 1945, the date of the Japanese surrender and the end of the Korean occupation.

Homeless Angel (1941) was the first Korean-Japanese co-production to be released on a large scale in Japanese cinemas. The film paints a bleak portrait of Korea under Japanese occupation.

Following page spread: *Miles Away from Happiness* (Jeon Chang-keun, 1941).

정착기

1945
1960

1945-1960
THE FOUNDATIONS OF KOREAN CINEMA

August 15, 1945 marked the end of World War II, but above all the end of the Japanese occupation of Korea. The country had been bled dry, while a new conflict loomed, with the division of land between the American forces south of the thirty-eighth parallel and the Soviet forces to the north. As for the few film infrastructures, they were almost entirely destroyed; most of the filming equipment had disappeared and film was in short supply.

However, ten days after liberation, cinemas reopened and the former Japanese exhibitors were replaced by Koreans, although no one knew what to show, or how. Some decided to rerun the rare Korean classics that had survived the war, while others showed old copies of imported foreign films, recalling byeonsa to accompany the screenings. Theatre groups revived kino drama while awaiting possible regulation of cinema exhibition.

The Americans began importing films on a massive scale—they showed over 400 feature films between 1945 and 1948—including many classics such as *In Old Chicago* (Henry King, 1937), *You Can't Take It with You* (Frank Capra, 1938), *Suspicion* (Alfred Hitchcock, 1941), and *Casablanca* (Michael Curtiz, 1942). They saw cinema as a means of educating Koreans about Western values, without taking into account the possible reticence of the population, raised on Confucian values, toward certain subjects such as crime, corruption, adulterous relationships, or capitalist greed. Ironically, most film prints passed through American-occupied Japan before arriving in Korea, worn and damaged and with Japanese subtitles.

In April and October 1946, the Americans finally introduced a series of regulations that abolished most of the bans imposed by the Japanese, while maintaining the authorization required for any film to be shown, in addition to the obligation of a double review, when the script was read and before the theatrical release for any new production.

The first signs of the future revival of Korean cinema came in the form of nine-minute short documentaries. The day after liberation, director Lee Byung-il took advantage of the general confusion to seize the rare film material still stored in the premises of the Choson Film Company, the former Japanese film institution. Between 1945 and 1948, along with other Korean technicians and filmmakers, he filmed scenes from the daily lives of his compatriots. To bear witness to the situation in the liberated country, the scenes were broadcast under the name *Liberation News* throughout the country (including the future North) as well as in Korean communities in Japan and the United States.

Some of the older generation of filmmakers returned to the cinema in 1946. Lee Gu-yeong directed the very first post-war feature film, *The Chronicle of An Jung-geun* (1946), the prelude to a series of biographical adaptations that sought to honor the emblematic figures of the Korean resistance and bear witness to the determination of the Korean people in their struggle for independence under Japanese occupation. A new generation of filmmakers, some of them trained in Japan, tried to diversify genres, such as Kim So-dong, director of the first talking horror film in 16mm, *Mok-dan Ghost Story* (1947).

After the division of the country in 1948, Rhee Syngman (1948–1960), president of the Republic of Korea (South), decreed a new series of laws for the cinema. The first of these prohibited "the broadcasting of any film with blurred images and imperfect sound," forcing producers to review technical standards that were often inadequate. Many Korean films of the time were still shot without sound and with 16mm hand-cranked cameras, whose haphazard handling led to problems with the film's running speed and caused blurred sequences.

The second rule prohibited any film that was not considered "artistic" or "reflective of the country's development," which opened up a number of possibilities for the censors. Despite these constraints, around 50 feature films were released between 1946 and 1950, including: *The Rose of Sharon* (An Cheol-yeong, 1948) and *A Diary of a Woman* (Hong Seong-ki, 1949), respectively the first documentary and the first feature-length fiction film in color; *The Blue Hill* (Yu Dong-il, 1949), the first musical, and *Pilot An Chang-nam* (No Pil, 1949), the first film to include aerial sequences. *A Fellow Soldier* (Hong Gae-myeong, 1949) marked the beginning of anti-communist films.

The start of the Korean War on June 25, 1950, brought the development of cinema to an abrupt halt. The United States mobilized a total of 1.8 million troops and attached great importance to film coverage of the conflict. They set up several departments across the country, some of which were coordinated by experienced directors such as Ahn Jong-hwa and Lee Phil-woo. Lee Gu-yeong directed the documentary *The Once Beautiful Seoul* (1950), and Yun Bong-chun *The Western Front* (1950) and *The Footmarks of the Barbarian* (1951). With *Assault on Justice 1* (1951), Han Hyung-mo made one of the most famous films, still studied to this day in Korean schools to understand the issues of the Korean War.

The filming of these documentaries and news reports trained a new generation of future technicians and directors, including Shin Sang-ok. The film industry moved from the capital, Seoul, which had been occupied by the North Koreans, to other major cities in South Korea: in 1951, *A Bouquet of Thirty Million People* (Shin Kyeong-gyun) was shot in Masan; in 1952, *Nakdong River* (Jeon Chang-keun) was shot in Busan; and in Daegu, *The Evil Night* (Shin Sang-ok), *The Night of Horror* (Son Jeon), and *The Street of Sun* (Min Kyoung-sik). The 17 feature-length fiction films made between 1950 and 1953 were either anti-communist or shinpa melodramas focusing on the conflict and the misfortunes of Koreans. Several major

---

Previous page: *A Hometown in My Heart* (Yun Yong-gyu, 1949).

정착기

directors, such as Choi In-kyu, Lee Myeong-u, and Park Gi-chae, were kidnapped by the North Koreans and many of the rare copies of pre-war films that still existed were destroyed in the renewed bombardments.

The conflict ended with the signing of an armistice on July 27, 1953, marking the end of the fighting but not the end of the war, which continues to be a reality. The fighting caused more than 3 million deaths and as many refugees. The peninsula was devastated, with over 70 percent of Seoul destroyed. Korea became one of the poorest countries in the world.

However, film production resumed as soon as the conflict ended, with around 15 feature films shot in 1954 and 1955. In 1956, President Rhee Syngman announced tax exemptions to encourage producers to reinvest in the industry. This measure, and the subsequent successes of *The Story of Chun-hyang* (Lee Gyu-hwan, 1955) and *Madame Freedom* (Han Hyung-mo, 1956), heralded the beginnings of a remarkable revival, with film production rising from 15 films in 1955 to 111 in 1959.

Troops of the First US Cavalry Division pass jubilant Koreans north of Seoul, October 1950.

LIBERATION FILMS

After the end of the Japanese occupation of Korea on August 15, 1945, three former directors quickly revived the film industry with two types of film: the liberation film, dedicated to the great figures of the resistance under the Japanese occupation, and the enlightenment film, to raise public awareness of the country's reconstruction.

Hurrah! For Freedom (Choi In-kyu, 1946) is often considered to be the very first film to be released after the occupation, no doubt because of its title and the fact that it has survived to the present day, even though it is in fact the third feature film to be distributed in cinemas. It marks a kind of "redemption for good behavior" for Choi In-kyu, director of the propaganda works *Sons of the Sky* and *Love and Pledge* in 1945, by telling the story of a fictitious Korean resistance fighter who plans an attack in the final days of the Japanese occupation. The film was a huge success, with over 150,000 viewers.

Today, only an incomplete 53-minute version of the original 100 minutes still exists. Rumor has it that the film was still complete when it was re-released in 1976, to commemorate the thirtieth anniversary of the country's liberation, but that it was censored by Park Chung-hee's regime, cutting out all the scenes involving two actors who had joined North Korea after the country's division.

The first real post-war feature film, *The Chronicle of An Jung-geun* (Lee Gu-yeong, 1946), retraced the life of the Korean independence militant, famous for having assassinated Ito Hirobumi, governor of occupied Korea, in 1909, before the annexation. This film is at the origin of a series of biographical adaptations of the great figures of the resistance, which seek to forge the national identity of a country in the midst of reconstruction.

Yun Bong-gil, the Martyr (Yun Bong-chun, 1947) tells the story of the activist who detonated a bomb at Emperor Hirohito's celebration on April 29, 1932, killing several high-ranking Japanese dignitaries. *Yu Gwan-sun* (Yun Bong-chun, 1948) was adapted from the biography of a schoolgirl known as the Korean Joan of Arc who, having lost her parents during the independence movement of March 1, 1919, organized peaceful marches across the country before being arrested and dying in prison on September 28, 1920, as a result of torture. This film was adapted several times, again by Yun Bong-chun in 1959 and 1966, and by Kim Kee-duk in 1974.

The liberation film experienced a revival after the Korean War with the rise of anti-Japanese sentiment, encouraged by President Rhee Syngman. It was one of the main themes of his policies between 1956 and 1960. In fact, the president extolled his own—albeit, in reality, only limited—role in the fight against the Japanese in the commissioned film *Rhee Syngman and the Independence Movement* (Shin Sang-ok, 1959), released just before the 1960 presidential elections.

The success of the blockbuster *King Gojong and Martyr An Jung-geun* (Jeon Chang-keun, 1959), which brought together several thousand extras, kick-started a series of big-budget historical dramas about resistance fighters. These included *The Daehan Empire and Min Yeong-hwan* (also known as *A Blood Bamboo*, Yun Bong-chun and Nam Hong-il, 1959) and *Nameless Stars* (Kim Gang-yun, 1959), a spectacular account of the student demonstrations in Gwangju against the Japanese occupiers in 1929.

The liberation film has gradually given way to modern melodramas based on the tragedies of ordinary people in the post-war period in Korea and the rest of the world. Nevertheless, there have been several recent films about resistance fighters on their birthdays: *Yu Gwan-sun* (Jo Min-ho, 2019) pays tribute to the hundredth anniversary of the tragic death of the Korean Joan of Arc, while the film adaptation of the

popular stage musical *Hero* (JK Youn, 2022) celebrates the 150th anniversary of the birth of An Jung-Geun.

A sub-genre of the liberation film of the immediate post-war period is the enlightenment film, which aims to raise public awareness of the need for collective reconstruction of the country. It was inspired by the *narodniki* agrarian socialist movement, founded by Russian populists at the end of the nineteenth century with the aim of educating and helping peasants in remote rural areas.

This concept, promoted by the famous resistance writer Yi Kwang-su after the relaxation of Japanese censorship in 1919, inspired the activist Shim Hoon: imprisoned for his participation in the March 1, 1919, movement, he became a writer and even an actor, replacing the lead actor at short notice in the film *Eternal Love of Su-il and Sun-ae* (Lee Gyeong-son, 1926). Shim Hoon also directed one of the jewels of the golden age of nationalist cinema, *At Daybreak* (1927).

In 1935, Shim Hoon published *Evergreen Tree,* the story of a young teacher and an educator who went to the countryside to teach. This novel is truly the origin of the illumination trend in Korean literature and cinema. Shim Hoon had planned to bring his novel to the screen, but died of typhoid fever in 1936 at the age of 35. Shin Sang-ok and Im Kwon-taek each made a version, unfortunately for propaganda purposes, in 1961 and 1978, under the title *The Evergreen Tree*.

The enlightenment genre inspired a series of films, such as *My Liberated Country* (Jeon Chang-keun, 1947), which tells the story of a former prisoner under Japanese occupation who returns home to help rebuild his native village, and *A New Oath* (Shin Kyeong-gyun, 1947), which follows three ex-prisoners who help revive the economy of a fishing community (marrying, in the process, three local damsels for a happy ending).

Dawn of Nation (1947) was one of a series of so-called liberation films celebrating the end of the Japanese occupation.

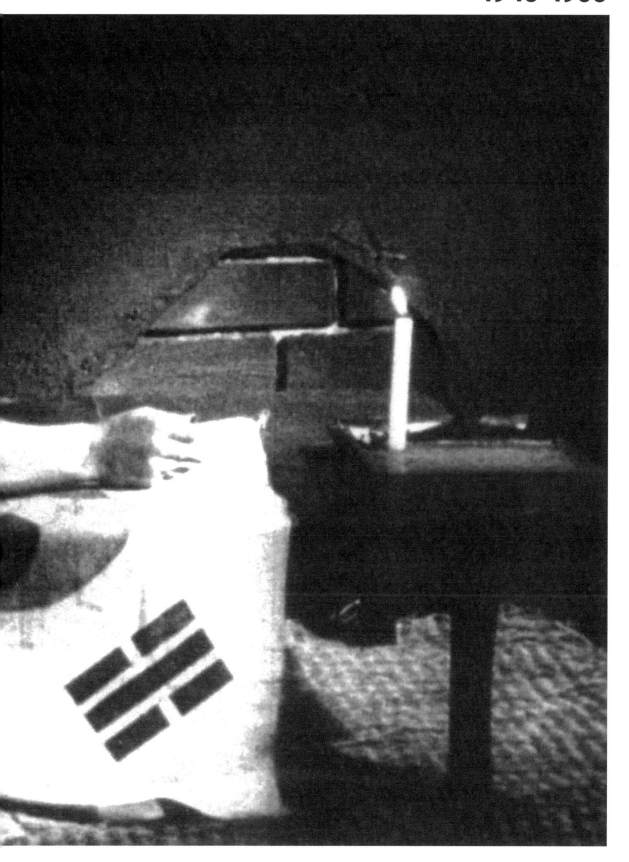

The orphans film—a sub-genre of the enlightenment film—seeks to raise awareness of the tragic plight of the 2 million children living alone. *The Angel Heart* (Kim Jeong-hwan, 1947) encourages viewers to support the orphanage centers set up throughout the country. *A Seagull* (Lee Gyu-hwan, 1948), a true masterpiece of cinema from this period, paints a particularly realistic portrait of a woman who defies all challenges (and the advances of her many suitors) to help abandoned children.

The enlightenment film was still in evidence in the 1950s, with major works such as *The Street of Sun* (Min Kyoung-sik, 1952), a neorealist melodrama shot on location in a slum on the outskirts of Seoul, where a man improvises as a teacher to educate the children. *Nakdong River* (Jeon Chang-keun, 1952) and *Light of Hometown* (Jang Hwang-yeon, 1953) take up the theme of characters who return to their native village to take part in collective reconstruction.

The enlightenment film genre was gradually supplanted by that of modern melodramas, before a brief period of revival in the 1970s, serving as a propaganda tool for Park Chung-hee's policies, with productions such as *Soil* (Kim Ki-young, 1978); since then, this genre has completely disappeared from Korean film production.

Previous page spread: *Hurrah! For Freedom* (1946) was the third film—and not the first, as is often stated—to be released in Korean cinemas after liberation. Its emblematic title makes it a true symbol of this period and perfectly encapsulates the sentiments of Koreans at the time.

HISTORICAL FILMS

The resounding triumph in 1955 of the third adaptation of *The Story of Chun-hyang* (Lee Gyu-hwan), a pansori, with more than 180,000 admissions, followed by the success of *Yangsan Province* (Kim Ki-young, 1955), *Sad Story of a Head Cutter* (Kim Seong-min, 1955), and *The Wedding Day* (Lee Byung-il, 1957) led to a craze for historical films in Korea, which in 1959 accounted for more than half of the 111 films produced. It was one of the leading genres of the 1960s and remains extremely popular, having produced some of the greatest successes of contemporary Korean cinema.

The first historical films of the second half of the 1950s were adaptations of popular novels and plays. They helped shape national identity by reminding Korean audiences of the glorious empire of the great kingdoms. They are nicknamed "royal court films" and are, for the most part, dialogue heavy, set behind closed doors to avoid the high cost of sets and costumes.

These films, shot in 16mm with post-synchronized sound, suffered in comparison with the American blockbusters of the same period, shot in 35mm or 70mm, CinemaScope, and Technicolor. Producers reacted swiftly with the release of *The Princess Seon-hwa* (Choe Sung-kwan, 1957), the very first Korean 35mm film in color, *Life* (Lee Kang-cheon, 1957) in CinemaScope format, *The 12-Stringed Instrument* (Gwon Yeong-sun, 1964) in stereophonic sound, *A Man of Great Strength: Im Gyeok-jeong*, 1968) in 3D, and *The Love Story of Chun-hyang* (Lee Seong-gu, 1971) in 70mm.

But the success of American blockbusters with even more colossal budgets, such as *The Ten Commandments* (Cecil B. DeMille, 1956) and *Ben-Hur* (William Wyler, 1959), prompted Korean producers in turn to make blockbusters with thousands of extras. *King Gojong and Martyr An Jung-geun* (Jeon Chang-keun, 1959), a liberation

film with a colossal budget of 72 million hwans, marked the genre's definitive transition toward large-scale historical epics. *The Way of Hwarang* (Jang Il-ho, 1962) thus became the first Korean film to feature 10,000 extras, 300 horses, and 50 boats; and *King Jin-shi and the Great Wall of China* (Gwon Yeong-sun, 1962), a production that brought together 120,000 (!) extras and re-created the Great Wall of China, with a set 33 meters high.

The historical film quickly became synonymous with grand spectacle, attracting ever-increasing audiences. The producers soon found themselves overwhelmed by the inflation of their own budgets. Faced with this situation, they agreed with cinema exhibitors to concentrate the release of historical blockbusters during the main holiday periods—New Year, Korean (Lunar) New Year, and Harvest Festival—to attract as many admissions as possible and try to make a return on their investments. This practice is still in use today, with the release of the main blockbusters concentrated during these periods alone.

The production of historical films reached its peak between 1960 and 1969, with over 250 feature-length films made during this period alone. However, the genre declined in the second half of the decade, as audiences tired of repetitive formulas and turned their attention to new film genres. The phenomenal success of the first two *James Bond* features led to a wave of spy films, with the 1966 releases of titles such as *The International Spy* and *The International Gold Bar Incident* (Jang Il-ho, 1965 and 1966), which replaced the historical film in the coveted holiday slot for the first time.

Considered to be the greatest director and producer of the decade, Shin Sang-ok sought to respond to the decline in public interest. He began his career with two so-called classic historical films, *Dream* (1955) and *The Youth* (1955),

---

The Street of Sun (1952) was a feature-length film made during the Korean War and a flagship "enlightenment film" of the liberation period.

before contributing to the golden age of Korean cinema with the blockbusters, shot in Cinema-Scope and Technicolor, *Prince Yeonsan* (1962) and its sequel, *Tyrant Yeonsan* (1962). Additionally, he made *Seong Chun-hyang* (1961), which became the biggest success in the history of Korean cinema at the time, with 380,000 admissions. Shin Sang-ok reacted to the decline of this period by making the first direct sound film, *Monarch* (1968), which enabled the real voice of the star of the time, Kim Ji-mi, to be heard for the first time.

As this technological advantage alone was no longer enough to move the crowds, Shin Sang-ok sought to diversify the genre with a series of adaptations of Asian legends, such as *The Snake Woman* (1969) and *A Thousand-Year-Old Fox* (1969). He also tried to compete with the Westerns and martial arts films in vogue at the time, incorporating more violence and sex into his films. His efforts paid off with the triumph of *The Eunuch* (1968), one of the biggest hits of the decade, with 320,000 spectators. Even so, the film earned him an arrest for "outraging public decency" because of the excessive number of nude shots.

The historical film suffered a definitive decline in the 1970s, becoming a mere propaganda tool under Park Chung-hee's regime. From then on, the genre celebrated either great historical figures, such as General Yi Sun-sin in *Admiral Lee Sun-shin* (Lee Kyu-woong, 1971) and *Diary of War* (Jang Il-ho, 1978) to encourage national patriotism, or the political regime by comparing, for example, the modernization of Korea in the 1970s to the golden age of the reign of the fourth Joseon king in *Tripitaka Korean* (Jang Il-ho, 1978).

During the 1970s and 1980s, the historical film moved to the small screen, in the form of popular television series with several hundred episodes. In the cinema, it served only as a backdrop for low-budget erotic productions. The rare attempts to revive the genre in the 1990s, such

as *Eternal Empire* (Park Jong-won, 1994), ended in failure.

Television series were soon in decline too, with the end of the cult 800-episode production *500 Years of the Joseon Dynasty* (Lee Byung-hun, 1983–1990); but a new wave of more dynamic franchises, such as *Tears of the Dragon* (159 episodes, Kim Jae-hyung, 1996–1998), *Hur Jun* (64 episodes, Lee Byung-hoon, 1999-2000), and *Emperor Wang Gun* (200 episodes, Kim Jong-sun, 2000-2002), are revitalizing the genre and attracting new interest from a younger audience.

The worldwide success of *Crouching Tiger, Hidden Dragon* (Ang Lee, 2000) finally prompted the Korean producers to try their hand at the big screen again. *The Legend of Gingko* (Park Jae-hyun, 2000), *Bichunmoo* (Kim Young-jun, 2000), and *The Warrior* (Kim Sung-soo, 2001) had encouraging initial results, before the triumph of *Untold Scandal* (Lee Je-yong, 2003), with over 3 million admissions, and above all the triumph of *The King and the Clown* (Lee Joon-ik, 2005), with over 12 million spectators.

The revival of the 2000s was characterized by a diversification of genres within the historical film category: comedy in *Once Upon a Time in a Battlefield* (Lee Joon-ik, 2003) and *A Tale of Legendary Libido* (Shin Han-sol, 2008); eroticism in *Forbidden Quest* (Kim Dae-woo, 2006) and *Empire of Lust* (Ahn Sang-hoon, 2015); fantasy in *Jeon Woo-chi: The Taoist Wizard / Woochi: The Demon Slayer* (Choi Dong-hoon, 2009); and horror in *Monstrum* (Huh Jong-ho, 2018) and *Rampant* (Kim Sung-hoon, 2018).

The triumph of *The Admiral: Roaring Currents* (Kim Han-min, 2014), the biggest hit in the history of Korean cinema to date, with 17.6 million viewers, triggered a new wave of large-scale historical blockbusters, recalling the golden age

The King and the Clown (2005) was a historical in the Korean film revival of the early 2000s.

of the genre in the 1960s; but the failure of block-busters *Kundo* (Yoon Jong-bin, 2014), *Warriors of the Dawn* (Jeong Yoon-chul, 2017), *The Fortress* (Hwang Dong-hyuk, 2017), and *The Great Battle* (Kim Kwang-sik, 2018) sowed doubts among producers, who were once again reluctant to continue investing in this expensive genre. The Covid-19 pandemic put a temporary end to their cogitations by completely freezing production of the genre for two years.

MADAME FREEDOM— THE CINEMA OF HAN HYUNG-MO

While *The Story of Chun-hyang* (Lee Gyu-hwan, 1955) evoked the Korea of the past and triggered a wave of historical films, *Madame Freedom* (Han Hyung-mo, 1956) marked the beginning of the transition to modernity, both in form and content, and the origins of the flagship genre of modern melodrama.

Han Hyung-mo was born on April 29, 1917, in Uiju, in the province of North Pyongan. After studying art in Manchuria, he became a set designer on *Homeless Angel* (Choi In-kyu, 1941), before leaving to train at the Japanese Toho studios. On his return to Korea, he convinced Choi In-kyu to resume directing and became his chief operator on two propaganda films, *Children of the Sun* (1944) and *Love and Pledge* (1945). At the end of World War II, he worked on the liberation films *Hurrah! For Freedom!* (Choi In-kyu, 1946) and *A Hometown in My Heart* (Yun Yong-gyu, 1949), before directing the most famous documentary on the Korean War, *Assault on Justice 1* (1951).

Han Hyung-mo was a true pioneer of post-war Korean cinema. In 1949, he directed *Breaking Through the Wall,* one of the first two anti-communist films, along with *A Fellow Soldier* (Hong Gae-myeong, 1949). *The Hand of Destiny* (1954) was one of the first crime films in the history of Korean cinema and the very first

to include an on-screen kissing scene. *Hyperbola of Youth* (1957) was the first comedy, along-side *The Wedding Day* (Lee Byung-il, 1957). *The Devil* (1957) was the very first thriller, and *A Jealousy* (1960) the first film to feature a love story between two women.

While Han Hyung-mo was partly responsible for the diversification of cinematic genres, he also contributed to the improvement of many technical aspects, thanks to his exceptional sense of lighting and framing in films such as *Hurrah! For Freedom* and *An Innocent Criminal* (Choi In-kyu, 1946 and 1948). *A Hometown in My Heart* is a veritable masterpiece of technical ingenuity, having required different types of lighting depending on the scenes shot, using scraps of Kodak, Fuji, or Agfa film with different sensitivities. *Breaking Through the Wall*, shot entirely with a hand-cranked camera, is famous for its perfect image stability.

From *Hyperbola of Youth* onward, Han Hyung-mo preferred to work in the studio to better control the lighting. He transformed an old railway station, destroyed during World War II, into a film set equipped with a ceiling light to avoid cast shadows. For *Madame Freedom,* the director had the first dolly in the history of Korean cinema built, based on simple illustrations gleaned from foreign film magazines. This camera support on wheels and rails enabled him to make, for the time, particularly fluid movements during filming. He also built a homemade crane to film the many dance scenes from a height.

Although Han Hyung-mo's early films were already of high quality, *Madame Freedom* represented a veritable revolution in Korean cinema, both in form and content. It was adapted from an extremely popular serial novel, published daily in 215 chapters in the newspaper *The Seoul Shinmun* between January 1 and August 6, 1954. The series caused a scandal because it dealt for the first time, and without taboos, with some of the consequences of the

massive influx of women from the surrounding countryside into the labor market in the 1950s to fill jobs left vacant by men who had fallen in the war.

Madame Freedom tells the story of the devoted wife of an illustrious university professor who accepts a job as a salesgirl in a boutique selling Western luxury goods. She discovers a hitherto unknown world: that of cafés, restaurants, and dance halls, where she does not long remain unmoved by the charms of her dance partner.

This resolutely contemporary film, which was a historic success with over 150,000 admissions, makes a profound change to the melodrama genre, abandoning the usual shinpa borrowings for more modern American influences. The usual subject of post-war woes is replaced this time by that of a middle-class Seoul family anchored in the modern world.

Han Hyung-mo continued to explore the theme of the free woman in most of his other films. In *The Pure Love* (1957), a young single woman stops at nothing to seduce a painter in a seaside resort. *A Female Boss* (1959) introduces the character of a flippant fashion magazine editor who rules her staff with an iron fist, including an attractive new employee. *My Sister Is a Hussy* (1961), the daughter of a judo teacher literally puts down all her suitors. Female audiences were fascinated by these portraits of strong women—and also by those of the men who were totally powerless in the face of this sudden emancipation.

The moral of Han Hyung-mo's films remains "safe," however, and might even shock modern viewers who fail to take account of the

---

In the tradition of modern comedies and melodramas, *A Female Boss* (1959) features strong women characters within "patriarchal morality."

historical context of Confucian society at the time: In *Madame Freedom,* for example, the heroine begs (on her knees!) her husband's forgiveness for "deserting the home"; the final sequence of *A Female Boss* shows the manager, so mischievous throughout the film, preparing dinner in traditional dress to welcome her former colleague who has become both her husband and the boss of her own former magazine. And in *My Sister Is a Hussy*, the judoka swaps her sports outfit for a *hanbok* to play the devoted wife at the end of the film.

Han Hyung-mo thus mischievously questions the profound changes in the society of his time, while remaining extremely attached to traditional Confucian values, even if these "morally acceptable" ends were undoubtedly motivated by the fear of possible censorship.

Curiously, Han Hyung-mo, who was so renowned for his incredible gift for innovation and diversification, was unable to adapt to the major changes in the Korean film industry in the 1960s and was quickly supplanted by a new generation of directors, such as Shin Sang-ok, Yu Hyun-mok, and Kim Ki-young. The image of the free woman, which he had helped to create, was quickly replaced by that of the good wife, sometimes strong-willed but always devoted to the father of the family, in the family dramas of the 1960s.

Han Hyung-mo tried his hand at various fashionable genres, such as the family drama with *A Dream of Fortune* (1961), the historical epic with *Prince Hodong* (1962), and the musical with *Let's Meet at Walkerhill* (1966) and *The Queen of Elegy* (1967), but the repeated failure of these productions prompted him to take early retirement at the end of the 1960s. As for *Madame Freedom,* the film saw a (mediocre) sequel in 1957, directed by Kim Hwa-rang, as well as a series of remakes by Kang Dae-jin in 1969, by Park Ho-tae in 1981 and 1986, and by Park Jae-ho in 1990, without anyone ever managing to match the genius of the original.

The original poster for *Madame Freedom* (1956), one of the most emblematic films of Korean cinema. The lettering was in *hanja* (Chinese characters), not in hangeul, as it is today.

MODERN MELODRAMAS

The success of Han Hyung-mo's *Madame Freedom* (1956) not only contributed to the revival of Korean cinema in the 1950s, it also gave birth to one of the most important genres in the history of Korean cinema: the modern melodrama. The Korean equivalent of Japanese shinpa melodramas, it anchors its tragic stories more firmly in contemporary Korean society. Whereas shinpa melodramas often feature an ethical dilemma based on the difference in social classes between the characters—for example, a courtesan falling in love with an upper-class man—modern melodrama focuses more on the personal desires of the characters, such as the female characters' quest for emancipation and freedom. This genre accounted for more than half of film production from the 1950s to the 1970s.

Melodrama is an artistic movement that originated in nineteenth-century popular theatre, combining tragedy, comedy, and drama. It is characterized by an emphatic style, an exaggeration of emotions, and a simplification of dramatic devices to create artificially tragic situations, with the aim of appealing to the sensibilities and emotions of the audience. *Orphans of the Storm* (David Wark Griffith, 1921) marked the definitive transition of melodrama from theatre to cinema.

Although the beginnings of Korean cinema under the Japanese occupation were influenced by shinpa melodramas, the massive import of American films after 1945 rapidly developed the genre, imbuing Korean cinema with the codes of classic melodramas such as *Sunset Boulevard* (Billy Wilder, 1950), *From Here to Eternity* (Fred Zinnemann, 1953) and *A Star Is Born* (George Cukor, 1954), followed by the flamboyant *All That Heaven Allows* (Douglas Sirk, 1955), *An Affair to Remember* (Leo McCarey, 1957), and *Some Came Running* (Vincente Minnelli, 1958).

Unlike the Americans, who even then saw their cinema as an export product that miti-gated the negative aspects of their culture and their country, the Koreans began by drawing on the misfortunes and difficulties of the post-war period and the division. *Melodrama* therefore enabled them, at first, to translate into images their extreme sense of helplessness in a ravaged country.

Many of the screenplays of the 1950s were set around the tragic day of June 25, 1950, the date on which the Korean War began. Couples were often separated by the enlistment of the main male character as a soldier, *The Everlasting Love* (Min Kyoung-sik, 1955); by panic when the population went into exile, *The Unforgettable People* (Yu Jae-won, 1957); or by the kidnapping of one or other of the protagonists by North Korean soldiers, *Where to Go* (Kim Seong-min, 1958). Other films explore the consequences of war, with a female character struggling to provide for her family while awaiting the eventual return of her husband, *The River of Temptation* (Yu Du-yeon, 1958). Sometimes the lovers manage to reunite, *Land of Love* (Kim Seong-min, 1954), but most of the time the man has (re)married, leaving his fiancée or wife in misfortune, *Mother* (Jeong Il-taek, 1959).

Most of these melodramas are still influenced by the shinpa movement, with female characters torn between happiness and sacrifice. *Madame Freedom*, in 1956, represented a decisive transition toward modern melodrama, tackling taboo subjects such as feminism, marriage, and adultery for the first time, while at the same time criticizing traditional Korean society and its rigid social norms.

The success of *Madame Freedom* thus led to a wave of modern melodramas, including *Wife and Mistress* (Kim Seong-min, 1957), *A Woman's War* (Kim Ki-young, 1957), and *Wild Chrysanthemum* (Lee Yong-min, 1957). Hong Seong-ki quickly forged a reputation as the father of modern melodrama, with the success of *The Star in My Heart* and *Over the Mountain and Sea* (both 1958), respectively first and fourth

1945–1960

at the box office that year. His *Lover* (1956) and *A Youth's Theatre* (1959), aimed at a younger audience, foreshadowed the youth films of the second half of the 1960s.

Hong Seong-ki's success declined at the end of the 1950s with the emergence of a new generation of directors, including Shin Sang-ok, who made a series of melodramas based on the character of the strong woman rather than the devoted mistress, such as *Confessions of a College Student* (1958), *It's Not Her Sin* (1959), *Dongshimcho* (1959), and *Sister's Garden* (1959). Shin Sang-ok also, for the first time, gave a central place to the father character, outlining the future sub-genre of the 1960s family drama.

Contemporary melodrama remained one of the leading genres throughout the 1960s, with titles such as *Sorrow Even Up in Heaven* and *Affection* (Kim Soo-yong, 1965 and 1966) and *Six Daughters* (Bae Seok-in, 1967), all topping the box office in their year of release and ranking among the biggest hits of the decade. Melodrama also included the genres of literary, anti-communist, family, and youth films.

Most of the melodramas of the 1960s were adaptations of radio plays, soap operas, early television series or color remakes of the black-and-white films of the 1950s—a boon for producers, who not only saved on the costs of writing new scripts, but also took advantage of the established popularity of the original material to boost their chances of future success. The average budget of these productions is also 10 to 50 times lower than that of historical or war films, ensuring better profits for their investors.

Contemporary melodramas mainly target women, pejoratively nicknamed the "Handkerchief Army," because they let their tears flow in the darkness of the cinema when faced with the

tragedies of the heroines. The gradual disaffection of female cinema-goers in favor of the small screen marked the beginning of the genre's decline between 1970 and 1990.

Contemporary melodrama was reborn at the same time as Korean cinema with the success of *The Letter* (Lee Jung-gook) and *The Contact* (Chang Yoon-hyun), in 1997, and *A Promise* (Kim Yoo-jin), in 1998, which topped the box office in their respective years of release. These were romantic melodramas, modeled on the popular k-dramas (television series) of the time and often featuring actors from the small screen making their first steps on the big screen. These films also targeted younger audiences, with triangular romances and/or one of the characters suffering from an incurable disease.

Christmas in August, the third biggest hit of 1998, marked the debut of director Hur Jin-ho. He revolutionized the genre with a series of films, including *One Fine Spring Day* (2001), *April Snow* (2005), and *Happiness* (2007), which were distinguished by their unprecedented treatment of more internalized feelings and many unspoken words, rather than the exaggerated tragedy of the past. His films are among the contempo-

Even the Way Is Far Away (1960) is a melodrama of its time with characters wearing Western dress. The film is also famous for its scenes shot in France and Italy.

97

rary classics of the genre. Their popularity led to a series of other increasingly successful contemporary melodramas, such as *A Moment to Remember* (John H. Lee, 2004) with 2.5 million admissions, *You Are My Sunshine* (Park Jin-pyo, 2005) with 3 million, *Maundy Thursday* (Song Hae-seong, 2006) with 3.1 million, before the triumphs of *Miracle in Cell No.7* (Lee Hwan-kyung, 2013) with 12.8 million and *Ode to My Father* (JK Youn, 2014) with 14 million.

The genre experienced a further decline in the second half of the 2010s, with young audiences now preferring blockbuster entertainment. Contemporary melodrama nevertheless continues to exist in the form of popular TV k-dramas.

Sister's Garden (1959) was part of the first wave of blockbuster modern melodramas. Star Choi Eun-hee (left) appeared in almost all of husband-director Shin Sang-ok's films.

창의적 착시기

1960

1961

1960-1961
AN ENCHANTED CREATIVE INTERLUDE

Rhee Syngman was elected president of South Korea in 1948, with the support of the United States. However, his terms in office were marked by an authoritarian exercise of power and were confronted by numerous political and economic challenges, notably the Korean War (1950–1953) and a difficult economic situation, with a per capita gross national product that was among the lowest in the world. To avoid being outvoted by his own party, in 1952 he introduced a constitutional reform that provided for his election by direct universal suffrage rather than by the assembly.

From the outset, Rhee Syngman's government was plagued by corruption and electoral fraud. The continuing US military presence after the Korean War aroused great discontent among the population. In 1956 and 1960, constitutional reforms were introduced to guarantee Rhee Syngman's re-election once again, sparking a wave of demonstrations across the country, led by workers' and students' groups, known as the April Revolution. Under pressure from these protests, Rhee Syngman was forced to resign on April 26, 1960.

Yun Po-sun was elected president in August 1960, but his term of office was hit by an economic and social crisis that led to a military coup on May 16, 1961. General Park Chung-hee became head of the Supreme Council for National Reconstruction and dissolved the National Assembly. He was finally inaugurated president on December 17, 1963, after new general elections, establishing an authoritarian regime that lasted until his assassination in 1979.

Film production was affected by the political situation, with the number of films produced falling from 111 in 1959 to 92 in 1960, then to 86 in 1961. On the other hand, this period also saw a degree of freedom of expression for a few months, which led to the production of two genuine masterpieces: *The Housemaid* (Kim Ki-young, 1960) and *Aimless Bullet* (Yu Hyun-mok, 1961).

Kim Ki-young's *The Housemaid* was inspired by a tragic incident that took place in the 1950s. A young maid, infatuated with the father of the family, kills his two children. The director was reluctant to adapt the story for fear of censorship and began by making a trilogy in the neo-realist style, consisting of *The First Snow* (1958), *A Defiance of a Teenager* (1959), and *A Sad Pastorale* (1960), to bear witness to the problems of his time.

Kim Ki-young, increasingly moved by the challenging reality of women from impoverished rural areas who are exploited in Seoul as workers, servants, or prostitutes, finally decided to make *The Housemaid* in 1960. The film tells the story of a young maid from the countryside who seduces the master of the house before gradually destroying the family. Although the film began as a contemporary melodrama, it quickly evolved into a psychological thriller and then a horror film about a woman who will do anything to climb the social ladder.

The film is a masterpiece as a psychological thriller, but also as a profound metaphor for its time. The family home, westernized and modernized, becomes the symbol of the ambition for power of certain plebeian classes in Korea in the 1950s and 1960s. The maid, relegated to the kitchen on the ground floor, is constantly on the lookout for social advancement and tries to climb the stairs leading to the first floor where a piano is enthroned, symbolizing the social success and westernization of the bourgeois family. In this room, the father of the family spends most of his time smoking and listening to music, embodying the role of the dominant male in patriarchal Korean society.

The film was released on November 3, 1960, at a time when censorship was being relaxed under the presidency of Yun Po-sun. It became one of the biggest hits of the year, with over 100,000 tickets sold. The film held up a social mirror to its audience, arousing both support and confusion. Some female viewers admit to crying out of fear and cursing "the servant girl" on the screen. The actress Lee Eun-sim, who played the lead role, never managed to separate her image from that of her character, bringing her career to a premature end after the failure of her next films, *The Modern Grandma* (Baek Ho-bin, 1964) and *Graduation Love Class* (Lee Hyung-pyo, 1964), which were shunned by audiences because of her presence on the screen.

Kim Ki-young used the main storyline of *The Housemaid* (1960) in his later films *Fire Woman* (1971) and *Fire Woman 82* (1982). *Insect Woman* (1972) and *The Carnivorous Animal* (1984) are two other versions with subtle variations. As you look back over the years, all these films are scathing critiques of the domineering patriarchy of Korean society at the time they were made. Im Sang-soo directed an official remake, *The Housemaid,* and a variation, *The Taste of Money*, in the official competition at the Cannes Film Festival, one in 2010 and the other in 2012; while Bong Joon-ho paid a vibrant tribute to Kim Ki-young's classic with his *Parasite* (2019).

Yu Hyun-mok adopted a formal approach that is diametrically opposed to that of Kim Ki-young. After starting out with meticulously prepared studio films such as *Crossroad* (1956), *Lost Youth* (1957), and *Forever with You* (1958), he felt a visceral need to shoot a film on location in the city of Seoul, to bear witness to the political upheavals that were shaking South Korea under the presidency of Rhee Syngman. *Aimless Bullet* (1961) was shot in the midst of the president's impeachment in April 1960.

Previous page and following page spread: The *Housemaid* (1960) is now considered one of the most important Korean films of all time, inspiring generations of directors, including Bong Joon-ho for his world-famous Oscar-winning *Parasite* (2019).

The film is based on a short story by Lee Beom-seon, one of the most influential writers of the post-war period in Korea. It tells the story of a North Korean refugee family in Seoul, whose main character, an accountant, struggles to support his pregnant wife and two children. His brother, a former war veteran, is unable to reintegrate into society. His sister works as a prostitute for American soldiers and his mother suffers from post-traumatic stress disorder.

Aimless Bullet (1961) is a chilling, defeatist portrait of Korea in the 1950s—and thus of Rhee Syngman's political record. The war had shattered families: Parents had lost their loved ones and their children had returned traumatized from combat. The new generation has nothing left and is throwing itself wholeheartedly into the arms of American soldiers and westernization. The film includes numerous scenes of demonstrations and horrific views of the slums and devastated districts, with young mothers hanging with their babies under the Cheonggyecheon footbridge in the middle of a chase with the police.

When it was released on April 13, 1961, *Aimless Bullet* was a huge hit with audiences and critics alike, and was dubbed the *Citizen Kane* of Korean cinema, in homage to Orson Welles's legendary 1941 film. However, on May 16 of the same year, Park Chung-hee came to power. The film was immediately withdrawn from cinemas by the new authorities, who considered its vision of Korean society too dark. The censors accused Yu Hyun-mok of pro-communism for having created the character of the traumatized mother, whose repeated incantations of "Let's go" would encourage viewers to flee to North Korea. The film was finally allowed to reappear two years later, when it was selected for the San Francisco Film Festival.

This first case of severe censorship, following the military coup, marked the end of the short period of creative freedom. It also heralded the film policy to come under the presidency of Park Chung-hee: although the film industry was enjoying a veritable golden age, with up to 229 films produced per year, it was subject to severe restrictions. Films such as *The Housemaid* (1960) and *Aimless Bullet* (1961) were no longer possible until another tiny window of freedom of expression opened up during the transitional period between the Park Chung-hee and Chun Doo-hwan regimes in the early 1980s.

Aimless Bullet (1961) became famous for its neo-realist, almost documentary-style direction, with scenes shot in the natural settings of the streets of Seoul to capture the atmosphere between the two political regimes.

황금기

1961
1971

1961-1971
THE GOLDEN AGE
OF KOREAN CINEMA

The 1960s saw the first golden age of Korean cinema, with production rising sharply. The number of films produced rose from 92 in 1960 to 229 in 1969, while cinema attendance reached 178 million admissions, a record only beaten in 2012. However, the situation was still precarious due to the relatively limited number of cinemas, which rose from 344 in 1962 to 690 in 1970. The decade also saw major technical developments, with the gradual use of 35mm color film and the tentative emergence of CinemaScope and 3D films.

Under the impetus of producer-director Shin Sang-ok, the first film empire was created. Melodramas dominated the market, accounting for almost half of all productions, but diversified into sub-genres such as family dramas and youth films, and comedy-dramas. New genres are also taking off, including martial arts, animation, science fiction, horror, and even monster films.

Magazines specializing in film, the arts, and fashion began to publish lengthy articles on the hottest stars, contributing to the advent of the star system. Kim Ji-mi, Moon Hee, Nam Jeong-im, and Yoon Jeong-hee gradually replaced the previous generation of actresses, consisting of Choi Eun-hee, Jo Mi-ryeong, and Moon Jung-suk. Similarly, Shin Young-kyun and Park Nou-sik were taking over from the likes of Kim Seung-ho and Choi Moo-ryong. The star couple of Um Aing-ran and Shin Seong-il are a fine example of this new era: They appeared together in 35 films made between 1963 and 1964,

and enjoyed great success with the film *The Barefooted Young* (Kim Kee-duk, 1964). Their relationship, both in real life and on screen, was widely covered by the growing tabloid press. Their wedding was one of the most talked-about events of the decade.

Despite an unstable political situation, Korean cinema enjoyed tremendous growth. On May 16, 1961, the government was overthrown by a military coup led by Park Chung-hee, who was sworn in as president on December 17, 1963, and implemented an ambitious economic development plan to pull Korea, one of the poorest countries in the world at the time, out of its difficult situation. Park saw the cinema as an industrial sector in its own right, and therefore devised a production and distribution system inspired by the Hollywood model.

A law governing cinema was enacted in 1962 with the aim of protecting and promoting Korean culture, which was considered a "national treasure." It required Korean production companies to have at least three cameras and fully equipped film sets measuring 700 square meters, and to employ three directors, four technicians, and around ten actors and actresses on a full-time basis. To encourage domestic production, the studios were required to release around 15 films a year, while imports were limited to a third of local production. This measure is a real revolution in an industry where American films were responsible for three-quarters of box office receipts. Every public success, every selection at the growing number of national and international festivals, and every award won by a Korean film enabled its producers to benefit from additional import quotas. This policy had the effect of considerably reducing the number of foreign films, from 208 in 1960 to 51 in 1964.

The South Korean government had a clear objective: to create a system of major studios modeled on the Hollywood system by encouraging local, pro-regime production under strict control. This meant that every film project had to be submitted to a censorship committee when the script was presented and before the film was released in cinemas, just as it was under the Japanese occupation. This protectionist policy required "quality" films: educational, anticommunist, and in line with the country's policies. Any work that undermined moral values, was critical of the regime, or was pro-communist was banned.

Although this system enabled the creation of a genuine production and distribution network for the first time in the history of Korean cinema, it had one major drawback: It favored quantity over quality. The studios engaged in mass-production, with the idea of benefiting from additional import quotas, because American films were practically the only ones that guaranteed a return on investment. At least, this system also enabled new and future great directors to make their first steps, such as Kim Keeduk, Im Kwon-taek, and Lee Man-hee.

With the introduction of these requirements, the number of Korean production companies fell sharply, from 71 to 16 in 1962 and just 4 in 1963. As the studios were unable to meet the standards imposed, they were forced to collaborate with independent producers, known as *daemyeong*, who paid a fee to the official studios to produce films under their name and distribute them in cinemas. This practice was deemed illegal and banned by a new law in 1966, when studies revealed that of the 189 films released in 1965, 130 were daemyeong productions. This decision showed the limits of the system, which was confirmed by the bankruptcy of the last four surviving studios in the early 1970s.

Because of the shortage of scriptwriters and the financial risks associated with original and little-known subjects, producers turned to existing material that was familiar to the public. As well as color remakes of Korean and foreign classics, they drew inspiration from literature, theatre, and television series. The proliferation of newspapers and radio stations encouraged the film adaptation of many literary and radio dramas. Songs, both old and new, served as inspiration for melodramas based on simple titles or the lyrics of a hit song, sometimes with the musical stars in the lead, on the model of the American musicals, which enjoyed great popularity at the time.

Previous page: *Confession of an Actress* (Kim Soo-yong, 1967).

Films were produced at a frenetic pace, taking less than four weeks from script development to theatrical release. The most prolific filmmakers, such as Kim Soo-yong (59 films between 1960 and 1969), Jang Il-ho (40) and Kim Kee-duk (40), shot up to 10 films a year. In the early 1960s, the studios were still simple sheds that were unheated in winter, as evidenced by the many films in which one can see the breath condensing from the actors' mouths. The lack of infrastructure and equipment meant that directors of different films had to share a single camera and pass it among them between takes. The stars worked on up to four films a day, reading their lines from prompts as they filmed. They were immediately dubbed by professionals "crammed" into the few sound-recording booths, who were instructed to adopt "soft voices," often very different from those of the actors. The film *Confession of an Actress* (Kim Soo-yong, 1967) offers a good insight into the film industry and the difficult shooting conditions of the time.

Films were distributed by six exhibitors throughout the country, who decided on their programming by "pre-buying" titles simply on the basis of a reading of the script. This method enabled the producers to obtain the funds they needed to make the films, but it limited their creative freedom, because of the repeated demand for hit formulas and the use of popular actors to minimize the risks of commercial failure. Until the early 1990s, each film was only released in one of the main cinemas in the major cities, before being repeated in smaller cinemas on the outskirts and in the provinces. The number of copies per film was limited to 16 to avoid a monopoly situation for the most eagerly awaited titles. In 1966, a tightening of the cinema law obliged exhibitors to show Korean films for at least 90 days a year.

Despite the many constraints on the Korean film industry at the time, the 1960s saw the birth of some of the masterpieces in the history of Korean cinema, including *The Houseguest and My Mother* (Shin Sang-ok, 1961), *The Coachman* (Kang Dae-jin, 1961), *The Seashore Village* (Kim Soo-yong, 1965), and *The General's Mustache* (Lee Seong-gu, 1968).

Previous page spread: Extension work on the old road junction in the Samgakji district of Seoul in the late 1960s.

The fifth Grand Bell awards ceremony in 1966 crowns *Seashore Village* (1965) as the best film of the year.

THE SHIN SANG-OK EMPIRE

Shin Sang-ok (1925–2006) is one of the most important directors in the history of Korean cinema, having made a confirmed 74 films,[1] including several classics. He is also known for creating the country's first major studio, diversifying film genres, and multiplying international collaborations. He never stopped pushing the boundaries to put Korea on the world cinema map.

Born in 1925 in Chungju, Shin Sang-ok left for Japan to study fine arts during the last years of the occupation, discovering cinemas from elsewhere—notably France. On his return to Korea, he began working on propaganda posters. He joined Choi In-kyu's studio (*Hurrah! For Freedom*, 1946), where he was hired as a set painter and gradually worked his way up to become his assistant. In the early 1950s, during the Korean War, he directed his first feature film, *The Evil Night* (1952), which is unfortunately considered lost. He also made the ambitious docudrama *Korea* (1954), during which he met the actress Choi Eun-hee, with whom he formed one of the most emblematic couples in Korean cinema. She appeared in almost all his films until their divorce in 1978.

After attracting attention with his first historical films, such as *Dream* and *The Youth* (both released in 1955), Shin Sang-ok directed one of the best crime films in the history of Korean cinema, *The Flower in Hell* (1958), which unfortunately remains his only foray into this genre. He founded his own production company, Shin Films, and enjoyed his first period of success with *Confessions of a College Student* (1958), *It's Not Her Sin* (1959), *Dongshimcho* (1959), and *Sister's Garden* (1959), which contributed to the golden age of contemporary melodramas in the 1950s, featuring strong female characters, following in the footsteps of the success of *Madame Freedom* (Han Hyung-mo, 1956). Close to the Liberal Party, he agreed to direct the ambitious historical epic *Rhee Syngman and the Independence

Movement* (1959) to promote President Rhee Syngman's re-election campaign. However, the film got him into trouble when, in 1960, it was revealed that it had been financed by disguised public funds.

Shin Sang-ok quickly bounced back by becoming a precursor of several emblematic film genres of the 1960s in Korea. He directed the successful family drama *A Romantic Papa* (1960), the historical epic *Chunhyang* (1961), which set a box office record with 380,000 viewers, and the special-effects fantasy productions *Madam White Snake* (1960) and *A Thousand-Year-Old Fox* (1969). He tried his hand at literary adaptations with *The Evergreen Tree* (1961) and *Deaf Samryong* (1964) and directed Korean film classics such as *My Mother and Her Guest* (1961) and *The Memorial Gate for Virtuous Women* (1962). The repeated success of his productions earned him the nickname Prince of Korean Cinema.

Shin Sang-ok not only made films but he also created the first Korean film empire inspired by Hollywood studios. Over the years, he assembled several film sets, film processing laboratories, sound recording and postproduction studios. By 1963, Shin Films owned more than half of Korea's film infrastructure and employed more than 250 people, three times as many as its main competitor. In 1967, it acquired Anyang Studios, considered at the time to be the largest studio in Asia. Over the course of the 1960s, Shin produced more than 200 films, serving as a veritable model of expertise for its competitors. Its Anyang Academy of Cinema and Arts center, dedicated to the cinema professions, trained many technicians and directors, while the Shin Film Acting Studio, managed by his wife and actress, Choi Eun-hee, between 1970 and 1978, gave birth to a new generation of stars.

Shin Sang-ok owes much of his success to his close links with General Park after the release of *The Evergreen Tree* (1961). His reasons for mak-

ing the film are contradictory: some claim that Shin deliberately created a propaganda tool to repent for his former affiliation with Rhee Syngman's Liberal Party, while others say that the future president Park appropriated the film to use as an example of his economic development plan, by widely distributing it in the countryside villages. In any case, this feature-length film, adapted from a 1936 short story by Shim Hoon about a couple of teachers who return to their home village to "educate" the rural population, is a tacit expression of Shin's support for government policy.

In 1963, Shin Sang-ok directed *Rice* (1963), this time a genuine propaganda film for Park's election campaign. The film was based on a true story about the creation of a new irrigation system to save a village from famine. The film was a success despite the irrigation project's failure in reality. The anti-communist blockbuster *Red Scarf* (1964), partly financed by the United States, aimed to promote the air force, with battle scenes of ultramodern fighter planes, although at the time Korea only had propel-

ler aircraft. Thanks to these productions, Shin Sang-ok received considerable support from the state throughout the 1960s, particularly in the form of major financial backing when he acquired Anyang Studios in 1967.

Shin Sang-ok also worked extensively abroad, being one of the few Korean distributors to sell his films throughout Southeast Asia. During the second half of the 1960s, he worked closely with Hong Kong's Shaw Brothers studios on a number of co-productions and helped introduce several foreign film genres to Korea, such as Sergio Leone's spaghetti Westerns and King Hu's early martial arts films. These films inspired him to create Korean adaptations, including the (incorrectly) self-proclaimed "first Asian Western,"[2] *Mounted Bandits* (1967), and the women-in-prison films *Girls in the Tiger Cage 1* and *2* (both 1976).

Director Shin Sang-ok and his wife, star Choi Eun-hee, were one of the first and most legendary film couples.

In the second half of the 1960s, Shin Sang-ok broke away from General Park's policies and publicly criticized the increasingly restrictive film laws. This position got him into trouble: First he was charged with concealing the import of foreign films by simply replacing the original names in the credits with fictitious Korean names; then he was arrested for "offending public decency" because of the scenes of female homosexuality underlying the historical drama *Eunuch* (1968). In 1974, Shin "forgot" to inform the Ministry of Information that his film *A Boy at His Age of 13* (1974) had been sent to the Berlin Festival, where it was selected. In 1975, Shin Sang-ok lost his producer's license for good when he deliberately reinstated two seconds of a censored shot of a topless actress in the trailer for *Rose and Wild Dog* (1976). Riddled with debt, he considered going into exile.

As fate would have it, Shin Sang-ok went in search of his ex-wife, Choi Eun-hee, who had disappeared six months earlier in Hong Kong, and was kidnapped himself by the North Korean secret service in July 1978. Supreme Leader Kim Jong-il had ordered their kidnappings to help him raise the quality of his country's cinema to international standards. Shin Sang-ok spent five years in prison for trying to escape twice, before finally being reunited with his ex-wife, whom he was forced to remarry. He then made seven films in three years, including *Pulgasari* (1985), a vague remake of the Japanese monster movie *Godzilla* (Ishiro Honda, 1954), the only one of his North Korean productions to receive worldwide distribution.

In 1986, the couple managed to slip past their guards during a trip to Europe to scout locations for a new film and took refuge in the American embassy in Vienna. Shin Sang-ok returned to the cinema in 1992 under the pseudonym Simon Sheen, producing the low-budget children's action series *3 Ninjas*. Disney bought the franchise and contracted Shin to direct *3 Ninjas Knuckle Up* (1995). Back in Korea in 1994,

his rare forays into cinema were failures. He died of hepatitis on April 11, 2006, and was awarded Korea's highest artistic distinction, the Cultural Golden Crown, the day after his death.

1. Some accounts suggest that he also co-directed several productions by his assistants, such as *The Sino-Japanese War and Queen Min the Heroine* (Lim Won-sick and Rha Bong-han, 1965).
2. The first Asian audiovisual productions inspired by "American Westerns" existed as early as the 1940s, notably in the form of Thai advertising films, and then in Japanese cinema in the 1950s and 1960s.

Producer, director, importer, and distributor of foreign films, Shin Sang-ok reigned supreme over Korean cinema from the 1950s to the 1970s.

FAMILY DRAMAS

During the 1960s, melodrama was the main genre on the big screen, accounting for more than half of the 1,500 films produced during that decade. The most interesting sub-genre to emerge was the family drama, which reflected both a cinematic evolution and the transition of post-war Korean society to an era of modernity. Whereas the melodrama of the 1950s was systematically centered on the female character—either as a victim or as a symbol of emancipation—the family drama focused on the father figure, a first in the history of Korean cinema.

Korean films made between the 1920s and 1960s are characterized by a strange absence of the father figure, either physical or moral. In the best cases, he is vaguely present, leaving his sons to act, and his wife and daughters to manage the family's day-to-day life. At worst, he is the cause of all his family's misfortunes, cheating on his wife, arranging his children's marriages against their will, even abandoning the home. This portrayal of the father was a metaphor for the powerlessness felt by the men who were unable to prevent the virtual disappearance of the Korean nation under Japanese colonization, and who played only a passive role in the liberation and division of Korea.

For the first time in the history of Korean cinema, the family drama places the father at the center of attention, but often in an unflattering light: an unreliable character, often in financial difficulty, unable to provide for his family. Although attached to traditional values, he disagrees with his children's modern lifestyle, but remains concerned for their well-being. The family drama thus becomes a metaphor for the family model that is desirable for rebuilding a nation that has been bled dry but is on the cusp of an incredible economic explosion.

The family drama is inextricably linked with the actor Kim Seung-ho (1918–1968). A stage actor in the 1930s, he made his film debut in *Hurrah! For Freedom* (Choi In-kyu, 1946) and went on to play a series of roles in the second half of the 1950s. He first came to prominence with his portrayal of a greedy merchant in *The Wedding Day* (Lee Byung-il, 1957), before going on to shine in the first family dramas of the 1960s, such as *A Romantic Papa* (Shin Sang-ok, 1960) and *Mr. Park* (Kang Dae-jin, 1960), for which he won the Best Actor award at the Asia-Pacific Film Festival. His many roles as a patriarch earned him the nickname Father of Korean Cinema. He might be compared to John Wayne for his imposing presence and unique charisma. He appeared in over 350 films between 1955 and 1968, before dying of a cerebral hemorrhage.

Kim Seung-ho's reputation as the patriarch of family dramas is no accident. Indeed, in the years preceding *A Romantic Papa* (1960), he often appeared in the role of father in melodramas such as *The Money* (Kim So-dong, 1958), *The Seven Daughters* (Park Si-chun, 1958), *The Real Estate Agent* (Park Seong-bok, 1959), or *Street of the Sun* (Kim Hwa-rang, 1959). However, the film that really marked the beginning of the genre was *A Romantic Papa* (1960), adapted from a popular radio soap opera and inspired both by Japanese *shomin-geki*,[1] for its content, and by Hollywood cinema for its form. The story follows a father who is unable to admit to his wife and five children that he has been made redundant. Although the film features some intergenerational conflicts, it focuses mainly on the character of the patriarch, who struggles to provide for his family but is saved by their solidarity.

Actor Kim Seung-ho (left) starred in many family dramas in the early 1960s, including *The Coachman* (1961), the first Korean film to win an award at any major international film festival.

Playing the father of a modest family in *Mr. Park* (Kang Dae-jin, 1960), Kim Seung-ho confirmed his status as a father of Korean cinema, this time wearing traditional clothes, after the Western outfits worn in his previous film, *A Romantic Papa*. In this new role, he plays a stubborn father who clashes with the modern aspirations of his children: The eldest wants to marry an unemployed friend, the youngest wants to marry a richer man, and his son is thinking of going to work abroad. *Mr. Park* is a pioneering film, tackling the social problems of the time head-on through the point of view of

a working-class family. The image of the dirty, grimy brick-maker with his children dressed in Western clothes is symbolic of Korean society in transition at the time.

Some family dramas, such as *View from an Alley* (Park Jong-ho, 1962) or *Salary Man* (Lee Bong-rae, 1962), follow the classic pattern of the conservative father clashing with his offspring's modern ideas, but others explore new horizons. For example, *Under the Sky of Seoul* (1961), the first film by director Lee Hyung-pyo, who had been Shin Sang-ok's assistant, is a metaphor for the confrontation between East and West,

pitting a practitioner of traditional Korean medicine (played by Kim Seung-ho) against a young Western doctor (and future son-in-law). In *Petty Middle Manager* (Lee Bong-rae, 1961), another masterpiece of the genre, three generations cohabit under the same roof, opening the way to new conflicts evoking different periods of Korean history while tackling the delicate theme of corruption among the wealthy classes.

Although most family dramas are dramatic comedies with happy endings, some fall back on the pure melodrama of previous decades. *The Coachman* (1961) is the final part of a book trilogy by Kang Dae-jin on the daily life of the poorer classes, following *Mr. Park* (1960) and *Fishermen* (1961, now lost). In this film, Kim Seung-ho plays a widower bringing up his four children alone, working as a coachman in Seoul, where horse-drawn carts are gradually being replaced by cars. This time, the drama focuses less on intergenerational conflict than on the cruel consequences of modern society, such as a battered wife, a cheated wife, and a delinquent son. The ending is rather happy, with one of the first big-screen depictions of a blended family unit. Furthermore, *The Coachman* was the very first Korean film to win an Honourable Mention at the Berlin International Film Festival in 1961.

A Dream of Fortune (1961) is a rather curious film by *Madame Freedom* director Han Hyung-mo. Starting out as a comedy, the film takes a tragic turn in the second half. It's the story of a teacher, played by Kim Seung-ho, who is struggling to repay the loans on his council house on the outskirts of Seoul and falls victim to a swindler. The consequences are disastrous and recall the model of the father responsible for his family's misfortunes in the melodramas of the 1950s. The tone of family dramas has changed over the years, in line with the gradual disillusionment of the Korean people under Park Chung-hee's regime, and increasingly undermining the model image of the patriarch. *The Body's Way* (1967) is an adaptation of the novel by Hungarian writer Lajos Biro and a remake of director Jo Keung-ha's 1959 film of the same name. Kim Seung-ho plays the father of a wealthy family of four children. Trapped, he is robbed of a large cheque after spending the night with the thief. Unable to admit the truth to his family, he disappears completely, never returning home to let his eldest son take over as head of the family. *The Body's Way* marks the end of the golden age of the 1960s family drama. Incidentally, Kim Seung-ho died one year to the day after the film's release.

1. *Shomin-geki* ("modern theatre") is a neo-realist film genre popularized in the 1930s by classic directors such as Kenji Mizoguchi, Mikio Naruse, and Yasujiro Ozu; it tells the story of the lives of working- and middle-class families.

The Wedding Day (1957) is considered to be the first Korean comedy and a landmark film in 1950s–1960s Korean cinema.

COMEDIES

Comedy is a real case study in Korean cinema. Its origins date back to the 1910s, in the form of imported French shorts, with Max Linder, and American shorts, with Charlie Chaplin, Buster Keaton, and Harold Lloyd. However, comedy was largely ignored by Korean cinema until the 1950s, with the exception of an ill-fated attempt in 1926 with the film *Fool* (Lee Phil-woo), an adaptation of the very first manwha, *The Vain Efforts of an Idiot* by Noh Soo-hyun. The failure of this film and the general absence of comedy in Korean cinema until the 1950s can be partly explained by the relative lack of circus culture in Korea, which was at the origins of American burlesque cinema, and by the difficult period of Japanese occupation, which favored melodramas.

In the 1950s, comedy began to make an appearance in Korean cinema with the simultaneous release of two films on February 11 and 12, 1957: *The Wedding Day* (Lee Byung-il, 1957) and *Hyperbola of Youth* (Han Hyung-mo, 1957). The

first is an adaptation of a popular modern Korean play by Oh Yeong-jin (1943) about a greedy merchant who replaces his daughter with a maid on the eve of an arranged marriage, after learning that his future son-in-law is an invalid. However, he is caught in his own deception, as the son-in-law is in perfect physical condition and had set up this ruse to test the integrity of his future father-in-law.

The success of *The Wedding Day* can be explained by the public's attraction to historical films and by Kim Seung-ho's remarkable performance. This is the first Korean film to win the Best Comedy prize at the fourth Asian Film Festival. This recognition is a source of pride for the Korean nation, which had been hampered by its lagging cinematographic technology, but above all it is the consecration of a genre hitherto ignored by the public. The success of this film led to a series of historical comedies, including *Heung-bu and Nol-bu* (Kim Hwa-rang, 1959) and *Chunhyang* (Lee Kyeong-chun, 1960).

Hyperbola of Youth (1957), released during the Korean New Year, was promoted as the "first

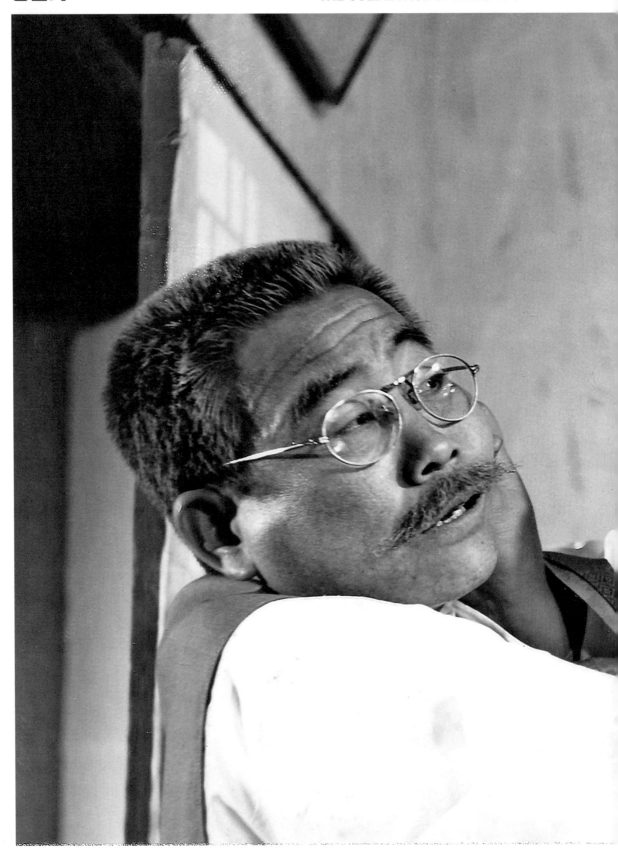

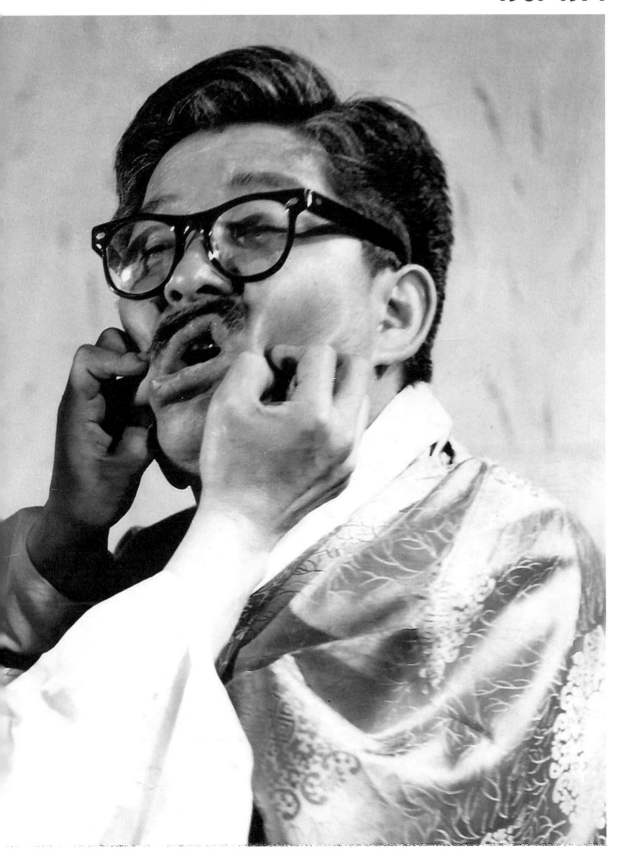

ever family comedy." This film by director Han Hyung-mo, famous for his meticulous American-style direction and for the phenomenal success of his previous feature, *Madame Freedom* (1956), was particularly eagerly awaited. The script is simple: Two friends from different social backgrounds swap lives and end up marrying each other's sisters. The film features a cast of attractive young actors, popular musicians and comedians from the variety shows of the time, who contributed greatly to the golden age of Korean comedy in the 1960s.

During the 1950s, *akgeug* (variety shows combining song and comedy acts) were developed to entertain American troops and Korean audiences. The success of *Hyperbola of Youth* encouraged performers to make the transition from stage to screen. The scripts of many of the films told the personal stories of the performers and their audiences, who were often poor people who had come from the countryside to try their luck in the capital. Some actors adopted a local dialect and dubbed their dialogue in different versions of the movie for different regional audiences. This unprecedented complicity between performers and audiences accelerated the popularization of cinema; many of the comedies of the second half of the 1960s were specifically aimed at the poorer classes, who frequented the cheaper cinemas on the outskirts of the capital.

Among the wave of comic artists, Yang Seok-cheon (1921–1990) and Yang Hoon (1923–1998) were the first to make a successful transition to the cinema. They started out in variety shows when, in 1948, they created the comedy duo Skinny and Fatty, whose humor was inspired by the famous American model Laurel and Hardy. Their popularity exploded in 1955 with a monthly television show. They made their film debut in *Hyperbola of Youth* (1957). Building on this success, they went on to make a series of slapstick films under the direction of director Kim Hwa-rang, including *The Unknown Future*

(1958), *Get Rich Quick* (1958), and *Skinny and Fatty Go to Bootcamp* (1959). After several box office failures, they continued their careers on television.

Other actors, such as Kim Hee-kap and Koo Bong-seo, played secondary roles just as important as those of the main stars, and their names sometimes even appeared in the titles of films, as in *The Upstart* (Kim Soo-yong, 1961), whose original title translates as *The Sudden Fortune of Koo Bong-seo*. Kim Hee-kap (1923–1993) appeared in over 350 films in the 1960s alone, earning him the nickname of the Korean Charlie Chaplin. His greatest success was the five-part franchise *Paldogangsan* (1968–1972), which was adapted into a TV series in 1974. Koo Bong-seo (1926–2016), who appeared in 233 films, 980 radio plays, and 786 episodes of the cult TV show *Smile and Luck Will Come* between 1969 and 1985, is known as the Godfather of Korean comedy. He is best known for being used as a scapegoat for the characters played by Seo Young-choon in a series of comedy films on the theme of cross-dressing.

Seo Young-choon (1928–1986) is considered the greatest comic star in the history of Korean cinema. He began his career as a duo with Baek Geum-nyeo in 1950s variety shows but became especially famous on television in the 1960s for his outspokenness and for comedic lines that became common parlance. His incredible performance as a cross-dressing woman in *Woman Is Better* (Kim Ki-pung) made the film one of the biggest hits of 1965 and launched the cross-dressing comedy sub-genre, inspired by the American film *Some Like It Hot* (Billy Wilder, 1959), with titles such as *A Male Housekeeper 1* and *2* (1968 and 1970), *The Male Beauty Artist* (1969), and *A Man and a Gisaeng* (1969), all directed by Shim Wu-seob. Seo Young-choon also parodied James Bond in several films in the second half of the 1960s, including *Salsal Doesn't Know* (Kim Hwa-rang, 1966), *Bizarre* (Kim Dae-hui, 1967), *Laughable Sweeping* (Shim

Wu-seob, 1969), and *Three Black Leopards* (Kim Eung-chun, 1971).

During the 1960s, so-called popular comedies accounted for up to 12 percent of annual film production; humor also infiltrated other film genres, such as musicals, family melodramas, historical and fantasy films, and even educational films such as *A Birth Control* (Eom Sim-ho, 1960) and *Do As You Wish* (Lee Hee-jung, 1969), which, under the guise of comedy, raised awareness of contraception.

During the 1970s, the tightening of censorship under the Park Chung-hee regime led to a large-scale migration of comedians to television. Comedy became inseparable from the small screen, but experienced its darkest period in the cinema, with fewer than 100 films produced between 1970 and 1990.

The comedy genre underwent a notable revival at the time of South Korea's transition to democratization and rapid economic growth, at the end of the 1980s. It began with Lee Myung-se's first films, *Gagman* (1989) and *My Love, My Bride* (1990), followed by the success of *Mister Mama* (1992) and Kang Woo-suk's *Two Cops 1* and *2* (1993 and 1996). *My Sassy Girl* (Kwak Jae-young, 2001) definitively established comedic hybrids that combined comedy with action, romance, or horror, rather than as its own genre.

Previous page spread: Comic actor Koo Bong-seo (right), in a cult scene from *Frailty, Thy Name Is Man*.

Television made a dramatic entry into Korean homes in the second half of the 1960s.

YOUTH FILMS

The phenomenal success of *The Barefooted Young* (Kim Kee-duk, 1964) gave rise to the youth film. This genre ushered in a new era for Korean cinema, helped by the emergence of a younger audience that no longer identified with traditional Confucian values and no longer believed in the promises of a better world promoted by the Park Chung-hee regime. Young people's films were influenced as much by Japanese culture as by the American cinema of the 1950s, which featured rebels with big hearts and tragic destinies, as in *The Wild One* (Laszlo Benedek, 1953), *Blackboard Jungle* (Richard Brooks, 1955), and *Rebel Without a Cause* (Nicolas Ray, 1955).

In 1955, the Japanese writer Shintaro Ishihara (1932–2022) published *Season of the Sun*, a collection of short stories that launched a new literary movement in Japan: taiyozoku (tribe of the sun). This movement portrayed young adults at a loose end in a society that didn't understand them. Refusing to carry the burden of guilt for their parents' participation and defeat in World War II, the heroes of these stories spend their time smoking, drinking, and flirting. The success of *Season of the Sun* prompted its author to produce and direct five film adaptations in 1956, including *Season of the Sun* by Takumi Furukawa, *Crazed Fruit* by Ko Nakahira, and *The Summer of the Solar Eclipse* by Hiromichi Horikawa. However, these films were quickly judged too provocative for the conservative Japanese society of the time. The rape scene of a drugged student in *Punishment Room* (Kon Ichikawa, 1956) even forced the Nikkatsu production studios to make a public apology and put an end to taiyozoku films in favor of productions more in line with the moral standards of the time.

These films were inaccessible in Korea due to the ban on importing Japanese cultural products after the occupation. Nevertheless, in 1960, a relaxation of the law once again allowed Japanese literature to be published, and *Season of*

the Sun became one of the most popular novels among young readers. This was a golden opportunity for Korean cinema, which was short of scriptwriters, especially as Korea had never ratified the 1952 UNESCO Universal Copyright Convention. Plagiarism of Japanese novels became widespread, amounting to 80 occurrences in 1963–1964 alone. Due to the popularity of taiyozoku novels among young people, the first adaptations, both official and unofficial, quickly hit the screens.

In the 1950s, the very first films aimed at young people appeared under the direction of Yu Hyun-mok. A budding director with a passion for Japanese cinema, he drew inspiration from the taiyozoku movement to make *Crossroad* (1956), *Sadness of Heredity* (1956), and *Lost Youth* (1957). However, these films were not as successful as expected, perhaps because they were too innovative for a society in the throes of an identity crisis, torn between its past and its future. The family drama genre, which emerged in the early 1960s, was a first stage in the reclaiming of Korean history and the reconstruction of a family unit under the father figure; as for the rise of the youth film in the second half of the decade, it resounds as a reaction and a challenge to this promotion of traditional values by a new generation disorientated in a society in the midst of reconstruction.

The publication of the work of Yojiro Ishizaka (1900–1986), one of Japan's most influential post-war authors, marked the real beginning of the youth film genre. After the relaxation of the law on Japanese literature, his works were among the best-selling literary works in Korea. In 1963, three of his short stories were adapted into films: *An Alley Under the Sun* (1958) was made into *Private Tutor* (Kim Kee-duk), *Blue Mountain Range* (1949) became *The Blue Dreams Will Shine* (Yu Hyun-mok), and *He and I* (1961) was adapted into *The Classroom of Youth* (Kim Soo-yong).

Shin Seong-il, the lead actor in *The Class-*

room of Youth (1963), which was a great success with over 100,000 spectators, suggested to the director of the Academy Theatre the idea of an (unofficial) remake of the Japanese film *Trampled Innocense* (Ko Nakahira, 1963). The director was looking for a project to attract a young audience and convert his theatre, located in a popular shopping area, into a cinema. Eighteen days (!) later, *The Barefooted Young* (Kim Kee-duk, 1964) had a triumphant release. The film drew 150,000 spectators in Seoul, Hee-Jun Choi's title song became an instant classic, young people everywhere imitated the frenzied twist of one of the film's key sequences, and clothing shops sold out of the outfits worn by the film's actors.

The film manages to seamlessly integrate American and Japanese influences to create a Korean film that perfectly reflects its times, in a tragic romance between a disillusioned thug and a wealthy student. Parents may see the film as nothing more than teenage excess, but for young people it's a cry of anger against a society they no longer understand. This generation, which had not really experienced either the Japanese occupation or the Korean War, no longer recognizes itself in traditional Confucian values and fears an uncertain future under General Park's regime. On the other hand, the main character fully identifies with Shin Seong-il's disillusioned and rebellious James Dean–like character.

Actor Shin Seong-il was one of the key elements in the success of *The Barefooted Young* (Kim Kee-duk, 1964). Born in 1937, he began his career in the family dramas *A Romantic Papa* (Shin Sang-ok, 1960) and *Under the Sky of Seoul* (Lee Hyung-pyo, 1961). He quickly set out to distinguish himself from the image disseminated by other popular actors of the time, such as the "perfect son-in-law" Kim Jin-kyu or the "brute force" Shin Young-kyun, by relying entirely on his charisma. He specialized in the roles of rebellious youth, as in *Farewell Adolescence* (Kim

Soo-yong, 1962), *Angry Apple* (Kim Muk, 1963), and *College Girls in the Year of the Horse* (Lee Hyung-pyo, 1963), which quickly earned him the nickname of the Korean Anthony Perkins. The character of Doo-su, whom he played in *The Barefooted Young*, was a clever mix of Marlon Brando (shirtless) from *The Wild One*, James Dean (poses and looks) from *Rebel Without a Cause*, and Yujiro Ishihara (same outfit and haircut), an actor in taiyozoku productions. After this role, Shin Seong-il achieved the status of a Korean icon, appearing in over 500 films during his 50-year career, including 231 made between 1964 and 1968.

The triumph of *The Barefooted Young* sparked a craze for youth films between 1964 and

Angry Apple (1963) was one of the first feature films to introduce actor Shin Seong-il (lower right), in the role of a young rebel against Confucian society, and foreshadowed the youth film genre.

1968. In 1964, out of 136 films produced, 55 were aimed at this audience, 26 of which starred Um Aing-ran and Shin Seong-il. An official sequel, *Run with Bare Feet* (Lee Yong-ho), was released the same year, while Kim Kee-duk made three other unofficial sequels, *Burning Youth* (1966), *Dark-Haired Youth* (1966), and *Naked Fist* (1967). Although some of the productions were nothing more than carbon copies of the original tragic love stories between two young people from different social backgrounds, the genre quickly diversified with lighter themes to appeal to a wider audience. Specifically, the films were musicals, headlined by music stars to encourage people to buy their records. Hoping to fool the public, some producers even included the word *youth* in the titles of productions that were not youth films, including the vaudeville *A Youth March* (Shim Wu-seob, 1966) and the family drama *Father's Youth* (Jung Sung-moon, 1966).

After the Ministry of Information announced in 1966 that any film adapted from Japanese works would be automatically disqualified from national festivals—depriving producers of the possible reward of importing a foreign film—the youth film declined and was rapidly replaced by action and martial arts films aimed at young audiences.

LITERARY FILMS

From the outset, Korean cinema was mainly inspired by literature, in particular folk tales such as *The Story of Chun-hyang* (Koshu Hayakawa, 1923), *The Story of Jang-hwa and Hong-ryeon* (Kim Yeong-hwan, 1924), and *The Story of Shim Cheong* (Lee Gyeong-son, 1925). Although *The Pioneer* (Lee Gyeong-son, 1925), the first adaptation of a contemporary Korean novel, was a failure, the literary-inspired films that followed were successful, including *At Daybreak* (Shim Hoon, 1927), *Oh Mong-nyeo* (Na Un-gyu, 1937), and *Altar for a Tutelary Deity* (Bang Han-jun, 1939).

After the end of the Japanese occupation, professionals in the Korean film industry sought to define the "perfect Korean film" to help rebuild their country's identity. The critics of the time finally chose two literary adaptations as the best representatives: *A Seagull* (Lee Gyu-hwan, 1948) and *A Hometown in Heart* (Yun Yong-gyu, 1949). The first, based on a novel by Ham Se-deok (1915–1950), is an enlightenment film. With the story of a couple caring for war orphans in the countryside, it encourages Koreans to rebuild their country by supporting each other. The second, adapted from another novel by Ham Se-deok, highlights the tragic fate of 2 million orphans and abandoned children, telling the story of a boy placed in a monastery who seeks maternal affection from a war widow. These two films definitively established the literary film genre as a noble one.

The Korean War put a temporary end to adaptations, with the exception of *The Evil Night* (1952), directed by Shin Sang-ok. This self-produced film, shot over two years, was inspired as much by Kim Kwang-ju's novel as by the director's own life. It tells the story of a writer in distress who finds meaning in his life by listening to the confessions of a prostitute. In the second half of the 1950s, traditional adaptations came back into fashion with *The Story of Chun-hyang* (Lee

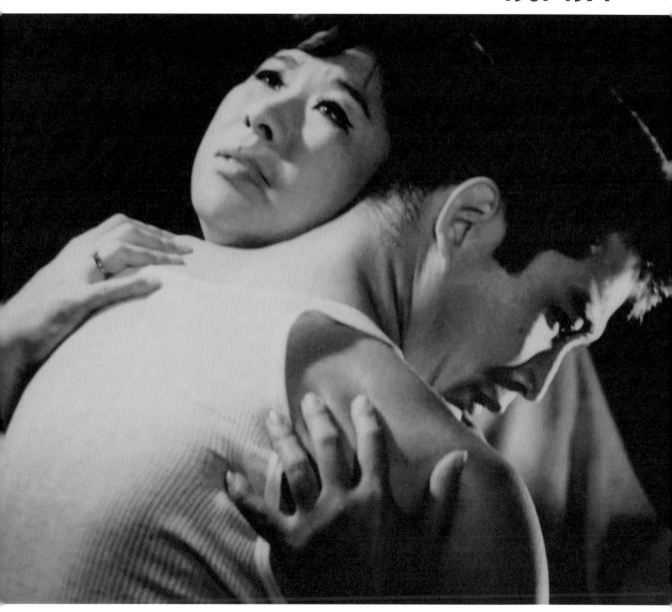

Gyu-hwan, 1955), *Dream* (Shin Sang-ok, 1955), *Idiot Adada* (Lee Kang-cheon, 1956), and others. The period was marked by a craze for the popular literature of Park Young-ri and Yi Kwang-su with *Love* (Lee Kang-cheon, 1957) and *A Drifting Story* (Gwon Yeong-sun, 1960).

Encouraged by the success of American literary adaptations in the 1950s, Korean producers embarked on similar projects. *Way of a Body* (Jo Keung-ha, 1959), a remake of *The Way of All Flesh* (Victor Fleming, 1927) and adapted from the Hungarian author Lajos Biro, paved the way for a series of adaptations of foreign works, such as *Katyusha* (Yu Du-yeon, 1960 / Leo Tolstoy's

Resurrection), *A Rainbow* (Yu Du-yeon, 1960 / *The Pastoral Symphony* [*La Symphonie pastorale*] by André Gide), *Pearl Tower* (Kim Muk, 1960 / *The Count of Monte Cristo* by Alexandre Dumas), *Jean Valjean* (Jo Keung-ha, 1961 / *Les Misérables* by Victor Hugo), and *A Gang of Rob-*

Previous page spread: Shin Seong-il's look is inspired by Marlon Brando and James Dean.

The Barefooted Young, a landmark Korean film of the 1960s and the introduction of the youth film genre. Shin Seong-il co-starred with Um Aing-ran, his future wife.

bers (Yu Sim-pyeong, 1961 / *Brigands* [*Die Räu-ber*] by Friedrich Schiller).

In the 1960s, President Park Chung-hee encouraged producers to adapt Korean literature to strengthen national identity. The first wave of films was inspired mainly by authors who had become famous under the Japanese occupation, such as Yi Kwang-su, Kim Dong-ni, and Hwang Sun-won, who emerged during a period of relaxed censorship after the demonstrations of May 1, 1919. These authors confronted Confucian values and modernized traditional themes of loyalty and peaceful country life with a more contemporary style that reflected the changing society in the 1960s.

Shin Sang-ok's first two masterpieces were *My Mother and Her Guest* (1961) and *The Memorial Gate for Virtuous Women* (1962). The first, adapted from the work of Chu Yo-sup (1902–1972), presents the dilemma of a war widow who must choose between staying with her mother-in-law and daughter or leaving to make a new life with a lover. This choice involves either respecting the Confucian value of eternal fidelity to her husband or "disowning" him for a new life. While the widow retained the power of decision in *My Mother and Her Guest*, in *The Memorial Gate for Virtuous Women* she is deprived of it, as her in-laws chase away her lover and the child she has had with him, forcing the widow to stay forever with her in-laws and the memory of her dead husband.

In 1965, the Ministry of Information set out to promote Korean culture worldwide by encouraging the production of films that could be selected for international film festivals. This initiative was inspired by the *bungei eiga* (literary adaptations) cultural policy launched in Japan in the 1920s. The aim was to elevate cinema from a form of popular entertainment to the status of an art form. This decision gave rise to films that have become classics of world cinema, such as *Rashomon* (Akira Kurosawa, 1950), *Sansho the Bailiff* (Kenji Mizoguchi, 1954),

and *Woman in the Dunes* (Hiroshi Teshigahara, 1964).

Seashore Village (1965), considered to be a masterpiece of Korean cinema in the 1960s, is the first example to emerge from this policy. It is a film by Kim Soo-yong, the second most prolific director in the history of Korean cinema, with 121 films made between 1959 and 1999, including 59 in the 1960s, and 10 in 1967 alone. The film is adapted from a short story by Oh Young-su and is set in an isolated fishing community. The first part of the film is almost documentary-like, with many scenes of folklore that appeal to both domestic and international audiences for their exoticism; the second part—which does not exist in the story—again confronts a widow with the dilemma of whether to stay with her in-laws or leave with a passing lover.

The success of *Seashore Village*, with over 150,000 spectators, led the Ministry to grant literary adaptations the same advantages as educational and anti-communist films, including financial support and the promise of additional import quotas for foreign films in the event of success. This measure triggered a veritable golden age for literary adaptations between 1967 and 1968, with 30 films made in 1967, more than three times the number of the previous year.

Directors enjoyed a degree of artistic freedom, since these films were subsidized by the state and were therefore no longer subject to the pressure of profitability, while the screenplays, based on novels approved by the regime, were less subject to censorship. This freedom manifested itself in the unbridled creativity of the directors. While the adaptations of the first half of the 1960s were mostly faithful adaptations of the novels, those of the second half clearly favored form. Directors no longer drew their inspiration from the novels written by authors during the Japanese occupation, but from more contemporary novels about male characters disorientated by the country's rapid modernization.

After the success of *Seashore Village*, Kim Soo-yong, who until then had been regarded as a simple craftsman content to make one commissioned film after another, revealed himself to be a true filmmaker. In 1967, he made three absolutely remarkable films—*The Fishing Boats Are Full*, *Burning Mountain*, and *Sound of Magpies*—which earned him the nickname of Father of Literary Adaptations.

His absolute masterpiece remains *Mist* (1967), a film largely inspired by Claude Lelouch's *A Man and a Woman [Un Homme et une femme]* (1966) and the works of Michelangelo Antonioni and Ingmar Bergman. It was one of the first Korean films to be openly inspired by the French New Wave and European cinema. This story of a married man in the midst of a personal crisis, who falls in love with a naive young woman during a stay in a small coastal village,

succeeded brilliantly in combining art and commerce, attracting over 136,000 spectators.

Lee Seong-gu (1928–2005) also benefited from this exceptional period of artistic creativity. He made an astonishing first film, *A Young Look*, in 1960, influenced by the Japanese New Wave, before creating a series of formally perfect but fundamentally commercial films. His formidable literary adaptations *The Sun and the Moon* (1967), *When the Buckwheat Blooms* (1967), and *A Young Zelkova* (1968) seem to have been a truly enchanted interlude in his career,

---

The public and critical success of *Seashore Village* marked the beginning of a golden age of literary adaptations in the 1960s.

with *The General's Mustache* (1968), based on the author Lee O-young, being his most accomplished masterpiece.

This incredible immersion into the disturbed mind of a writer unable to find his place in a rapidly changing society features a totally unstructured narrative, which begins with the hero's death before moving backward in a non-linear chronology. The film also includes the very first sequence drawn in a feature-length fiction film, by the father of Korean animation, Shin Dong-hun.

In 1968, the lack of selection in international festivals led to the end of subsidies and the end of the golden age of literary films. The genre did not disappear completely, however, and continued to produce many masterpieces in the decades that followed. The dark political period of the 1970s gave rise to a new sociorealist literary trend, finally adapted in the post-regime Park Chung-hee years of the 1980s with films such as *A Ball Shot by a Midget* (Lee Won-se, 1981) and *People of the Slum* (Bae Chang-ho, 1982).

The post-war generations, having had access to better education and having become more curious, formed a new reading public. In the 1980s, the success of a book was measured in millions of copies sold, whereas in 1975, 20,000 copies were enough. Adaptations of novels by contemporary authors such as Choi In-ho and Lee Mun-yeol were among the greatest cinematic successes of the 1980s and 1990s, with films such as *Whale Hunting* (1984) and *The Deep Blue Night* (1985) by Bae Chang-ho and *Our Twisted Hero* (1992) by Park Jong-won.

Previous page spread: *A Gang of Robbers* (1961) is the Korean adaptation of Friedrich Schiller's play *Brigands* [*Die Räuber*].

An Empty Dream (1965), one of the most surprising films of its time, is a tribute to German Expressionism.

IN THE MARGINS:
YU HYUN-MOK
AND LEE MAN-HEE

In the 1960s, the film industry was heavily regulated by the regime. The studios were monopolized, making the situation particularly difficult for more independent artists; despite this, some filmmakers managed to bypass the system to produce more personal projects.

Yu Hyun-mok, the famous director of the classic Korean film *Aimless Bullet* (1961), was responsible for 43 feature-length fiction films made between 1956 and 1994, including the masterpieces *The Daughters of Pharmacist Kim* (1963), *Guests Who Arrived on the Last Train*, and *Rainy Days* (1979). Although often misunderstood on their release, these films have been re-evaluated over time. Yu Hyun-mok was also behind the creation of the very first Korean film club, the Film Art Research Group, at Dongguk University in 1947, and of the Cine-poem association in 1963, dedicated to experimental cinema. In 1970, he founded the Korean Short Film Association to teach filmmaking. These initiatives formed the basis of the independent Korean cinema of the 1970s and 1980s.

Yu Hyun-mok, born in 1925, discovered his

passion for cinema while watching the French film *Crime et châtiment* [*Crime and Punishment*] (Pierre Chenal, 1935). He began his career as an assistant on *The Life of Hong Cha-gi* (Yim Woon-hak, 1948), became scriptwriter on *Final Temptation* (Chung Chang-wha, 1953), and then a director in 1956. His first feature films, *Crossroad* (1956), *Lost Youth* (1957), and *Forever with You* (1958), foreshadowed the youth film genre a decade ahead of its time. Fascinated by Japanese culture (banned in Korea between 1945 and 1998, though literature was re-authorized in the early 1960s), he adapted several Japanese novels, notably *Even the Clouds Are Drifting* (1959), *Wife's Confession* (1964), and *An Empty Dream* (1965).

Most of Yu Hyun-mok's films were flops, with audiences finding them "too intellectual." The filmmaker owed his career solely to the prizes he won at national festivals, which enabled his producers to obtain the right to import foreign films. Nevertheless, he was forced to juggle more personal projects, such as the masterpieces mentioned above, with commissioned films such as the historical epic *Lim Kkeok-jeong* (1961), the comedies *Express Marriage Operation* (1966) and *Three Henpecked Generations* (1967), and the anti-communist films *Nightmare* (1968) and *Flame* (1975). He also initiated a short-lived craze for segmented horror films, following the success of his *Grudge 1* and *2* (1967 and 1968).

The majority of his films are literary adaptations, made not just during the golden age of the genre, between 1965 and 1968, but throughout his career. Unlike his peers, he preferred novels to short stories, and good content to a single best-selling title. *The Daughters of Pharmacist Kim* (1963), for example, was part of the wave of "good father" stories popular at the time, but for the first time adopted an exclusively female point of view. Yu Hyun-mok takes up the subject, changing the conservative ending to assert that a good society should be egalitarian, as much matriarchal as patriarchal. The film also includes many traditional rituals, thus preceding by several years the wave of folk literary adaptations launched by *Seashore Village* (Kim Soo-yong, 1965).

Yu Hyun-mok often uses philosophy to denounce politics to better effect. The anti-communist production *Martyrs* (1965), for example, was merely a pretext for him to question human existence and belief in a superior divinity. He extended this reflection in his masterpiece *Guests Who Arrived on the Last Train* (1967), which, under the guise of a youth film, explores the human condition through the destinies of several characters in a society in the throes of transformation. In the anti-communist film *Rainy Days* (1979), he completely reexamined the ideological conflict between South and North Korea, questioning the difference between vice and virtue, with little regard for which side of the "border" individuals fall on.

The filmmaker also excelled in terms of form. *Forever with You* (1958), he designed his set specifically to suit the camera movements, rather than adapting his mise-en-scène to the location. In *The Daughters of Pharmacist Kim* (1963), he went completely beyond the limits of the CinemaScope frame, constantly playing

with different fields and even off-screen. In *Aimless Bullet* (1961), he mixed American and Japanese cinema, the French New Wave and Italian neo-realism.

The short films he made as part of his Cine-poem association led to the fascinating *An Empty Dream* (1965). A tribute to German Expressionism, this absolutely unique and experimental feature-length film is made up of a series of poetic sequences recounting the shared dream of two patients in dental surgery under anesthetic. They find themselves propelled into the immense studio setting of a city where they try to live out a forbidden relationship while escaping from a Machiavellian dentist. The film was a flop and earned the director a conviction for "offending public decency" because of a scene in which his leading lady was shown with her back topless.

After an initial creative break, between 1969 and 1978, to devote himself to teaching and making educational documentaries, Yu Hyun-mok left the film industry for good when import quotas were abolished in 1984. No producer was prepared to show him the slightest confidence in his personal projects in an industry in steep decline in the 1980s. The director then devoted himself full-time to teaching and publishing several books on cinema before his death in 2009.

Lee Man-hee (1931–1975) was one of the most important filmmakers in the history of Korean cinema. He made 51 feature films between 1961 and 1975, including ten in 1967 alone, several of which are considered classics.

Starting out as an assistant to Ahn Jong-hwa and Kim Myeong-je at the end of the Korean War, Lee Man-hee made several acclaimed films, such as *Kaleidoscope* (1961), *Dial 112: Help* (1962), and *Never Look Back* (1963), in which he honed a style fundamentally influenced by Hollywood cinema. The director was commissioned to make *The Marines Who Never Returned* (1963), a very big-budget anti-communist propaganda film, which he transformed into a magnificent paci-

fist pamphlet, to the despair of the studios that commissioned it. Fortunately, the film became the biggest box office success of 1963, saving him from immediate trouble, but two years later he was charged with "treason against national security" for showing North Korean soldiers in an all too human light in *Seven Women POWs*. He was imprisoned and tortured, and only regained his freedom by agreeing to shorten his film by around 40 minutes.

His meeting with cinematographer Lee Suck-ki and scriptwriter Baek Gyeol in 1966 was decisive for the rest of his career. Together, they took advantage of the golden age of literary films to embark on an exciting period of formal experimentation, attempting to externalize the inner torments of the main characters. *The Water Mill* (1966) was adapted from a short story by Na Do-hyang, but in the end the trio kept only the title and a vague storyline to literally visualize the progressive madness of the hero, who was in love with a ghost (or not). The

film blends classical Japanese cinema with German Expressionism in a series of shots that were unheard of in Korean cinema at the time.

Late Autumn (1966), adapted from Kim Ji-heon, follows a prisoner on leave, who begins a race against time to find her one-day lover before having to return to her cell that evening. In *Coming Back* (1967), Lee Man-hee uses urban landscapes to reflect the inner torments of a woman who cheats on her paralyzed husband with a journalist. *A Miracle* (1967) was the first Korean feature-length sound film without any music. *A Day Off* (1968) is certainly the absolute masterpiece of Lee Man-hee's cinema, following, broadly speaking, the wanderings of a rather flighty man who spends his day wan-

The Marines Who Never Returned (1963) became the benchmark of so-called anti-communist films. The Korean army provided more than 3,000 soldiers for the battle scenes.

dering the city in a vague attempt to raise the money needed for his girlfriend's abortion. The film, considered too dark, failed to pass the censors and was only released in 2005.

After a series of increasingly experimental film failures, Lee Man-hee was obliged by his producers to make only commissioned films. In 1971, he directed the kimchi Western *Break the Chain* (1971), which served as the inspiration for Kim Jee-Woon's future film *The Good, the Bad, the Weird* (2008). In 1974, he was fired from the shooting of the anti-communist film *Wildflowers on the Battleground* for once again denouncing the horrors of war. He died a few months later on the set of his last film, the literary adaptation *Road to Sampo* (1975), now considered one of the best films of the 1970s.

In *The Water Mill* (1966), a literary adaptation, the director took a completely different approach to the novel's plot and combined it with staging techniques from classical Japanese cinema and German Expressionism.

쇠락기

1971
1980

화려한 외출

*第3期映像빠리쟝느尹静姫가 熱演하는 反逆의 뉴·시네마!!

La Sortie Ravissante

尹静姫／李大根

製作・金泰洙
監督・金洙容

総天然色
CinemaScope

企劃・黄奇性／金庚洙 原作・金容誠 脚色・趙汶眞 撮影・鄭一成 照明・車正男 泰昌興業 株 製作・配給

1971-1980
THE DECLINE OF KOREAN CINEMA

The 1970s are often regarded as the darkest period in the history of Korean cinema. From 1968 onward, the United States began gradually withdrawing from its international military commitments, leading President Park Chung-hee to take measures to strengthen national security, fearing an attack from North Korea. In October 1972, he introduced the Yusin Constitution, which gave him absolute power with an unlimited number of presidential terms, renewable every six years. As a result, opponents were repressed, media were censored, and freedom of expression was almost non-existent.

In 1974, the film law was amended for the fourth time, bringing new regulations for the Korean film industry. The regime encouraged anti-communist, patriotic, and pro-government films that supported domestic policies and portrayed a happy image of the country. Censorship was stepped up considerably: In 1975, 80 percent of screenplays were subject to revision, compared with just 3 percent in 1970.

Film production fell sharply, from 209 films made in 1970 to just 96 in 1979. Although exhibitors were obliged to show Korean films 121 days a year, audience numbers fell sharply from 178 million to 70 million by the end of the decade, leading to the closure of many cinemas and a reduction in the number of screens from 690 to 472 nationwide. Imports of foreign films are still limited to a third of domestic production, and a new law reduced the number of additional quotas to just 5 additional titles per year. As a result, American film releases fell from around 60 titles at the start of the decade to around 30 in the following years, although most of these productions continued to attract on average three times as many viewers as Korean feature films.

The considerable drop in film production was not solely due to government measures: as part of the country's modernization plan, Park Chung-hee's regime encouraged the population to buy televisions on a massive scale to support the development of the national economic industry and, unofficially, to enable better dissemination of government propaganda. As a result, the percentage of households with a television set rose from less than 1 percent in 1966 to more than 50 percent in 1977.

These changes led to a massive migration of directors, actors, and actresses to the small screen. This was the golden age of variety shows, historical soaps such as *My Lady* (TBC, 1970–1971) and *Way of Women* (KBS, 1972), and the broadcasting of sporting events. The profile of cinema-goers was changing, between the disaffection of part of the public for the big screen and a wave of people arriving from the countryside to try to make their fortune in the city. Roughly 62 percent of cinema-goers were now men, and 66 percent were between the ages of 20 and 30, which favored the production of Korean Westerns and martial arts films.

Almost half of the 1,300 feature films produced during the decade were melodramas, with an unexpected revival of shinpa melodrama following the surprise success of *Love Me Once Again* (1968), with over 390,000 admissions, and its sequels *Love Me Once Again 2* and *3* (1969 and 1970) and *Love Me Once More* (1971), all directed by Jung So-young. Anti-communist and literary films recommended by the regime came second. This period also saw the emergence of a sub-genre that was as curious as it was unique in the history of Korean cinema: hostess films, made between 1974 and 1979, which accounted for eight of the ten biggest domestic box office hits of the decade.

The 1970s marked a period of transition for some of the leading directors of the previous decade. Former tycoon Shin Sang-ok found it increasingly difficult to keep his film empire, Shin Films, afloat and eventually lost his producer's license over censorship issues, before being kidnapped by North Korean secret agents. Director and author Yu Hyun-mok could no longer find his place in an increasingly controlled industry: He turned to teaching and making short educational films before making a fleeting return to the cinema in 1978. Lee Man-hee was shunned by his producers for the formal excesses of his literary adaptations of the late 1960s; he was forced to make commissioned films, such as *Break the Chain* (1971), and died after a final film of his own, the masterpiece *Road to Sampo* (1975).

The 1970s was therefore a purely commercial decade of film, during which one interchangeable production followed another under the strict censorship of the regime. It was the golden age of the three most prolific directors in the history of Korean cinema: Kim Soo-yong, considered to be the father of literary adaptations, made 39 films (out of a total of 121), including two absolute masterpieces, *Night Journey* (1977) and *Splendid Outing* (1978).

Im Kwon-taek consolidated his reputation as an honest craftsman by making 41 films (out of a total of 102). Gradually becoming aware of cinema as an art and no longer as mere entertainment, he began to choose his projects more carefully in the second half of the 1970s. *Genealogy* (1979) marked the start of a long series of masterpieces to come, earning him the nickname of Best Korean Director of All Time.

Go Yeong-nam was the most prolific director, making 54 films during the decade (out of a total of 109), including the masterpiece *The Shower* (1979).

A new generation of filmmakers attempted to revolutionize the industry: under the aegis of Ha Gil-jong, five professionals created the film collective Era of Image to make realistic films aimed at a typical young adult audience. Although their initiative was a relative failure, it sowed the seeds of the future New Waves of Korean cinema in the 1980s and 1990s.

In 1971, Lee Seong-gu attempted to raise the technical quality of Korean cinema by making *The Love Story of Chun-hyang*, the first 70mm production. However, the high cost of

---

Previous page: *Splendid Outing* (Kim Soo-yong, 1977).

film made it a unique experience. As for Jung Jin-woo, he tried to develop live sound recording after almost winning the Golden Bear for his film *Long Live the Island Frogs!* at the 1973 Berlin International Film Festival, against Satyajit Ray's *Distant Thunder*. The award that previously eluded him mainly due to the overdubbing of voices, as was still customary in Korea. He shot his subsequent films in direct sound and encouraged film professionals to do the same to match world standards and compete more successfully at international festivals.

A street in Seoul in the 1970s.

MARTIAL ARTS FILMS

During the 1970s, one of the most significant phenomena in Korea was the rise of a new film genre from Hong Kong, which would eventually make Hollywood tremble: kung fu films, popularized by the worldwide success of Bruce Lee. The history of Korean martial arts films is marked by the constant exchange with Hong Kong, which made it possible to produce more than 200 films in the genre in that decade.

Korean martial arts films are strongly influenced by Chinese chivalric stories from the Ming dynasty (1368–1644), which inspired one of the most important works of Korean literature, *The Story of Hong Gildong* (attributed to Heo Gyun, circa 1608–1613). This fictional biography tells the story of a young man who, at the head of a group of brigands, steals from the rich to give to the poor. Toward the end of the Qing dynasty (1644–1911), these Chinese novels were codified to give rise to the *wuxia* films, stories of knights errant who acquire superhuman skills through their experience in the martial arts.

The arrival of literacy and modern printing in Korea in the nineteenth and twentieth centuries sparked a new craze for Chinese wuxia novels. This movement was partly inspired by the success of the American film *Robin Hood* (Allan Dwan, 1922) and led producers in the 1920s to make the first Korean martial arts film, *The Captain of Bandits* (Lee Gyeong-son, 1926). The film's failure and the tightening of censorship under the Japanese occupation made it a unique case.

Meanwhile, in the Chinese Republic founded by Chiang Kai-shek, the wuxia movement, which emphasized individual values, was particularly popular with young people who no longer identified with Confucian traditions. The Chinese film industry, mainly based in Shanghai, naturally seized on the subject and produced a series of martial arts films adapted from novels. However, in the early 1930s, the government decided to ban the genre, prompting some producers, including the Shaw Brothers, to emigrate to Hong Kong to pursue their activities.

The Shaw Brothers studios, which dominated the Asian film industry in the 1950s, sought to collaborate with other countries, and saw Korea as an ideal partner because of its low costs and exceptional natural scenery. The first Korean–Hong Kong co-productions were launched at the end of the 1950s with melodramas such as *The Affection of the World* (Kim Hwa-rang, 1957), *Love with an Alien* (Jeon Chang-keun, Tu Kuang-Chi, Mitsuo Wakasugi, 1958), and *Nostalgia* (Chung Chang-wha, 1958).

In the 1960s, co-productions of anti-communist spy thrillers inspired by the *James Bond* franchise and shot partly in Hong Kong enjoyed a golden age with films such as *The International Spy* and *The International Gold Bar Incident* (Jang Il-ho, 1965 and 1966) and *Starberry Kim* (Go Yeong-nam, 1966).

During the 1960s, there was a revival of interest in literature in Korea, and Kim Kwang-ju (1910–1973) took advantage of this to translate a large number of Chinese and Taiwanese stories of chivalry, which he felt were closer to Korean culture than to Western culture. Kim Kwang-ju had directed a feature film entitled *Beautiful Devotion* (1933), before fleeing the Japanese occupation to settle in Shanghai, where he became the assistant to the Korean director Jeong Gi-tak, who had made martial arts films in particular. Kim Kwang-ju's intuition proved to be right. On his return to Korea, his translations of wuxia novels quickly became best-selling books and were successfully adapted as serials in newspapers and on the radio.

Korean martial arts films were commissioned to emulate the commercial success of Hong Kong productions, but they also allowed young up-and-coming filmmakers to refine their own style, such as Im Kwon-taek did with *A Precious Sword, a Knife of Thunder* (1969).

Historical Korean films such as *King's Secret Agent* (Yu Sim-pyeong, 1963), *Eight Swordsmen* (Lee Kang-cheon, 1963), and *Hwalbindang* (Gang Jung-hwan, 1965) already included scenes of swordplay and hand-to-hand combat, but it was only after the success of Hong Kong productions that Korean martial arts films really took off. It was at the 13th Asian Film Festival in Seoul that director-producer-distributor Shin Sang-ok discovered *Come Drink with Me* (King Hu, 1966). Although it was not yet well known at the time, this film is now regarded as a revolution in Chinese-language wuxia films and as the origin of worldwide interest in martial arts cinema. Shin Sang-ok decided to distribute it, seeing a great opportunity to capitalize on the craze for wuxia novels.

It was a triumph, with over 300,000 admissions. Shin Sang-ok distributed three other films, this time by Chang Cheh: *The Magnificent Trio* (1966), *The One-Armed Swordsman* (1967), and *Golden Swallow* (1968), which drew a total of over 700,000 spectators. These successes were accompanied by the re-publication of 30 wuxia novels by Taiwanese authors Wolong Sheng (1930–1997) and Sima Ling (1933–1989), reinforcing the craze for the martial arts film genre.

The Hong Kongers were involved in the first Korean martial arts films from the outset, notably providing the choreography for *Agile*

Tiger (Gwon Yeong-sun and Sun Ya-fu, 1969) and *Bandit* (Ahn Hyun-chul, 1969). For their part, Korean directors drew heavily on the first films imported from Hong Kong: *A Wandering Swordsman and 108 Bars of Gold* (Chung Chang-wha, 1968), *Night of Full Moon* (Im Kwon-taek, 1969), and *Sad Story of a Faithful Woman* (Choe Gyeong-ok, 1969) borrowed the model of *Come Drink with Me* by giving the lead role to a woman, while *The Great Swordsman* (Gang Beom-gu, 1968), *Armless Swordsman* (Lim Won-sick, 1969), and *One-Armed Master of the Wild* (Kim Yeong-hyo, 1970) imitated *The One-Armed Swordsman* and its hero.

Above all, Korean producers saw an opportunity to produce domestic films quickly and cheaply to meet the import demands of foreign films. All they had to do was include the name of a Korean director and three Korean actors in the credits to qualify their production as "domestic." They also used other tricks, such as shooting the same film in Korean and Hong Kong versions, alternating lead actors from the respective countries between takes, or even paying to add a Korean co-director to the credits of Hong Kong films. Some producers, such as Shin Sang-ok, simply added a few scenes shot in Korea to integrate them into Hong Kong films that had already been completed or replaced the names of Chinese actors with those of Korean actors. These factors explain why so many martial arts films were produced in such a short space of time in the 1960s and 1970s. In France, some Korean films, such as *Tomb for a Strongman* and *Close Kung Fu Encounter* (Kim Si-hyun, 1974 and 1975) or *Black Leopard* (also known as *The Taekwando Hero*) (Jung Kwang-woon, 1975), were even released as Hong Kong productions!

In return, Korean films also influenced Hong Kong cinema. In 1972, Huang Feng sent his young protégés, including future superstars Sammo Hung, Jackie Chan, and Angela Mao, on a four-month intensive hapkido course in Korea, where they made *Hapkido* [released as *Lady Kung Fu* in North America] (1972). The discovery of this film inspired Bruce Lee to include a hapkido master in his *Game of Death* (Bruce Lee and Robert Clouse, 1978), partly shot in Korea. Jackie Chan even decided to stay in Korea for two years after his internship to perfect his martial arts technique, returning later to appear in four Lo Wei productions shot on location: *The Killer Meteors* (1976), *To Kill with Intrigue* (Lo Wei and Kim Chin-tai, 1977), *Spiritual Kung Fu* (1978), and *Dragon Fist* (1979). Even King Hu, the famous Taiwanese writer-filmmaker behind the worldwide craze for martial arts films with *Come Drink with Me*, directed *Raining in the Mountain* (1979) and *Legend in the Mountain* (1979) in Korea.

The worldwide craze for martial arts films also encouraged many Korean talents to try their luck in Hong Kong. Chung Chang-wha directed *Temptress of a Thousand Faces* (1969), the first Hong Kong film to be officially sold in Europe, and *Five Fingers of Death* (*Tian xia di yi quan*) (1972), the first martial arts film to top the American box office on release. The film went on to become one of the ten biggest box office hits of the year in the United States and launched the worldwide martial arts film craze. Chung Chang-wha is nicknamed the Godfather of Korean Action Cinema.

Lee Doo-yong is considered Korea's most famous martial arts director. After the success of his first film, the melodrama *The Lost Wedding Veil* (1970), Hapdong Films asked him to direct a big-budget "taekwondo film." Lee Doo-yong organized an extensive cast, bringing together several hundred martial artists and selecting only the best twelve. The incredible success of his Bruce Lee film *Manchurian Tiger* (1974) rekindled interest in domestic martial arts films, and thirteen of the fourteen production companies in existence at the time began producing similar titles. Lee Doo-yong made five more such films in 1974 alone, including *Left Foot of Wrath*, starring Bruce Lee, and the diptych

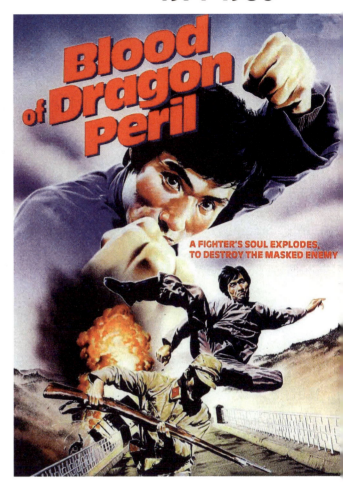

Returned Single-Legged Man 1 and *2*, inspired by the Hong Kong film *The One-Armed Swordsman*. But, bored with the genre, he redirected his career toward contemporary crime films inspired by American cinema, before making two world-famous masterpieces: *The Hut* (*Pimak*) (1981) and *Spinning the Tales of Cruelty Toward Women* (1984).

Korean martial arts films continued to enjoy great popularity in the 1980s, in contrast to the growing disinterest of international audiences, with the successes, notably, of *New Journey to the West* (Kim Jong-seong and Jin Jun-ryang, 1983) and *Fool 2* (Lee Doo-yong, 1986), with over 100,000 admissions. It was not until the end of the decade that the genre gradually gave way to more contemporary action films.

A few rare martial arts films have been produced more recently, such as *The Warrior* (Kim Sung-soo, 2001), inspired by the Chinese historical epics of the early 2000s, the formally remarkable *Duelist* (Lee Myung-se, 2005), *The City of Violence* (Ryoo Seung-wan, 2006), made in the wake of the worldwide success of *Kill Bill 1* and *2* (Quentin Tarantino, 2003–2004), and *The Swordsman* (Choi Jae-hun, 2020).

Thus, Korean cinema's first foray onto the world stage took place discreetly, camouflaged among martial arts productions often of mediocre quality or labeled as "Asian or Hong Kong productions."

Blood of Dragon Peril (1978) was a Korean movie made in co-production with Hong Kong. It was adapted from the popular manwha *Bridal Mask* (1974). It has been released worldwide as a sole Hong Kong production.

Following page spread: The real name of director *Rocky Man of Blood of Dragon Peril* was Kim Seon-gyeong.

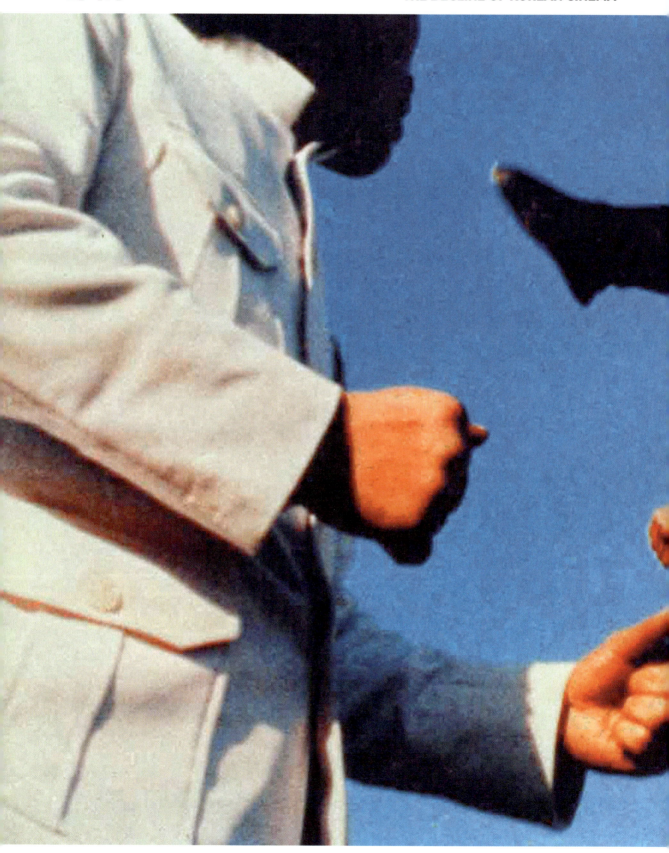

WESTERNS

In 2008, *The Good, the Bad, the Weird* (Kim Jee-woon), presented out of competition at the Cannes Film Festival, created quite a stir. It was one of the most expensive films in the history of Korean cinema, with a budget of around $17 million. While some critics consider it a mere "Asian curiosity" or "the first Korean Western," *The Good, the Bad, the Weird* is in fact a moving tribute to the Manchurian action films of the 1960s and 1970s.

In the 1960s, war films, with their impressive battle scenes and crowds, were expensive. Producers were looking for new, less expensive, and equally effective action genres. Among the thrillers, crime films, and gangster movies, a trend emerged: the Manchurian action film. At first, these productions recounted the sacrifice of independent resistance fighters in their struggle against the Japanese occupiers in the region of Manchuria before turning into veritable Korean Westerns in the second half of the 1960s.

Why Manchuria? This region has a rich and complex history, shared in ancient times between the proto-Korean and Siberian Tungus peoples. In the course of history, it came under the control of the Chinese in 108 BC, the Korean kingdom of Koguryo and the Korean-Tungus kingdom of Balhae until 926, before returning to Chinese rule. Despite this, Manchuria was often a source of fascination for ambitious Korean rulers eager to conquer new territories.

At the turn of the nineteenth and twentieth centuries, Manchuria was disputed by the Russians and Japanese, leading to the Russo-Japanese War of 1904–1905. After Japan's victory, the Korean peninsula became part of its empire, and Manchuria became a refuge for many Koreans fleeing the Japanese occupation. They settled as peasants or independence fighters. In 1931, Japan invaded the region and established the puppet state of Manchukuo. With the division of Korea in 1948, over 2 million Koreans found themselves isolated from their nation and stateless, and they later became Chinese citizens. The Manchurian land became a symbol of exile, resistance, heroism, and past glory for Koreans.

Among the first filmmakers to set their stories in Manchuria were Gang Beom-gu, Chung Chang-wha, and Kim Muk. From the 1950s onward, these three filmmakers sought to shake up the endless melodramas with more dynamic works. Gang Beom-gu directed *Harbin at Sunset* (1959), the first Manchurian action film, in which a young man sets out to find his resistance-fighter brother in Manchuria, and finds himself embroiled in a dark tale of stolen jewels involving dangerous Chinese. Chung Chang-wha followed up with *Horizon* (1961), about a former independence soldier who forms a secret society, the Black Dragons, to fight the Japanese in the city of Harbin. In 1961, Kim Muk released *At Daybreak,* recounting the Korean resistance fight against the Japanese occupiers in Manchuria. Although *Farewell to the Duman River* (1962), Im Kwon-taek's first feature, is not strictly speaking a Manchurian action film (the story takes place entirely in the vicinity of Manchuria), the epic final battle on skis predates the best similar scenes in Korean Westerns by several years.

The dozen or so films produced between 1962 and 1967 continued to follow the theme of Korean resistance to Japanese occupation in the symbolic region of Manchuria. Initially, these productions had only a vague connection with the Western, before undergoing a radical transformation in 1967. Cowboy films had always been very popular in Korea, from the first American imports in the 1910s and 1920s, through to the revival of cinema in the 1950s. However, the successive failures of *The Alamo* (John Wayne, 1960), *4 for Texas* (Robert Aldrich, 1963), and *Major Dundee* (Sam Peckinpah, 1965) in the early 1960s led to the decline of American Westerns.

Shin Sang-ok, a director-producer-distributor on the lookout for the latest global trends, spotted the first spaghetti Westerns. The Korean release of *A Fistful of Dollars* (Sergio Leone, 1964) attracted 350,000 spectators in Seoul alone, and sparked a veritable craze for the genre between 1967 and 1969—the year in which the regime banned their importation, after a final release, *Django* (Sergio Corbucci, 1966), due to the increasing violence in a twilight genre.

In 1967, Shin Sang-ok began work on *Mounted Bandits*, promoted (incorrectly) as the "first Eastern Western," followed by *Homeless* (1968), a fusion of Manchurian action films and the American Western *Shane* (George Stevens, 1953), in which a former resistance fighter arrives in remote Manchuria to help a woman and her son protect their farm from bandits. These films triggered a wave of some 20 Korean Westerns shot between 1967 and 1973. Most were "westernized" Manchurian action films, such as *Eagle of the Plains* and *One-Eyed Park* (Im Kwon-taek, 1969 and 1970), while others were blatant plagiarisms of American classics like *Six Terminators* (Gwon Yeong-sun, 1970) and *The Magnificent Seven* (Kim In-soo, 1971), copying the film

of the same title *The Magnificent Seven* (John Sturges, 1960), itself inspired by Japanese Akira Kurosawa's *Seven Samurai* (1954). *Female Bandits* (Choe Gyeong-ok, 1967) was the first to mix the Western with the martial arts film, another leading genre of the time, while *Outlaw on a Donkey* (Ahn Il-nam, 1970) was the first parody of the genre.

Curiously, in the late 1960s and, above all, in the early 1970s, the form of the films evolved along with their content. The fantasized Manchuria was gradually transformed from a humid climate into a desert region that increasingly resembled the American West. The courageous Korean resistance fighters of early Manchurian action films gradually give way to lonely, marginalized characters rebelling against a "totalitarian state." They end up in money stories involving Chinese or Japanese villains. Nevertheless, morality is always preserved, as any fortune acquired by the hero is systematically donated to Korean independence fighters. The

---

Mounted Bandits (Shin Sang-ok, 1967).

most discerning viewers will not fail to draw parallels between these marginalized people in a totalitarian state in their "individualistic race for wealth" and the economic situation in Korea in the 1970s.

Break the Chain (Lee Man-hee, 1971) represents both the culmination and the end of the Korean Western genre. Loosely inspired by *The Good, the Bad, and the Ugly* (Sergio Leone, 1966), the film recounts the frantic race for a statuette between a hitman, a thief, and a Japanese spy. None of the main characters is interested in the actual contents of the statuette, which conceals a list of the names of resistance fighters in Manchuria, who can determine whether they live or die depending on who recovers the precious object. The three heroes are obsessed solely with glory and money.

Break the Chain (1971) was a commissioned film for Lee Man-hee, who was then at the bottom of his career. This feature accumulates just about every genre cliché from dozens of previous films: absurd action scenes, caricatured characters dressed in leopard outfits, 1940s gangster suits, or leather jackets, firing Russian, German, and English pistols, or Japanese, Chinese, or American rifles. The film is a shining example of Korean cinema's ability to assimilate global influences and turn them into a purely national product.

Due to competition from martial arts films and increased censorship under the Yusin regime, the Korean Western disappeared as quickly as it appeared. Among the few titles still released after *Break the Chain*, Lee Doo-yong's *Manchurian Tiger* (1974) is more of a martial arts film set in a Western context, while *Janggo Is Red Hot* (Choi Yung-chul, 1986) is an embarrassing parody of *Django* set in 1980s Seoul. Since then, only *Crazy Lee* (Ryoo Seung-wan), 2008's *The Good, the Bad, the Weird*, and the Netflix series *Song of the Bandits* (Hwang Jun-hyuk, 2023) have paid tribute to the genre.

Previous page spread: *Six Terminators* (1970) is one of the many Korean Westerns that have shamelessly followed American models. In this case, it is a loose remake of *The Magnificent Seven*, itself inspired by the Japanese swordplay film *Seven Samurai* (Akira Kurosawa, 1954).

The Good, the Bad, the Weird (2008) is one of the few recent tributes to the so-called Manchurian action films of the 1960s and 1970s.

HOSTESS FILMS

One of the most striking cinematic events of the 1970s was the sudden, short-lived emergence of the hostess film. The films were a phenomenal success, accounting for eight of the ten biggest Korean box office hits of the 1970s, including *Winter Woman* (Kim Ho-sun, 1977) and *Heavenly Homecoming to Stars* (Lee Chang-ho, 1974), first and second on the list with 585,000 and 465,000 admissions, respectively. An astonishing genre under the darkest era of Park Chung-hee's presidency, combining the two elements usually most repressed by censors at the time: eroticism and social realism.

The economic development plan put in place by Park's presidency led to major changes in the Korean national economy in the 1960s and 1970s. Between 1961 and 1981, gross national income rose from $471 to $1,549, while the main export industries of agriculture, mining, and fishing were replaced by textiles. This sector, which employed mainly women workers, helped to increase the proportion of women in the workforce from 26.8 percent in 1960 to 45.7 percent in 1976.

Industrialization led to a massive rural exodus, with the population of Seoul doubling from 2.5 million in 1960 to 5 million in 1970. During this period, the Park regime encouraged sex tourism, leading to a sharp increase in the number of tourists: Japanese tourists, for example, rose from 96,531 in 1971 to 649,707 in 1979, 85 percent of whom were men traveling alone. Unfortunately, many women from rural areas became victims of unscrupulous trafficking networks.

Newspapers and magazines of the time covered the sex worker phenomenon extensively, with the emergence of the first tabloids, such as *Sunday Seoul* (1968–1991), which sold like hotcakes by publishing sensationalist interviews with these women, first anonymously, then openly. Some prostitutes enjoyed great success by publishing their memoirs, such as Oh

Mi-young's *Miss O's Apartment* or Yoon Go-na's *Barmaid Number 77 / I Am Lady Number 77*, which were adapted for the cinema in 1978 by Byun Jang-ho and Park Ho-tae. Of the 2,918 literary works published between 1970 and 1985, 102 were autobiographies or fiction dealing directly with bar hostesses.

The phenomenon was a boon for third-generation authors, who emerged at this time. This name refers to writers who published novels in Korean for the first time, rather than in the Japanese of the occupation period. Among them, Cho Seon-jak, Cho Hae-il, and Choi In-ho often described the tragic fate of people who had fallen victim to the industrialization of the 1970s and who lived "on the margins of society," such as prostitutes.

Lee Chang-ho, former assistant director to Shin Sang-ok, was one of the first to believe in the potential of these subjects. He landed the rights to Choi In-ho's *Heavenly Homecoming to Stars*, the most popular novel since the publication of *Madame Freedom* in 1952, and convinced his friend Ha Gil-jong to produce it in 1974. Lee Chang-ho made this first film completely on instinct, using photographs cut from clandestinely acquired Japanese film magazines to direct his cinematographer Jang Seok-jun. He also spent 40 days fine-tuning the soundtrack with conductor Lee Jang-hui, a rare practice at a time when music was generally recorded in just a few days.

The film opened to 465,000 spectators, making it the highest-grossing film in the history of Korean cinema. Although this success is partly attributed to the popular novel on which it is based, it is above all the film's social-realist approach, dynamic direction, and innovative soundtrack that appeal to audiences. The main character, Kyeong-ah, embodies the archetypal "sacrificial woman" of Korea's patriarchal society in the 1970s, tossed from adulterer to abusive husband in a series of failed relationships, before ending up as a bar hostess to support

her mother, who has stayed in the country. The love of a painter can no longer save her from her tragic fate.

The success of *Yeong-ja's Heydays* (Kim Ho-sun, 1975) the following year, with 361,000 admissions, consolidated what was initially called the youth film, in reference to the young age of this emerging new generation of directors. The story, adapted from a novel by Cho Seon-jak, follows the misadventures of Yeong-ja, a naive and innocent young maid, who is abused by her boss's son, exploited in a textile factory, loses an arm in a car accident, and ends up as a bar hostess. She finally marries a disabled man, more out of pity than love, as he, like her, is marginalized in an increasingly individualistic and competitive economic society.

Director Kim Ho-sun confirmed the success of his hostess films with his next two, *Cuckoo's Dolls* (also known as *Women's Street*, 1976) and above all *Winter Woman* (1977), which became—in turn—the biggest hit in Korean cin-

ema history, with 585,000 admissions. *Cuckoo's Dolls* depicts the lives of several prostitutes in a red-light district, while *Winter Woman* focuses on the story of Lee-hwa, who decides to "sleep" with lonely strangers as an offer of comfort in Korea's changing society.

Other films in the same genre came out in the wake of cultural changes, such as *A Woman I Betrayed* (Jung So-young, 1978), *Yeong-ah's Confession* (Byun Jang-ho, 1978), and *Woman on the Asphalt* (Moon Yeo-song, 1978). They are seen as a reflection of Korean culture and society at the time, addressing themes such as rural exodus, poverty, unemployment, loneliness, sexuality, and social inequality. The heroines of these films also raise important questions about the status of women, victims of stigmatization, and discrimination in Korea's patriarchal society.

The 1972 floods in Seoul.

The term *hostess* is rather overused. While *Wedding Dress of Tears 1* and *2* (Byun Jang-ho, 1973 and 1974) feature a prostitute as the main character, they are defined as melodramas, while the genre classics *Winter Woman* (1977), *A Rose with Thorns* (Jung Jin-woo, 1979), and *Heavenly Homecoming to Stars 2* (Ha Gil-jong, 1978) do not include any hostess characters. Eventually, over the years, the hostess film became synonymous with any vaguely erotic film featuring a female character who falls victim to patriarchal society. These productions are increasingly opportunistic and focused on prostitution, losing the satirical and critical dimension of the genre's classics.

The advent of hostess films is rather curious in the highly censored Korean film industry of the 1970s. The genre constitutes a transgression not only for its scenes of nudity and sexuality, but also for its depictions, strictly forbidden by film law, of prostitutes, red light districts, and slums. The explanation could lie in a desire on the part of Park Chung-hee's regime to relax censorship on sexuality at the height of his presidency, in order to divert public attention from the real problems of society, a method also employed by the Philippine regime of Ferdinand Marcos in the 1970s, and Suharto's Indonesian regime in the 1990s, with the same type of erotic productions being released during the darkest years of their rule.

But the directors of the time were also resourceful. They loaded their scripts with as many pernicious elements as possible and negotiated "lighter" versions that were still daring by the standards of the time. As for the authorization to film in areas that were in principle off-limits, the filmmakers were always careful to include examples of the "success" of Park's policies, such as the modernization of railroads and road networks, or the new districts of downtown Seoul, to appease the censors.

The success of hostess films declined sharply in the early 1980s, following the failure of several sequels to the genre's greatest classics: *A Woman I Betrayed 2* (Hong Seong-ki, 1980), *Heavenly Homecoming to Stars 3* (Lee Gyeong-tae, 1981), and *26 x 365 = 0 II* (Choi Soo-ji, 1982). This decline in popularity did not, however, mean the end of erotic films in Korea: The genre evolved toward even more daring productions in the 1980s, which broke all box office records and were even exported to prestigious international festivals.

Vast construction sites in the 1960s and 1970s were part of President Park Chung-hee's modernization program to relieve congestion in downtown Seoul.

THE ERA OF
IMAGE REVOLUTION

Ha Gil-jong is considered one of the most important directors of the 1970s, if not of all time. He sought to revolutionize the industry during the most sinister political period of Park Chung-hee's presidency: first through his films, then by co-creating the collective movement Era of Image to attempt to trigger a Korean New Wave. Although most of his films were commercial failures on release, they have since been widely reappraised. His death at the age of 37 from a heart attack prevented him from realizing his ambitions but helped to forge his legend.

Born in Busan in 1941, Ha Gil-jong was deeply affected by the death of three of his friends during the April Revolution in 1960. He decided to go into exile in the United States, where he became one of the first Korean students to graduate from the University of California, in 1969. Strongly influenced by the hippie movement, he set out to revolutionize Korean cinema with his first feature film, *The Pollen of Flowers* (1972). Loosely inspired by Pier Paolo Pasolini's *Theorem* [*Teorema*] (1968), the film tells the story of a wealthy bisexual businessman's lover, who is invited to spend a weekend with the latter's family, triggering a series of tragic events. This is a thinly veiled satire of the consequences of Park Chung-hee's regime, with the action taking place in a villa nicknamed the Blue House (the equivalent of the White House, in America) and the lover representing the Korean people, on whom the wealthy corrupt family unleashes its physical and mental wrath.

The film fell victim to censorship, which intensified under the Park regime in the 1970s,

Love with My Whole Body (1973) marks screenwriter Hong Pa's transition to directing and astonishes with its daring formal and narrative approach.

and was released in a truncated version of 30 minutes. Ha Gil-jong tried to get around the problem by setting his second film, *Fidelity* (1974), under Japanese occupation, thus justifying the violence of the story by the cruelty of the occupier. The film is loosely based on the Thai tale *Ghost of Mae Nak* and tells the story of a soldier returning from war who discovers (belatedly) that his wife and daughter are in fact ghosts, since they were massacred by the Japanese. The film again falls victim to censorship, with 20 minutes of explicit sexual scenes removed.

Ha Gil-jong then directed *The March of Fools* (1975), a youth film considered a safe haven from the censors. However, his story of three students in revolt against society was deemed "subversive and dangerous to public morals," and resulted in a further 20-minute cut. The film was nevertheless a great success, with over 153,000 viewers, partly because it was adapted from a novel by the popular writer Choi In-ho (*Heavenly Homecoming to Stars*), and partly because of its dynamic direction and engaging soundtrack.

Building on his success, Ha Gil-jong, together with film critic Byun In-shik and directors Lee Chang-ho, Kim Ho-sun, Lee Won-se, and Hong Pa, founded the film collective Yeongsang sidae (the Era of Image). This movement was inspired by various currents in cinema: Italian neo-realism, the French, Japanese, and German New Wave, British Free Cinema, and American New Cinema. The collective's aim was to use cinema as a means of resistance against political and cultural oppression, producing films aimed at young adults that challenged social conventions.

In July 1975, the collective published a manifesto in the press, which stated, in particular: "A film should be a spear, capable of tearing down the walls of authoritarianism. Have we ever had a New Wave in this country? We, the 'protectors of the image,' declare with this man-

ifesto that we will create new aesthetic values by uniting our different ideals." But unlike the KAPF, the first (proletarian) film collective in the history of Korean cinema, in the 1920s, the Era of Image did not adopt a political ideology; rather, it attempted to propose "a different kind of cinema," drawing inspiration from associations of the 1960s and 1970s, such as Cine-poem in 1963 and the Korean Short Film Association in 1970, created by director Yu Hyun-mok and involving Byun In-shik and Ha Gil-jong.

Among the collective's members, film critic Byun In-shik is best known for his 1972 essay *The Rebellion of Film Aesthetics* [*Yonghwamiui Panran*]. In it, he expresses his disappointment with Korean cinema, which, in his view, has never succeeded in freeing itself from the shackles imposed by the Japanese occupiers, contenting itself with tirelessly producing shinpa melodramas and plagiarisms of Nipponese literature.

Another member, Hong Pa, made a name for himself as a screenwriter, but failed to break through as a director, with the successive failures of his *Love with My Whole Body* (1973) and *Mystic* (1974). Lee Won-se, Kim Soo-yong's former assistant for ten years, notable for the literary adaptations *Seashore Village* (1965) and *Mist* (1967), began directing films in the early 1970s, penning three of the six movies in the popular anti-communist spy thriller franchise *Special Investigation Unit* (1973–1975).

Lee Chang-ho, meanwhile, directed the biggest hit in Korean film history on its release, *Heavenly Homecoming to Stars* (1974), launching the wave of hostess films.

The fifth member of the collective, Kim Ho-sun, consolidated the genre with the success of *Yeong-ja's Heydays* (1975), his own film.

The collective began by publishing a quarterly film magazine inspired by the Parisian *Cahiers du Cinéma,* before launching an appeal to recruit new members and spot potential talent. More than 900 people responded, including future directors Lee Say-mean (*The Rose and*

the Gambler, 1983), Lee Hwang-lim (*Moonlight Melody*, 1985), Jang Gil-su (*Love Song of Lethe*, 1987), and Chung Ji-young (*North Korean Partisan in South Korea*, 1990), as well as actors Kim Myeong-soo (*JSA—Joint Security Area*, Park Chan-wook, 2000) and Yim Sung-min (*Between the Knees*, Lee Chang-ho, 1984).

The collective's aim was clear: to make films for young adults that were different from the usual cinematic standards. Lee Chang-ho explored the musical comedy genre with an original script, *Yes, Good-Bye for Today* (1976). Kim Ho-sun continued to work in the hostess genre with *Cuckoo's Dolls* (1976) and *Winter Woman* (1977). Hong Pa tried his hand at two intimate melodramas, one about student love, *Wood and Swamp* (1975), and the other about marital problems, *Fire* (1978). Lee Won-see experimented further with form, deconstructing narrative structures in *The Flower and the Snake* (1975), along the lines of French filmmaker Alain Resnais's work of the period.

Attempting to produce a success to replenish the collective's coffers, Ha Gil-jong made the somewhat conventional comedy *Wanted: Girl* (1976), the story of a young man from the countryside looking for a wife in the city. After the failure of this film, he directed (the incredible) historical feature *The Ascension of Han-ne* (1977), in which a mentally challenged man brings home

a mysterious woman, who becomes the target of the village shaman's wrath. Under the guise of an erotic fable, the film denounces the Misin tapa movement, which violently repressed folk religious beliefs under Park's regime in the 1970s. *The Ascension of Han-ne* was completely banned from release, and only rediscovered years later. This film foreshadowed the erotic historical film genre of the 1980s by a decade.

The repeated failure of these films, as well as Lee Chang-ho's arrest in 1975 for alleged use of marijuana, led to the collective's dissolution in 1978, after only three years of existence. One of the reasons for this failure probably lay in the directors' inability to "break down the walls of authoritarianism" during the strictest period of Park's regime: the second half of the 1970s was marked by strong repression of youth, with bans on gatherings, long hair, bell-bottoms, and miniskirts. Many artists were arrested under false pretenses, to prevent any form of popular

The Ascension of Han-ne (1977) foreshadowed the historical erotic films of the 1980s but was banned after its release for its sensuality and mocking political allusions.

protest. The collective's films were simply too far ahead of their time.

After the failure of the Era of Image, Ha Gil-jong directed two new adaptations of works by author Choi In-ho: *Heavenly Homecoming to Stars 2* (1978) and *Byeong-tae and Yeong-ja* (1979), an unofficial sequel to his *The March of Fools*. Unfortunately, these films failed to recapture the creative momentum of his early years.

Although the Era of Image collective and Ha Gil-jong's cinema may not have revolutionized the cinematic landscape at the time, their legacy is immense. In particular, they encouraged future generations of filmmakers to use their art to question and transform society. Their films were instrumental in the emergence of independent cinema in the 1980s and the Korean New Wave in the early 1990s.

ANTI-COMMUNIST FILMS

The very first anti-communist film, *A Fellow Soldier* (Hong Gae-myeong, 1949), was released just one year after the August 15, 1948, transfer of power from the US military government to President Rhee Syngman. It was a blockbuster financed by the United States, with over 20,000 extras and impressive battle scenes. The film tells the story of two brothers who flee the tyranny of North Korea to become policemen and soldiers in South Korea to fight communism. The first independent anti-Communist production, *Breaking Through the Wall* (1949), marks the debut of Han Hyung-mo, future director of *Madame Freedom* (1956), which tells the story of two brothers-in-law, one a Communist and the other a soldier, who end up challenging each other to a duel.

These films were the starting point for a series of 17 anti-communist films shot between 1950 and 1956, to which we can add the many documentaries made during the Korean War (1950–1953). Although they reflect a Korean policy aligned with that of the American government in a joint effort to "demonize communist ideology" in a country still traumatized by the recent division, these productions initially resemble more classic melodramas with North Korean characters manipulated by the "evil" Chinese and their Soviet allies. In *The Hand of Destiny* (Han Hyung-mo, 1954), for example, the heroine is a North Korean spy torn between her love for a South Korean and her loyalty to her new homeland, while the enemy soldiers in *The Battle Line of Freedom* (Kim Hong, 1955) are presented as victims "instrumentalized" by the regime.

The film *Piagol* (Lee Kang-cheon, 1955) sparked controversy as the first anti-communist feature film to take sides by adapting the true story of a Communist partisan unit trapped in the South after the armistice was signed in 1953. On its release, the director, Lee Kang-cheon, was

accused of violating the 1948 National Security Law, which forbids any sympathy for the North Korean regime. After redacting certain scenes and shooting a new ending to show the North Korean heroine deciding to stay in South Korea, *Piagol* was finally authorized for theatrical release.

Lee Man-hee suffered a radically different fate ten years later under Park Chung-hee's regime: *Seven Women P.O.Ws.* (1965) tells the story of a North Korean unit that rescues South Korean female soldiers held prisoner by the Chinese army. Accused of violating the National Security Act with his "overly humanist" portrayal of the enemy, Lee Man-hee was this time imprisoned and tortured. His film was finally authorized for release under the title *The Return of the Female Soldiers*, in a version cut by 40 minutes. This was a warning to filmmakers at the time about the risks involved in portraying North Koreans in a positive light.

Rhee Syngman's policy of leaning more toward an anti-Japanese attitude in the second half of the 1950s reduced the number of anti-communist films to be released between 1956 and 1961, but they returned in force under the presidency of Park Chung-hee (1962–1979). The aim was to prove loyalty to the American allies at the height of the Cold War, as well as to repudiate North Korea, which was economically superior at the time.

Five Marines (Kim Kee-duk, 1961) is a tribute to South Korean soldiers, based on the original idea of a general close to President Park. It was the first genuine Korean

Brotherhood or *The Brotherhood of War* (*Taegukgi*, Kang Je-gyu, 2004), an anti-communist film, became the biggest hit of all time on its release in Korea.

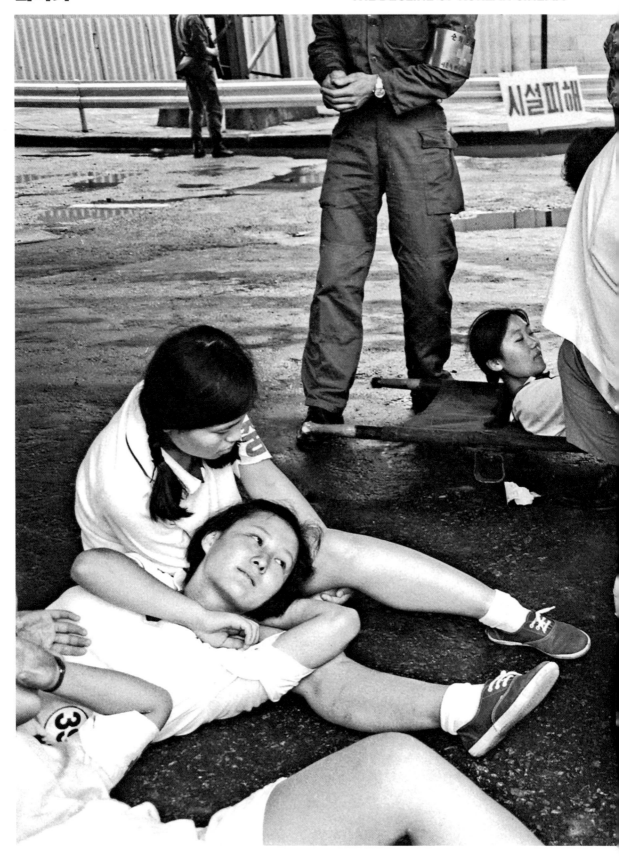

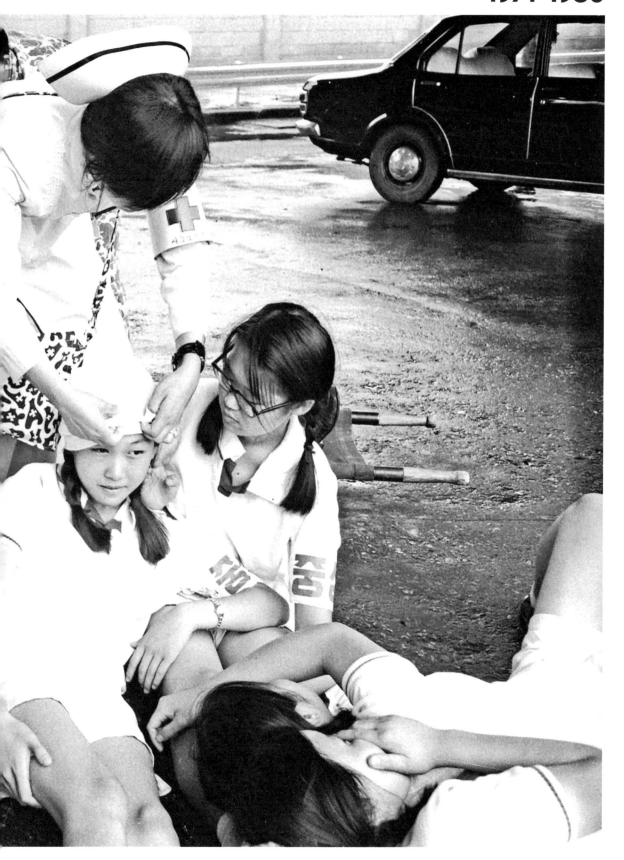

war film, with many battle scenes made with the support of the army. The film was a public success, with 50,000 admissions, and was quickly followed by two other productions, *The Marines Who Never Returned* (Lee Man-hee, 1963) and *Red Scarf* (Shin Sang-ok, 1964), which attracted over 200,000 spectators each. War films such as *The Fighting Lions* (Kim Muk, 1962), *YMS-504 of the Navy* (Lee Man-hee, 1963), and *The Incheon Landing Operation* (Jo Keung-ha, 1965) were a hit with viewers, who were less interested in the anti-communist message than in the promise of big-screen entertainment.

In 1966, the creation of two special awards for Best Anti-Communist Screenplay and Best Anti-Communist Film at the Grand Bell Awards (the Korean equivalent of the American Oscars) led to a significant increase in the number of productions, from 12 in 1964 to over 40 in 1968. In addition, the mobilization of 320,000 South Korean soldiers to support the American army in the Vietnam War inspired films such as *Operation Tiger* (Kim Muk, 1966) and *Female Vietcong No. 18* (Gang Beom-gu, 1967), which were shot directly on location in real-life conditions, causing injury and even death to several technicians.

Anti-communism quickly infiltrated all Korean film genres: melodrama and war films first, then comedies such as *The Unknown Future* (Kim Hwa-rang, 1958) or *Honeymoon Train of Haptragi* (Hwang Oe-cheon, 1962), as well as literary films such as *Descendants of Cain* (1968) and *I'll Become a Man* (1969), both directed by Yu Hyun-mok. But anti-communism infiltrated above all spy thrillers, a popular genre since the success of the first *James Bond* films, Terence Young's *Dr. No* (1962) and *From Russia with Love* (1963). After the revelation of several cases of North Korean secret agents infiltrating the South, these entertainments took on a more serious tone, notably with the *Special Investigation Unit*

franchise (1973–1976). Five of the six movies were based on true stories of North Korean female spies.

After the attempted assassination of Park Chung-hee on January 21, 1968, by a 31-strong North Korean commando unit, followed by the capture of the *USS Pueblo* two days later, anti-communist measures became coercive. President Park Chung-hee now considered cinema an essential propaganda tool, and allocated 120 million won to produce six anti-communist films, a budget well above the average for the time. These films, including *Testimony* (Im Kwon-taek, 1974), *Wildflowers on the Battleground* (Lee Man-hee, 1974), *I Won't Cry* (Im Kwon-taek, 1974), and *A Spy Remaining Behind* (Kim Si-hyun, 1975), are typical examples of the propaganda of the time, with numerous scenes of destruction and violence to depict the supposed cruelty of the North Koreans. They were shown in schools to "educate" young viewers.

The public failures of these films put an end to any further attempts to produce works of similar scope, and the assassination of President Park in 1979 marked the end of the golden age of anti-communist film. In the years that followed, the genre evolved, with films such as *Rainy Days* (Yu Hyun-mok, 1979) and *Jjako (Pursuit of Death)* (Im Kwon-taek, 1980), which humanized the communists without fear of censorship, and showed the futility of ideological conflict. Although the regime of Chun Doo-hwan (1980–1988) initially continued to produce anti-communist blockbusters partly co-financed by the army, such as *Abenko Green Berets* (Im Kwon-taek, 1982) or *South and North* (Kim Ki, 1984), the abolition in 1985 of prizes for anti-communist works at the Grand Bell Awards ceremony precipitated the end of the genre.

The first relaxation of censorship under the presidency of Roh Tae-woo (1988–1993) saw the emergence of the directors of the first Korean

New Wave, who dared to tackle hitherto taboo subjects, such as the conflict between North and South Korea. *North Korean Partisan in South Korea* (Chung Ji-young, 1990) made history as the first feature film since 1955's *Piagol* to present North Koreans as human beings rather than enemies. Based on the autobiography of a war reporter who infiltrated the partisans to depict their daily lives from the inside, the film was a huge success, drawing 320,000 spectators.

North Korean Partisan in South Korea gave birth to the division film sub-genre, which dominated the box office in the following years. *The Taebaek Mountains* (Im Kwon-taek, 1994) focuses on the conflicts between leftists and anti-communists between 1945 and 1953. Unlike the propaganda films of the past, which focused solely on the struggle between good and evil, these films are concerned with ideological differences and the tragic consequences of the country's division.

Previous page spread: A compulsory civil defense training course, given monthly to high school girls to teach them first aid in the event of a North Korean attack.

Five Marines (1961), the first feature film by Kim Kee-duk, was a "grand spectacle" of entertainment that paved the way for future anti-communist films.

Shiri (Kang Je-gyu, 1999) represents a turning point not only in the history of Korean cinema, but also in the evolution of the genre. The film was a huge success, with 6 million viewers, and contributed to the revival of the film industry by launching a series of blockbusters. *Shiri* focuses on entertainment and pure spectacle, with gunfights that are virtually unheard of in contemporary Korean society, where firearms are banned. Some of the story's North Korean characters are portrayed with great humanity, such as a female spy who must make the agonizing choice between her love for a South Korean and her duty to her homeland.

The early 2000s also saw an easing of tensions between the two Koreas, symbolized by the historic meeting between South and North Korean leaders Kim Dae-jung and Kim Jong-il at the 2000 Inter-Korean Summit. This event led to a wave of film productions focusing on the rapprochement of the two countries, such as *Love: Impossible* (Jung Cho-shin, 2003), which tells the love story of a South Korean archaeologist and the daughter of a North Korean diplomat in China. *Welcome to Dongmakgol* (Park Kwang-hyun, 2005) tells the story of peaceful cohabitation between North and South Korean soldiers in a remote village in 1950.

Korean blockbusters were evolving toward increasingly grandiose productions, such as *JSA—Joint Security Area* (Park Chan-wook, 2000), *Silmido* (Kang Woo-suk, 2003), and *Brotherhood* (Kang Je-gyu, 2004), which adopted a typically Hollywood script structure and staging for local stories of Korea's division. Despite this evolution, anti-communist films did not disappear completely, as witnessed by the war films *71-Into the Fire* (John H. Lee, 2010), *Northern Limit Line* (Kim Hak-soon, 2015), and *Memories of War* (John H. Lee, 2016).

In the 2010s, Korean independent cinema went even further, daring to tackle for the first time certain injustices committed against North Koreans, with films like *Dance Town* (Jeon Kyu-hwan, 2010) and *The Journals of Musan* (Park Jung-bum, 2010), which deal with the difficult integration of refugees into South Korean society. *The Net* (Kim Ki-duk, 2016) details the violent interrogation of a fisherman who capsizes in South Korean waters.

Robot Taekwon V (1976), produced by director Yu Hyun-mok, marked the revival of Korean cartoons. It also set the trend for anti-communist and science-fiction animated films.

ANIMATION

The origins of animated films in Korea can be traced back to the importation, in 1914, of the series of American silent shorts *Colonel Heeza Liar* (John Randolph Bray, 1913–1917), quickly followed by the works of the "fathers of Japanese anime" Oten Shimokawa, Junichi Kochi, and Seitaro Kitayama. Korean animation got off to a rocky start, with two unsuccessful attempts: *Gaeggum* (literally, "dog dreams"), a feature-length debut announced in 1936 and starring a human-like dog character inspired by Disney films, never materialized. The Cartoon

Movie Production Company, founded by Kim Yong-hwan, a former assistant on Japanese propaganda animated films, went bankrupt before any projects were completed.

The early days of animation in Korea were marked by commercials such as the first *Lucky Toothpaste* (Mun Dal-bu, 1956), which extolled the virtues of various textile, pharmaceutical, and electronic products. These commercials, broadcast in cinemas and on television in the late 1950s, paved the way for the emergence of future animation professionals such as Shin Dong-hun, Lee Sang-ho, and Nelson Shin. The late 1950s saw the arrival of the first short films for children, such as *The Ant and the Grasshopper* (Han Seong-hak, Park Yeong-il, and Jung Do-bin, 1961), institutional films, such as *I Am Water* (Jung Do-bin and Park Yeong-il, 1963), and propaganda films.

In 1957, the success of Disney Studios' *Peter Pan* (Clyde Geronimi, Wilfred Jackson, Hamilton Luske, 1953) and the Korean children's film *Sorrow Even Up in Heaven* (Kim Soo-yong, 1965) prompted Seiki Studios to produce the very first animated feature. Shin Dong-hun's *A Story of Hong Gil-dong* (1967) is a transposition of his brother Shin Dong-woo's comic strip of the same name, itself adapted from a Korean literary classic. The production faced many obstacles due to a lack of expertise, infrastructure, and equipment. To cut production costs, the team salvaged US Army reconnaissance films, painstakingly scraping away the printed gelatin before applying the drawings directly onto the cleaned film. Despite these difficulties, *A Story of Hong Gil-dong* was a huge success, with over 200,000 viewers when it was released in 1967.

After a disagreement with his producers, Shin Dong-hun directed *Hopi and Chadol Bawi* (1967), an unofficial sequel to *A Story of Hong Gil-dong*. When the film's failure ended his directing career, he worked for television, directing the opening credits for *Horse-Year Bride* (Kim Kee-duk, 1966) and a magnificent animated sequence for *The General's Mustache* (Lee Seong-gu, 1968).

Park Yeong-il directed *Sun Wukong* (1968) and *A Golden Iron Man* (1968); Yong Yu-su made the official sequels to *A Story of Hong Gil-dong*, *General Hong Gil-dong* (1969) and *Prince Hodong and Princess of Nakrang* (1971). At the same time, renewed public interest in puppet theatre in the 1960s led to the production of *Heung-bu and Nol-bu* (Gang Tae-ung, 1967), falsely promoted as "the world's first stop-motion film," and *Kong-jui and Pat-jui* (Gang Tae-ung, 1978), both flops.

Many Korean animated features are inspired by Japanese productions.[1] *Treasure Island* (Park Yeong-il, 1968) is inspired by the manga *New Treasure Island* (Osamu Tezuka, 1947), while *Lightning Atom* (Yong Yu-su, 1971) is clearly influenced by the animated series *Astro Boy* (1963–1966). Similarly, *The War of the Great Monsters* (Yong Yu-su, 1972) is an imitation of Japanese *kaiju eiga* (monster movies), such as *Godzilla* (Ishiro Honda, 1954).

The Japanese anime *Magic Boy, Shônen Sarutobi Sasuke* (Akira Daikubara and Taiji Yabushita, 1959) was falsely promoted as "an American film" in a Korean dubbed version. *Golden Bat* (Takeo Nagamatsu, 1968) was touted as "the very first Korean-Japanese collaboration" by its distributor, Shin Sang-ok, when in fact it was simply a remake of several episodes of the original Japanese TV series, with the replacement of Japanese names by Korean ones in the credits.

In 1974, new film laws passed under the Yusin Constitution encouraged the production of anti-communist and literary films. These measures, combined with ever-increasing competition from television and exorbitant production costs—the budget for an animated film is ten times that of a traditional feature—put an abrupt end to the first golden age of Korean animation, between 1972 and 1976.

The genre was reborn in 1976 with the huge success of *Robot Taekwon V*, which attracted over 210,000 spectators. The project was initiated by cinematographer-producer Yu Hyun-mok and director Kim Cheong-ki, who were inspired by the craze for taekwondo after the first World Championships in 1973, and by the Japanese animated series *Mazinger G* (1972–1974), broadcast on Korean television. Their idea was to create a giant robot with the features of the revered Korean admiral Yi Sun-sin (1545–1598), who battles hordes of (North Korean) soldiers. This success sparked a series of anti-communist animated films for children, encour-

aged by the regime and shown in schools. These included the six sequels to *Robot Taekwon V* (Kim Cheong-ki, 1976–1996), *77 Group's Secret* (Park Seung-cheol, 1978), and *General Ttori* (Kim Cheong-ki, 1979).

The success of *Robot Taekwon V* also confirmed the craze for science-fiction animated films, which once again shamelessly plundered Japanese and American TV series, such as the main character—a cross between Batman and Superman—in *Black Star and the Golden Bat* (Han Heon-myeong, 1979), Wonder Woman in *Fly, the Princess of Wonder* (Kim Cheong-ki, 1979), and the Captain Future look-alike in *Space Three Musketeers* (Lim Jung-kyu, 1979). The creation of the first Korean Baseball League in 1982, the 1984 South Asian Games, and the organization of the 1988 Seoul Olympic Games gave rise to a series of sports-related animated films, including *Arm of Gold* (Choe Jin-woo, 1983), the *Dokgo Tak* franchise (Collective, 1983–1987), and *Run Hani!* (Hong Sang-man and Lee Hak-bin, 1988).

To meet the ever-increasing competition from the small screen and the first TV channel dedicated entirely to animation, Tooniverse, created in 1995, producers in the 1990s targeted a new, older audience with a series of innovative films, such as *Blue Seagull* (Oh Jung-il, 1994), the first film to include 3D sequences, and the erotic sketch film adapted from the eponymous webtoon *NudInude* (Collective, 1998).

In the 2000s, the animation genre experienced a revival with the release of ambitious feature films aimed at children, such as *My Beautiful Girl, Mari* (Lee Sung-gang, 2002) and *Oseam* (Seong Baek-yeop, 2003), and films for teenagers, such as *Wonderful Days* (Kim Moon-saeng, 2003) and *Aachi & Ssipak* (Jo Beom-jin, 2006), and for adults, such as *The King of Pigs* and *Seoul Station* (Yeon Sang-ho, 2011 and 2016), the latter being an animated prequel to his future cult film *Train to Busan* (2016). Although these attempts were sometimes successful,

they never really established Korean animation on a global scale.

On the other hand, the Koreans developed a fine reputation as "TV series subcontractors": they acquired their skills in the 1960s, coloring the productions of American studios Hanna-Barbera (*Tom & Jerry*, *Scooby-Doo*), before consolidating their expertise under the impetus of Nelson Shin. A director of animated commercials in the late 1950s, he is above all the inventor of the special lightsaber effect in the *Star Wars* saga of the 1970s. He succeeded in convincing the Americans to outsource their series, such as *The Simpsons*, *Spiderman*, and *My Little*

Aachi & Ssipak (2006), a feature film aimed at adult audiences, was banned from Korean cinemas for its violence.

Pony, to Korea at lower cost. The new know-how acquired for these productions led to the emergence of original Korean TV franchises in the 2000s, including the world-famous *Pucca* (since 2000), *Pororo the Little Penguin* (2003–2021), and *Larva* (2011–2019).

    1. After the end of the Korean occupation in 1945, the distribution of Japanese cultural products was strictly forbidden; only children's literature and animated series were allowed from the 1960s onward.

The animated film *The King of Pigs* (2011), aimed at adult audiences because of its themes such as bullying, became a live-action TV series in 2022.

제2의 창의적 시기

1980

1981

1980-1981
A SECOND ENCHANTED CREATIVE INTERLUDE

The assassination of Park Chung-hee by KCIA director Kim Jae-kyu on October 26, 1979, ushered in a brief phase of democratization, before a new military coup d'état organized by future president Chun Doo-hwan on December 12, 1979, restored martial law. The Gwangju Uprising, a popular student and trade union movement for democratization that began on May 18, was violently suppressed, with thousands of demonstrators shot dead by the military. A statement by President Jimmy Carter on May 23, urging the Korean government to restore order, was seen by the Korean people as US support for the military regime and fueled anti-American sentiment for decades to come.

Lee Chang-ho and Lee Won-se, former members of the Era of Image collective, saw this period of political confusion as a small window of opportunity for creative freedom. Their starting point was once again the realization that the film industry was still sclerotic with unrealistic productions, most of which were shot for the sole purpose of meeting compulsory film production quotas. They took the opportunity to try their hand at making a series of sociorealist films more rooted in reality, with the idea of presenting a true image of Korea and, at the same time, denouncing a certain political reality.

In 1980, after a four-year period of inactivity due to his arrest for alleged marijuana use, Lee Chang-ho returned to directing with *Good Windy Day*. The film follows the story of three friends who come to Seoul from the countryside to seek their fortune. They settle in an outlying neighborhood threatened with destruction by the city's rapid development. The film stands out for its realistic portrayal of some 15 characters, whose intertwined destinies denounce the sharp socioeconomic inequalities of the period in this underprivileged neighborhood, now destroyed.

Taking advantage of the confused situation of the time, *Good Windy Day* passed the censors unhindered and became a hit, with over 100,000 spectators. The realistic, endearing characters and dynamic direction won over audiences. Lee Chang-ho quickly followed up with *People of Dark Streets* (1981), an adaptation of the first part of a novel that depicts the precarious situation of several characters in Korean society in the early 1980s. Lee Chang-ho had planned to make a trilogy of the original story, to multiply the points of view on social inequality.

People of Dark Streets tells the tragic story of a prostitute. The first half of the film offers a detailed portrait of her daily life, while the second part explores, in flashback, her past and the reasons that led her to leave the countryside for Seoul. The film represents a transitional work in Lee Chang-ho's filmography, but also in Korean cinema, taking its place between the hostess films of the 1970s and the erotic productions of the 1980s, while providing a fundamentally social-realist view of its time.

Despite the film's resounding success, with 255,000 spectators, Lee Chang-ho found himself prevented from directing the two sequels to complete his initially planned trilogy. The new censorship committee set up under the presidency of Chun Doo-hwan rejected his scripts, thus putting an end to the short period of creative freedom. Frustrated, Lee Chang-ho shot *Declaration of Fools* in 1983, a film that amply expresses his despair at the new military regime. The film opens with a (fictional) suicide scene in which the director throws himself off a building in downtown Seoul.

During the filming of *Good Windy Day,* Lee Chang-ho convinced his assistant Bae Chang-ho to start making social-realist films of his own, in order to launch a movement. Bae Chang-ho adapted Lee Dong-cheol's bestseller *People of the Slum* (1982), which depicts the harsh reality of daily life for an abandoned and remarried woman and her six-year-old son in one of Seoul's slums at the time, before the sudden reappearance of her ex-husband.

The first half of the film almost resembles a sociological documentary, with local residents playing themselves on screen, while the second half focuses more on the mother's drama. Unfortunately, filming ended after the new regime came to power, forcing the director to cut 50 scenes and pledge not to show his film at international festivals, so as not to portray Korea in a negative light abroad.

At the same time, Lee Won-se, who was part of the Era of Image collective with Lee Chang-ho, filmed the adaptation *The Ball Shot by a Midget* (1981). The director moved the novel's original plot, set in a Seoul slum, to a coastal salt-producing village, to show that socioeconomic problems affect the whole country. The film tells the story of a man marginalized by dwarfism who struggles to support his family. His wife becomes a bar hostess, and their situation worsens when their basic seaside shack is threatened to make way for a middle-class housing project.

The film explores in depth the socioeconomic disparities of Korea in the early 1980s. As filming once again came to an end after Chun Doo-hwan's inauguration, censorship had a considerable impact on the film, with the deletion of several key scenes. Despite these cuts, *The Ball Shot by a Midget* remains a masterpiece as it stands, poignantly testifying to the social inequalities of the time.

The period of relative artistic freedom not only encouraged young directors to tackle sociorealistic subjects, but also led veteran filmmakers to consider tackling subjects previously considered taboo.

Under the guise of a police investigation

Previous page spread: *People of the Slum* (1982) was shot in the natural setting of a real slum.

into the alleged murder of a cult leader, the film *Son of Man* (Yu Hyun-mok, 1980) actually explores the conflict between Korean religious tradition and materialistic modernity. The director highlights the marginalization of individuals in the face of Seoul's rapid development, including numerous shots of the city in the throes of change. Such a project would have been unthinkable under Park Chung-hee's presidency, but Yu Hyun-mok took advantage of the political turmoil to mislead his producers, telling them he was shooting a simple literary adaptation to satisfy their film quotas.

In *Jjagko (Pursuit of Death)* (1980), Im Kwon-taek for the first time portrays a North Korean as a human being, rather than as a "monster," as in traditional productions of the genre. The film tells the story of a former South Korean officer and a notorious communist guerrilla who, 30 years after their first confrontation, find themselves in a rehab center for the homeless. Although the film passed the censors and (ironically) won the award for Best Anti-Communist Film, a key scene was cut toward the end, in which the two former enemy brothers agree that the conflict between the Koreas is solely the result of power games between the American and Soviet superpowers.

These films testify to the true creativity of certain directors, who express themselves and present works radically different from the usual productions when the political situation allows them to do so. They also inspired other high-quality social-realist productions during the decade, despite increased censorship, including *A White Feathered Gull* (Jung Jin-woo, 1983) and *The Blazing Sun* (Hah Myung-joong, 1984). But above all, they gave the Minjung student movement the courage to produce independent films on the margins of the system, such as *O Dreamland* (Lee Eun, Jang Dong-hong, and Chang Yoon-hyun, 1988) and *The Night Before the Strike* (Lee Eun, Lee Jae-gu, Chang Yoon-hyun, and Jang Dong-hong, 1990).

Despite being heavily censored, *The Ball Shot by a Midget* (1981) denounced the marginalization of certain populations during Korea's modernization and remains a masterpiece.

위기

1981
1992

1981-1992

THE CRISIS YEARS

On August 27, 1980, Chun Doo-hwan was elected president by the National Conference for Reunification, with his inauguration following in February 1981. Unfortunately, this new era did not bring the much-hoped-for democratization, but the continuation of another military regime that perpetuated the economic policies of its predecessor while restricting freedom of expression. Any political or pro-communist allusion, any sociorealistic representation likely to tarnish Korea's image abroad was once again banned, putting an abrupt end to films such as *Good Windy Day* (Lee Chang-ho, 1980) or *People of the Slum* (Bae Chang-ho, 1982), which had attempted to offer a different kind of cinema in the early 1980s.

The legislative framework for the film industry underwent several changes. It was no longer necessary to advocate the revitalization reforms of the Yusin Constitution. The number of compulsory screening days for Korean films was increased from 121 to 165. The quota system of three films produced for one imported film was replaced by the obligation for every production company to shoot at least one Korean film per year. However, the "quality film" label continued to exist until 1985, in the form of a $20,000 endowment awarded in the event of a prize at the annual Grand Bell Awards ceremony—the Korean equivalent of the American Oscars—or selection at a foreign festival, thus initially perpetuating the tradition of films

shot quickly and cheaply in an attempt to win this award.

The film industry was also faced with the arrival of color television in December 1980, which led to a further decline in cinema attendance, from 53 million in 1980 to 42 million in 1982. The typology of cinemas changed: The number of large cinemas with over 1,000 seats fell from 447 in 1980 to 259 in 1989, while the number of 100- to 200-seat cinemas increased from 9 in 1982 to 434 in 1989.

In 1984, under pressure from the United States, a new law (effective 1986), which authorized any company to produce Korean films and even to import as many foreign titles as desired against a simple deposit of $200,000, encouraged an increase in the number of independent structures, from 20 in 1984 to 109 in 1989, and enabled film production to rise from 81 to 110 films shot annually.

The first years of the decade were marked by renewed interest in martial arts films, thanks to the growing popularity of Hong Kong superstar Jackie Chan. The prodigious success of his film *Drunken Master* (Yuen Woo-Ping, 1978), with over 890,000 viewers, triggered a wave of martial arts comedies aimed at young adults, including the popular *Aekwon Fighting Skill* franchise (four films, Lee Hyung-pyo, 1980–1983) and *5 Pattern Dragon Claws* (Kim Si-hyun, 1983). The reboot of the 1970s *Highschool Joker* series, *Wild College Boys* (Kim Eung-chun, 1983), revived the teen school film genre, while the dozens of special-effects cartoons and fantasy productions released every summer tried to win back middle-schoolers.

The most popular genre remains melodrama, with over a third of total film production. *Love Me Once Again '80* (Byun Jang-ho, 1980), a remake of the cult *Love Me Once Again* (Jung So-young, 1968), the fifth biggest hit of the decade, revived the shinpa sub-genre. Anti-communist films continued to be supported by the regime in the early 1980s, particularly after the North Korean assassination attempt on President Chun in 1983 but disappeared when the awards for Best Anti-Communist Screenplay and Best Anti-Communist Film at the annual Grand Bell Awards were abolished in 1985.

The horror film now drew its inspiration from a variety of global film genres: The first Korean zombie film, *A Monstrous Corpse* (Gang Beom-gu, 1981), a remake of the Spanish-Italian *Let Sleeping Corpses Lie* (Jorge Grau, 1974); the first "real" Dracula, with *Dracula in a Coffin* (Lee Hyung-pyo, 1982) and *Ghost Training Center* (Choi Ki-poong, 1988), inspired by the success of Hong Kong jumping vampire films; and the car action film *Fool 4—Dune Buggy* (Bang Kyu-sik, 1988) became the very first Korean feature film in Dolby stereo.

The relaxation of censorship on the representation of sexuality led to a flood of erotic productions. *Madame Aema* (Jeong In-yeop, 1982) was the first big hit, attracting over 315,000 viewers. This became Korea's longest-running film franchise, with a dozen sequels and over 200 similar titles released in the 1980s and 1990s. Although often of mediocre quality, they were the six biggest successes of the decade, although they failed to dethrone the box office record of 585,000, still held by *Winter Woman* (Kim Ho-sun, 1977).

Lee Chang-ho and Bae Chang-ho are the two most important filmmakers of the decade. The former was behind the hostess films of 1974, then the wave of sociorealistic films of the early 1980s. He made two of the biggest erotic hits, *Between the Knees* (1984) and *Er Woo Dong: The Entertainer* (1985), and directed the sports comedy adapted from a manwha (Korean comic strip), *Lee Chang-ho's Baseball Team* (1986), which finished in eighth place. Bae Chang-ho, his former assistant director, took first and third place in the decade's rankings, with *Deep Blue Night* (1985) and *Whale Hunting* (1984), with 495,000 and 426,000 admissions, respectively.

Although in steep decline, Korean cinema was nevertheless making a name for itself for the first time on a global scale, due to selection and awards at the world's three most prestigious film festivals. In 1981, Lee Doo-yong became the very first Korean director to receive a Special Jury Mention at the Venice Film Festival, for *The Hut* (*Pimak*), before being selected

---

Previous page: *Mandala* (*Two Monks*) (Im Kwon-taek, 1981).

in the Un Certain Regard (art films by young directors) section of the Cannes Film Festival in 1984, with *Spinning the Tales of Cruelty Toward Women*. Im Kwon-taek's *Mandala* (1981), *Village in the Mist* (1984), and *Gilsodom* (1986) were screened three times at the Berlin International Film Festival. *Why Has Bodhi-Dharma Left for the East?* (Bae Yong-kyun, 1989) was selected in the Un Certain Regard section, before becoming the first Korean film to win a Golden Leopard at the Locarno (Switzerland) International Film Festival.

A nationwide protest movement, the June Democratic Uprising, mobilized hundreds of thousands of demonstrators between June 10 and 29, 1987, to force the government to hold the first democratic elections. This pressure led to the election of Roh Tae-woo, Chun Doo-hwan's designated successor, on December 16, 1987.

Under Roh Tae-woo's presidency (1988–1993), the legislative framework, again revised in 1989, authorized Americans to open agencies in Korea and deal directly with Korean cinemas. *Fatal Attraction* (Adrian Lyne, 1987) was the very first film to be distributed under these new conditions by United International Pictures, a joint venture between Universal, Paramount, and Disney studios. The film, which benefited from an extensive marketing campaign, was a huge success. The release provoked numerous protests from professionals in the Korean film industry, unhappy with this new competitor; an urban legend even claims that producers released snakes in some cinemas to dissuade viewers from seeing the film.

The ever-increasing importation of foreign productions, whose number rose from 26 in 1984 to 264 in 1989, precipitated the decline of Korean cinema, unable to compete with American blockbusters. This was the darkest period for the film industry since the 1950s, before its revival in the late 1990s.

Previous page spread: On September 29, 1988, at the Seoul Olympic Games, Gabriela Sabatini faced Manuela Maleeva in the women's singles tennis semi-final.

Come, Come, Come Upward (Im Kwon-taek, 1989) was one of many Korean films selected for international festivals in the 1980s. It won its lead actress, Kang Soo-yeon (left), the Best Actress award at the 1989 Venice Film Festival.

FESTIVAL FILMS

Korean cinema seems to have been (re)discovered only through its repeated international successes over the last 20 years. Yet its presence on the international scene goes back much further, with its first dazzling recognition in the early 1980s, when its local industry was in steep decline.

The Wedding Day (Lee Byung-il, 1957) was the first Korean feature film to win an award at an international film festival, winning Best Comedy at the fourth Asian Film Festival. The event was founded in 1953 by President Nagata Masaichi of Japan's Daiei Studios, with the aim of strengthening ties between Southeast Asian countries and enhancing Japan's reputation. He teamed up with Run Run Shaw, director of the prestigious Shaw Brothers studios in Hong Kong, to convince the four other biggest Japanese producers of the time (Toho, Shochiku, Shin Toho, and Toei), as well as leading producers from the Philippines, Taiwan, Singapore, Indonesia, and Malaysia, to present their latest releases at a 12-day event held each year in a different Asian country.

Over the years, director-producer Shin Sang-ok has played an increasingly important role in the organization of the event. He takes advantage of the festival to enter his own productions in competition, strengthen his contacts with Asian studios, launch co-productions, and keep abreast of the latest film trends in other member countries for distribution in Korea. His films *My Mother and Her Guest* (1961) and *Prince Yeonsan* (1962) won Best Film and Best Set, respectively, at the ninth edition of the festival held in Seoul in 1962, arousing immense pride among Koreans.

Unfortunately, the festival, which still exists under the name Asia-Pacific Film Festival, doesn't have much influence beyond Southeast Asia. But the Korean awards won over the decades, including Best Film for a *Petal* (Jang Sun-woo, 1996), *A Little Monk* (Joo Kyung-jung, 2002), and *Brotherhood* (Kang Je-gyu, 2004), have brought Korean cinema sustained attention in Asia.

Kang Dae-jin's *The Coachman* (1961) became the first Korean film to win an award at one of the world's three most prestigious film festivals, winning the Silver Bear at the Berlin International Film Festival in 1961. Alas, the selection of *To the Last Day* (Shin Sang-ok, 1960) at Berlin in 1962 was also the last for another 20 years.

Nevertheless, the Koreans kept on trying to export their films: *The Bell Tower: Missing Another Dawn* (Yang Ju-nam, 1958) was produced with the sole aim of being selected for the San Francisco International Film Festival, testifying even then to the Koreans' growing awareness of the need to promote their culture worldwide. In 1965 and 1974, the Park government set up two major financial support programs to encourage the production of "quality films" for foreign markets. But these attempts were in vain, despite the undoubted quality of films such as *Seashore Village* (Kim Soo-yong, 1965), *The General's Mustache* (Lee Seong-gu, 1968), and *The Road to Sampo* (Lee Man-hee, 1975).

Nevertheless, Korean cinema regularly takes part in "smaller" festivals: at the Sydney Festival, with *Even the Clouds Are Drifting* (Yu Hyun-mok, 1959) and *The Coachman* (Kang Dae-jin, 1961); in San Francisco, with *The Evergreen Tree* (Shin Sang-ok, 1961) and *Martyrs* (Yu Hyun-mok, 1965); in Frankfurt, with *Love Affair* (Shin Sang-ok, 1963); in Melbourne, with *Deaf Samryong* (Shin Sang-ok, 1964) ; in Edinburgh, with *A*

The Bell Tower: Missing Another Dawn (1958) was the first Korean film to be considered for the San Francisco International Film Festival. Unfortunately, it failed and has since been relatively (and unjustly) forgotten.

Woman in the Wall (Park Jong-ho, 1969); and at the Sitges International Fantastic Film Festival, with *Woman of Fire* (Kim Ki-young, 1970), where actress Yun Yeo-jong won Best Actress, ahead of her Best Supporting Actress Oscar for *Minari* (Lee Isaac Chung, 2020), in 2021.

The 1980s saw the first worldwide recognition of Korean cinema. At a time when the industry was in full decline, Lee Doo-yong and Im Kwon-taek placed several of their films at the three biggest international festivals. The former received the Jury's Special Mention for his *The Hut* (*Pimak*) (1981) at the Venice Film Festival in 1981 before becoming the first South Korean director to be selected in the Un Certain Regard section at the Cannes Film Festival, in 1984, with his *Spinning the Tales of Cruelty Toward Women*.

Im Kwon-taek became a regular at the Berlin International Film Festival, consecutively screening *Mandala* (1981), *The Village in the Mist* (out of competition, 1984), and *Gilsodom* (1986). In 2005, he became the first Asian filmmaker to win a Golden Bear for lifetime achievement. His films *The Surrogate Woman* (1986), *Come, Come, Come Upward* (1989), and *Adada* (1988) won Best Actress awards in Venice and Moscow for Kang Soo-yeon and Shin Hye-soo, respectively, and in Montreal for Shin Hye-soo.

Why Has Bodhi-Dharma Left for the East? (Bae Yong-kyun, 1989) was selected in the Un Certain Regard section, before becoming the first Korean film to win a Golden Leopard at Locarno. Shot over seven years on the margins of the Korean film industry, it also became the

A Seoul cinema poster announces some of the films in the 19th Asia Pacific Film Festival.

Following page spread: *Why Has Bodhi-Dharma Left for the East?* (1989) was the first Korean film to win a Golden Leopard at the Locarno Film Festival and to be distributed in the United States.

very first Korean film to have an official theatrical release in the United States, in 1990. In the same year as *Why Has Bodhi-Dharma Left for the East?*, another Korean feature, *Chilsu and Mansu* (Park Kwang-su, 1988), also won the Grand Prix Semaine de la Critique at Locarno. Unfortunately, this initial worldwide attention was not followed up in practice. Few of these award-winning films were released in cinemas to raise international awareness of Korean cinema, and festival selections were once again rare in the 1990s.

The success of the Busan International Film Festival, created in 1996 and quickly dubbed the Asian Cannes Film Festival, finally drew the attention of international critics and festival programmers to such future stars as Hong Sang-soo (*The Day a Pig Fell into the Well*, 1996), Kim Ki-duk (*Crocodile*, 1996), and Lee Chang-dong (*Green Fish*, 1997). In 2000, the Cannes Film Festival selected four Korean feature films in its various sections: *Chunhyang* (Im Kwon-taek) in the Official Competition; *Virgin Stripped Bare by Her Bachelors* (Hong Sang-soo) in Un Certain Regard; *Peppermint Candy* (Lee Chang-dong) in the Directors' Fortnight; and *Happy End* (Jung Ji-woo, 1999) in Critics' Week.

Between 2000 and 2023, Cannes programed a total of 60 Korean feature films in its various sections, and awarded several of them, including *Painted Fire* (Im Kwon-taek, 2002, Best Director), *Old Boy* (Park Chan-wook, 2003, Jury Prize), and *Decision to Leave* (Park Chan-wook, 2022, Best Director). Korean films also made their mark at other festivals, winning Best Director and Best Actress awards for Lee Chang-dong and Moon So-ri for *Oasis* (2002), the Golden Lion for Kim Ki-duk for *Pieta* (2012) at the Venice Film Festival, the Grand Prix for *My Beautiful Girl, Mari* (Lee Sung-gang) at the 2002 Annecy (France) International Animated Film Festival, and Hong Sang-soo's Silver Bear for *The Novelist's Film* at the 2022 Berlin International Film Festival.

The supreme recognition was most certainly the Palme d'Or at the 2019 Cannes Film Festival and the four Oscars for Best Film, Best Director, Best International Film, and Best Screenplay, in 2020, for *Parasite* (Bong Joon-ho), exactly a century after the official debut of Korean cinema.

THE "3 S" POLICY— EROTIC FILMS

In the early 1980s, several sequels to classic hostess films such as *A Woman I Betrayed 2* (Hong Seong-ki, 1980), *Heavenly Homecoming to Stars 3* (Lee Gyeong-tae, 1981), and *26 x 365 = 0 II* (Choi Soo-ji, 1982) were flops. However, five of the decade's biggest successes were once again erotic productions, testifying to the genre's evolution, closely linked to the times.

Chun Doo-hwan's presidency was a precarious one. After seizing power in a military coup in 1979 and dissolving the National Assembly before his inauguration, he faced strong public disapproval for perpetuating the previous military regime and for his involvement in the brutal suppression of the Gwangju Uprising in May 1980. To maintain his power, he adopted the ancient Roman formula *Panem et circenses*, adapting it to the "3 S's": Sex, Screen, and Sports.

Chun Doo-hwan undertook numerous initiatives to entertain the Korean people: Right from the start of his mandate, he introduced color television and, in May 1981, he founded the Gukpung Festival, which took place one week after the first anniversary of the Gwangju

Between the Knees (1984) is one of the landmarks of 1980s erotic cinema. It is also famous for its profound anti-American sentiment at a time when much of the Korean population was denouncing the country's cordial relations with the United States.

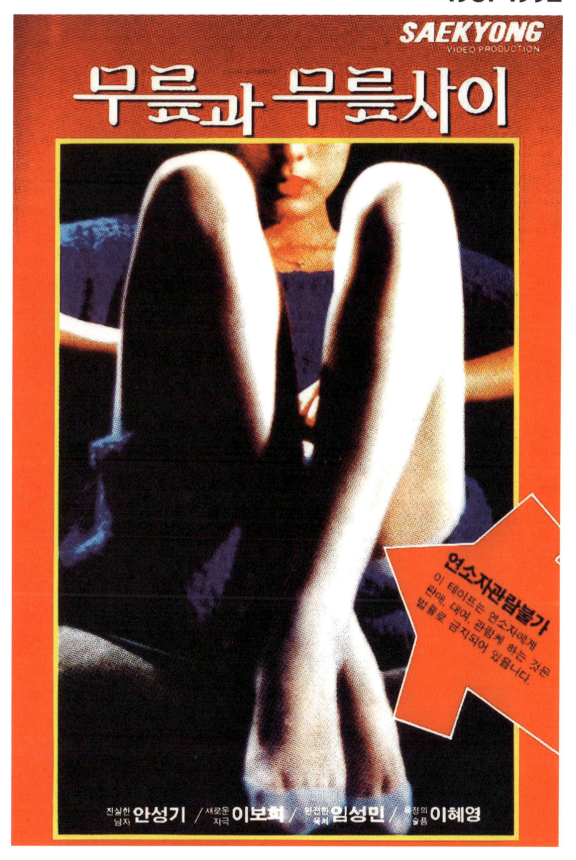

Uprising. The event attracted the biggest music stars of the day for a series of concerts, and over 6,000 students from 197 universities for a singing competition. In 1982, he created the Korean Baseball League, and from 1984 onward, the media gave extensive coverage to preparations for the 1986 Asian Games and the 1988 Olympic Games in Seoul. The censorship on the depiction of sex in films was relaxed.

This decision led to the immediate appearance of resolutely erotic films. *Madame Aema* (Jeong In-yeop, 1982), released concurrently with the lifting of the curfew that had been in force since the 1979 coup d'état, became a huge success, ranking sixth in the 1980s box office with 315,000 admissions. The film was inspired by *Emmanuelle* (Just Jaeckin, 1974), which drew 9 million viewers when it was released in France and contributed significantly to the worldwide popularity of erotic cinema in the 1970s.

Unlike the original story, in which the heroine is a married woman in an open relationship, Lee Ae-ma is a wife totally devoted to her husband, even if he is unfaithful and imprisoned for violence. However, she eventually "breaks free," first by reconnecting with a former lover, then by embarking on a passionate relationship with an artist. This choice of a middle-class woman demonstrating (sexual) independence is the first representation of its kind in cinema since *Madame Freedom* (Han Hyung-mo, 1956).

While the first film ends with Aema's decision to conform to Confucian tradition by returning to her husband, the second *Madame Aema* movie presents the protagonist right from the opening sequence as a "new woman," who now dares to live her sexuality to the full. Subsequent offerings borrowed more and more Western

Spinning the Tales of Cruelty Toward Women (1984) was selected for the Un Certain Regard section of the Cannes Film Festival.

codes, including from the American series *Red Shoe Diaries* (66 episodes, Collective, 1992–1997), which directly influenced the Korean franchise by making Aema a devotee of sadomasochism in *Madame Aema 7* (Suk Do-won, 1992), then bisexual in *Madame Aema 8* (Suk Do-won, 1993), at a time when Korean society still considered monogamous heterosexuality to be the norm.

Madame Aema became the longest-running franchise in Korean cinema history, with a dozen sequels produced to date, the latest being *Madame Aema 2016* (Kim Mi-yeon, 2016), released directly on a streaming platform. A disagreement between producers gave rise to two "unofficial" versions of the series, *Emma in Paris* (Jeong In-yeop, 1988) and *Gypsy Emma* (Lee Seok-ki, 1990), new successes with over 100,000 viewers, transposing their plot to "exotic" French and Spanish settings.

The success of *Madame Aema* led to the production of over 200 similar erotic films, shot quickly and cheaply in the 1980s and 1990s. Producers competed with increasingly provocative posters and titles vaguely reminiscent of international hits, such as *Tango in Seoul* (Park Yong-joon, 1987), reminiscent of *Last Tango in Paris* (Bernardo Bertolucci, 1972), and *Dangerous Passions* (Park Ho-tae, 1989), reminiscent of *Fatal Attraction* (Adrian Lyne, 1987).

The following erotic films were among the biggest box office hits of the 1980s: *Prostitute* (Yu Jin-sun, 1988) came second with 432,000 viewers; *Er Woo Dong: The Entertainer* (1985) and *Between the Knees* (1984), both directed by Lee Chang-ho, came fourth and ninth, respectively, with 373,000 and 238,000 viewers; and *Seoul Rainbow* (Kim Ho-sun, 1989) came tenth with 261,000 viewers. In addition to *Madame Aema, Red Cherry* (Park Ho-tae, 1982) and *Mountain Strawberries* (Kim Su-hyeong, 1982) are two other successful franchises, shot between 1982 and 1994. Despite lower box office receipts, these two series were among the best-selling videos in the late 1980s and early 1990s.

Renowned directors also began making erotic films, often under pressure from their producers. Lee Chang-ho, for example, directed *Widow Dance* in 1983, marking his transition to the genre. This adaptation of a novel continues his exploration of the condition of women victims of Korean patriarchal society, begun in his hostess films of the 1970s, here with the portrait of three widows marginalized by their social status.

In *Between the Knees* (1984), he tackles the rise of anti-Americanism following the fate of a woman traumatized after her physical assault by a Westerner (to a Michael Jackson song). *Er Woo Dong: The Entertainer* (1985) is a historical-erotic in the tradition of Lee Doo-yong's *The Hut* (*Pimak*) (1981) and *Spinning the Tales of Cruelty Toward Women* (1984), the story of a young woman who falls in love with an upper-class man and becomes a prostitute, eventually committing suicide.

While early erotic successes such as *Madame Aema* (1982) were set against the backdrop of contemporary Korean society, *Er Woo Dong: The Entertainer* (1985) stands out for its meticulous reconstruction of fifteenth-century Korea. This film marked the advent of a new sub-genre of low-budget historical erotic films, such as the *Byun Kang-soi* trilogy (Um Jong-seon, 1986–1988), *Potato* (Byun Jang-ho, 1987), and *Revenge* (Kim In-soo, 1989), and more ambitious productions like *Mulberry* (Lee Doo-yong, 1986), and above all *The Surrogate Mother* (Im Kwon-taek, 1987). The latter, the tragic story of a surrogate mother from an underprivileged background during the Joseon period (1392–1910), toured the world's film festivals. The fundamentally erotic cinema of the 1980s not only ensured some of Korea's biggest box office successes, but also some of the first worldwide recognition of Korean cinema.

1980S BLOCKBUSTERS: LEE CHANG-HO AND BAE CHANG-HO

Two filmmakers, Lee Chang-ho and Bae Chang-ho, whose careers were closely intertwined, not only left their mark on the history of South Korean cinema, with five of the ten biggest box office hits of the 1980s, but also laid the foundations for the Korean New Wave, which emerged at the end of the decade. Lee Chang-ho, born in 1945 in Seoul, was the son of a film "censor," whom he often accompanied to work to watch unedited versions of Korean and foreign films. After studying architecture, in 1965 he became assistant to director and producer Shin Sang-ok, on films such as *Homeless* (1968), *Eunuch* (1968), and *A Thousand-Year-Old Fox* (1969).

Lee Chang-ho regretted the overabundance of anti-communist war films in the cinema of the 1970s, which in his eyes were only panegyrics to President Park. Although an admirer of Lee Man-hee's films, he disliked their overly melodramatic endings and conformism, aspiring to a more realistic cinema. In 1974, he directed *Heavenly Homecoming to Stars,* his first feature film shot with a handheld camera. The film was a huge success, triggering the wave of hostess films. He then joined the Era of Image collective hoping to "revolutionize" cinema. Unfortunately, he was banned from filming in 1975, having been unjustly accused of using marijuana.

It was at this time that Bae Chang-ho proposed that Lee Chang-ho should become his assistant. Born in 1953 in Daegu, Bae Chang-ho

---

Declaration of Fools (1984) is a cult work of Korean cinema in the 1980s and one of director Lee Chang-ho's greatest successes. The film was largely improvised with the actors during shooting and served as the filmmaker's cry of revolt against the censors of the time.

developed his passion for cinema thanks to his film-loving mother. After studying business, he worked for the multinational Hyundai, writing screenplays in his spare time. The two men finally collaborated in the early 1980s: Bae Chang-ho assisted Lee Chang-ho on *Good Windy Day* (1980) and *People of Dark Streets* (1981) before making his own successful film, *People of the Slum* (1982), which enabled Bae Chang-ho to launch his own career as a filmmaker.

For his part, Lee Chang-ho, frustrated at not being able to make the two planned sequels to his film *People of Dark Streets* due to increased censorship, shot *Declaration of Fools* in 1983. Freely inspired by a novel by Lee Dong-cheol (already author of *People of the Slum*), the film is above all the fruit of the director's spontaneous ideas and improvisations with the actors. It follows the wanderings of two outcasts and a

prostitute across Korea, expressing the disarray of the Korean population under the authoritarian regime.

The producers, frightened by the result, refused to release the film. Lee Chang-ho decided to circulate a copy in universities, where the film quickly gained a cult following. On its theatrical release a year later, *Declaration of Fools* attracted over 100,000 viewers, thanks to word-of-mouth. Lee Chang-ho went on to make three successful erotic films, *Widow Dance* (1983), *Between the Knees* (1984), and *Er Woo Dong: The Entertainer* (1985).

At the height of his popularity, Lee Chang-ho decided to set up his own production company, Pan Films. This was a decision he later said he regretted, as he was now obliged to look after his own investments and work less spontaneously. He set about adapting a sports manhwa, *Lee Chang-ho's Baseball Team* (1986), which recounts the love rivalry between two young baseball players at a time when the sport was enjoying great popularity in Korea.

Although the film was the eighth biggest hit of the decade, with 287,000 admissions, it disappointed its fans by being too commercial. The sequel, directed by Jo Min-hee in 1988, attracted just 40,000 spectators. As for his subsequent commercial productions—the melodrama *Y Story* (1988), the slapstick comedy *Miss Rhino and Mr Korando* (1989), and the historical drama *Myong-Ja Akiko Sonia* (1992)—they went completely unnoticed. Lee Chang-ho attempted a return to auteur films with *The Man with Three Coffins* in 1987, a critically acclaimed work considered one of the best of the decade, but it failed to find its audience either.

After the resounding failure of *Declaration of Genius* (1995), an unofficial sequel to his cult film *Declaration of Fools* (1984), Lee Chang-ho retired from cinema. He turned to Christianity, and in 1997 founded the Bucheon International Fantastic Film Festival (BIFA), now Asia's largest genre film event. In 2013, he returned

to directing, with *God's Eye View*, the story of a fake missionary kidnapped by Islamic rebels in Cambodia, which once again went completely unnoticed.

After his first film, *People of the Slum* (1982), Bae Chang-ho directed the film adaptation *Tropical Flower* (1983), based on Choi In-ho's novel *Heavenly Homecoming to Stars*. This thriller, loosely inspired by *Rear Window* (Alfred Hitchcock, 1954), stars a voyeur played by actor Ahn Sung-ki, who spies on his neighbor, increasingly isolated in her small apartment in modernizing Korea. The film appealed above all to young audiences, who identified with the female character's progressive isolation, and was a notable success, with 155,000 admissions.

Bae Chang-ho once again targeted a young adult audience with the adaptation of another novel by Choi In-ho, *Whale Hunting* (1984). This film, which narrates the tragicomic

misadventures of a disillusioned student, a homeless man, and a prostitute, became a veritable phenomenon for young people just as disoriented as the main characters in a society muzzled by power, and was a huge success, becoming the third biggest hit of the decade, with 426,000 spectators.

Bae Chang-ho continued his success with *Deep Blue Night* (1985), which recounts the tragic fate of a Korean who leaves to seek his fortune in the United States. This film, too, appealed to the aspirations of the young people who made up his audience, many of whom at the time were dreaming of leaving their homeland. It was the biggest hit of the decade, with 495,000 admissions. Bae Chang-ho was dubbed the Steven Spielberg of Korean cinema, thanks to his repeated successes. His portrait was even painted on some cinema facades to draw crowds to his name alone.

After the failure of *Whale Hunting 2* (1985), shot under pressure from his producers, Bae Chang-ho completely rethought his career. He then entered the second period of his career, focused more on his artistic questioning than on commercial success. With *Hwang Jin-i* (1986), a remake of a classic historical film, Bae Chang-ho took an artistic turn at 180 degrees, offering a contemplative film with an extremely slow pace, which totally disconcerted his usual audience. Nevertheless, the filmmaker returned to success, attracting 192,000 viewers with his next romantic comedy, *Our Sweet Days of Youth* (1987), which tells the story of an excessively shy

---

Whale Hunting (1984) was the third-biggest hit of the 1980s, earning director Bae Chang-ho the nickname of the Steven Spielberg of Korean cinema for his ability to string together blockbusters.

man who succeeds in winning the woman of his dreams through the purity of his feelings.

This film was Bae Chang-ho's last public success. In 1990, his historical epic *The Dream*, which defines life as a waking dream, was another commercial failure. The director then decided to set up his own production company, to make personal projects on the margins of the system. In *Love Story* (1996), where he directs himself and his wife, he reconstructs the beginnings of their relationship. In *Road* (2004), Bae Chang-ho plays a blacksmith who questions the meaning of life. After the commissioned film *The Last Witness* (2001), Bae Chang-ho made his final film, *The Trip* (2009), a series of sketches on the themes of life and love.

IN THE MARGINS: THE CINEMA OF KIM KI-YOUNG

Kim Ki-young's presence in the section devoted to Korean cinema of the 1980s may seem strange, especially as the director rejects the films he made during this period. Yet he embodies this particular transitional period in Korean cinema better than anyone else. An emblematic figure in the Korean film revival of the 1950s and a successful auteur in the 1960s and 1970s, he was simply unable to adapt to the changes in the Korean film industry in the 1980s, like his fellow directors Kim Soo-yong and Yu Hyun-mok.

Kim Ki-young is also emblematic of this period, being one of the few Korean filmmakers to be rediscovered through the emergence of the video market. The re-release of several of his classics on VHS cassettes in the 1980s contributed to his rehabilitation as a true cult director for a whole future generation of filmmakers. Among them, Bong Joon-ho, who pays him a vibrant tribute with his future masterpiece *Parasite* (2019), totally influenced by *The Housemaid* (1960) and by Kim Ki-young's cinema in general.

Born in Seoul in 1919,[1] Kim Ki-young was the son of teachers. After failing the medical school entrance exam, he moved to Japan to become an ear, nose, and throat specialist. On his return to Korea, he married one of the actresses in the theatre troupe he had founded. She, in turn, became a doctor and spent her life paying off the debts associated with her hus-

---

Burying Old Alive (1963) curiously shares many similarities with the Japanese feature *The Ballad of Narayama* (1958), which was never distributed in Korea. It also foreshadows *The Ballad of Narayama* by Japanese filmmaker Shohei Imamura, which won the Palme d'Or at Cannes in 1983.

band's film activities. Indeed, Kim Ki-young was one of the few Korean filmmakers to operate on the margins of the film industry in the 1960s and 1970s. Too slow, too meticulous, and therefore too expensive, he turned down most commissioned films to concentrate solely on his own productions.

Along with Han Hyung-mo, Kim Ki-young is one of the directors to have contributed most effectively to the technological progress of Korean cinema. He is one of the few who systematically draws storyboards before shooting. His first feature, *The Boxes of Death* (1955), was shot with a hand-cranked camera and out-of-date film scraps but was the first Korean film with synchronized sound. From his second film, *Yangsan Province* (*The Sunlit Path*) (1955), he favored studio shooting with overhead lighting to avoid cast shadows. For *Woman of Fire* (1971), he broke 50 beer bottles to find the right shard to use as a filter. The peculiar hue of his films in general is for him a metaphor for the dark political period under Park Chung-hee's regime; he refused to use natural sources of lighting until the country saw better days.

He spent a great deal of time with his actors during the preparatory phases of his projects, to feed his characters with their life experience and to better understand how to direct them during filming. He was an exceptional talent scout, spotting future stars Kim Ji-mi, Ahn Sung-ki, Yoon Yeo-jung, Sunwoo Yong-nyeo, and Lee Hwa-si.

He considered a good film to be "one that reflects the essence of its time and adds something extra." Kim Ki-young's filmography can be summed up by the recurrence of several themes, treated differently according to the historical periods in which they are set. Human impulses are the common thread running through all his works. Kim Ki-young was firmly convinced that the DNA of Koreans is forever marked by the successive unfortunate periods of Japanese occupation, division of the country,

and military rule, driving them to do whatever it takes to ensure their own survival and social success.

After several melodramas typical of 1950s cinema, he set about a neo-realist trilogy dubbed A World of Violence: *The First Snow* (1958), *A Defiance of a Teenager* (1959), and *A Sad Pastorale* (1960), all deal with the struggle for survival of prostitutes, pickpocketing war orphans, and gang leader's mistresses in a devastated Korea. He returned to these types of story in his later films *The Sea Knows* (1961), the sketch film *Woman* (1968), *Transgression* (1974), and *Woman of Water* (1979).

His absolute masterpiece, *The Housemaid* (1960), marked the start of a cycle of films about domestic servants using their charm to seduce the masters of the house in an attempt to climb the social ladder quickly. This first film led to two remakes, *Woman of Fire* (1971) and *Woman of Fire 82* (1982), as well as the subtle variations *The Insect Woman* (1972) and *Carnivorous Animals* (*Beasts of Prey*) (1984). These versions, filmed over different decades, bear witness to the evolution of Korean society and growing socioeconomic inequalities: Domestic servants are less and less culpable, while householders become increasingly abusive, taking advantage of their privileged position to exploit their female employees even further.

Kim Ki-young's best film on human impulses is his little-known masterpiece *Burying Old Alive* (1963). Reminiscent of Japan's *The Ballad of Narayama* (Keisuke Kinoshita, 1958, and Shohei Imamura, 1983), this feature is inspired by the alleged ancestral ritual (in reality, a legend) whereby grown-up children abandoned their parents in the mountains so that they would no longer be a burden on the community. The plot of *Burying Old Alive* is as terrible as it is complex. A war widow agrees to marry one of the ten brothers of a large family in a small community. The village shaman predicts that her son, born of her previous union, will cause the ruin and

death of the siblings, so the men beat the young boy until he is crippled.

Gu-ryong, now an adult, falls in love with a woman, but because of his physical handicap, he can only marry a young, mute woman. The community suffers a period of drought, and the shaman orders Gu-ryong to abandon his mother in the mountains to ward off fate. On his return, he discovers that the woman he loved has been raped and killed by the ten brothers. When *Burying Old Alive* was released in 1963, it was stripped of many scenes and accused of depicting humans as barbarians, motivated only by their baser impulses, their own pleasure, comfort, and well-being. Critics, for their part, remained skeptical about certain sequences deemed "unrealistic."

Absurdity is a key element in the work of Kim Ki-young, who shares a taste for the grotesque with American director Robert Aldrich and Japanese filmmaker Shohei Imamura. Trained as a doctor, the filmmaker takes an entomologist's look at his characters, the bet-

---

Shot after a series of commissioned anti-communist films, *A Woman After a Killer Butterfly* (1978) is one of Kim Ki-young's most atypical works. The filmmaker seems to communicate all his despair in a sequence of surreal sequences that are completely incomprehensible, but very beautiful.

ter to dissect them. The title of *Insect Woman* (1972) is anything but coincidental, and many of his films contain references to insects, such as the poisonous butterflies in *A Woman After a Killer Butterfly* (1978), and the praying mantises in *Carnivorous Animal* (1985). Kim Ki-young also demonstrates a sense of morbid derision. Some of his films are among the most disturbing sequences in the history of Korean cinema: the final scene (now lost) of his second film, *Yangsan Province* (1955), is said to have shown the furtive resurrection of murdered young lovers who make love in their graves before reaching paradise in a ray of light. In *The Sea Knows* (1961), a soldier burned alive emerges from a pile of corpses to hug his mother; in *Insect Woman* (1972), a baby devoured by rats reappears with a rodent tail in a freezer. Finally, *Io Island* (1977) includes a final sequence of necrophilia.

But these scenes are never gratuitous. According to Kim Ki-young, they reflect the absurdity of society and of human life in general. Throughout his work, the director constantly questions "rationality." In *Insect Woman* (1972), for example, scenes completely unrelated to the plot—characters suddenly screaming in fright without the viewer ever knowing why, or shots of the protagonists' worried gazes on seemingly banal objects—serve only to create a sense of unease and confusion in the viewer.

The repeated failure of his productions

and the tightening of censorship in the 1970s forced Kim Ki-young to accept commissioned projects. He directed the literary adaptations *Transgression* (1974), *Soil* (1978), and *Woman of Water* (1979), as well as the anti-communist film *Love of Blood Relations* (1976). His films of the 1980s were all productions designed to fill quotas. Shot in just a few days, these feature films even sought to deceive viewers by using titles vaguely reminiscent of hits, such as *Free Woman* (1982), which refers to *Madame Freedom* (Han Hyung-mo, 1956), and *Hunting for Idiots* (1984), which is a mixture of two 1980s hits, *Whale Hunting* (Bae Chang-ho, 1984) and *Declaration of Fools* (Lee Chang-ho, 1984).

The rediscovery of Kim Ki-young through film clubs and video releases led to a first retrospective of his work, at the Busan Festival in 1997. On this occasion, the then previously unreleased film *An Experience to Die for: Be a Wicked Woman* (1990–1995), which the director had never wanted to show, too ashamed of the result, was presented. Other retrospectives followed, including those at the Cinémathèque de Paris in 2006 and the Berlin International Film Festival in 2008.

Kim Ki-young's masterpiece *The Housemaid* (1960) was given a prestigious restoration by the World Cinema Foundation under the aegis of Martin Scorsese. The director was about to make his comeback behind the camera with *Diabolical Woman*, his first film "with a happy ending," but tragically died with his wife in a fire in their home on February 5, 1998.

FILMS OF THE MINJUNG MOVEMENT

Since the birth of the traditional film industry, there have been several attempts to completely rethink it, but always without success, due to the different powers in place, first the Japanese occupation, then the military regimes. Nevertheless, the creation of the very first film club, the Film Art Research Group, founded in 1949 by Yu Hyun-mok, was followed in 1963 by that of the Cine-poem association, dedicated to experimental cinema, and in 1970 by that of the Korean Short Film Association. These organizations try to bring together film enthusiasts to watch films together, organize debates, and set up practical workshops for making short films.

The 1970s saw the emergence of a new generation of cinephiles in university circles, who increased initiatives to use cinema as a means of protest expression and to show their opposition to the usual caricatured representation of society in the standardized productions of the commercial film industry. In 1970, the Korean Small-Scale Film Club produced experimental short films in 8mm, and in 1971, the Chung-ang University Fine Arts Film Club brought together future professionals Lee Choon-yun, Kim Yu-jin, Kim Su-nam, and Jeong So-nyeo to rethink cinema. Between 1974 and 1978, Han Ok-hee founded the feminist group Kaidu Club in Seoul, which was responsible for the very first women's festival.

In the late 1970s, the Minjung movement, a series of student and trade union protests, brought together politically oppressed, economically exploited, socially marginalized, culturally despised, and religiously condemned people who dared to mobilize against the new military regime established by Chun Doo-hwan (1980–1988), to demand a transition to true democracy. This movement was the first to succeed in producing independent, committed works shot on the margins of the system. It was also at the ori-

gin of the first Korean New Wave and the beginnings of future independent cinema.

French and German cultural centers also played an important role in this movement, giving rise to a community later dubbed the Cultural Center Generation. Their members finally had access to screenings of uncensored foreign films that were impossible to see elsewhere. The Era of Image collective, founded by directors such as Ha Gil-jong and Lee Chang-ho, was the first to try to influence the traditional film circuit with their theories.

In 1982, the Seoul Cinema Collective (renamed Seoul Visual Collective in 1986, after the arrival of video) became part of a group of associations that adopted a real political discourse. The collective became famous with the publication of two essays, *For a New Cinema* (1983) and *On Film Movements* (1985), which were essential for Korean film buffs in the 1980s. These essays offered in-depth analysis of global film movements such as the French New Wave, German New Cinema, and Latin American New Cinema, with the aim of encouraging similar movements in Korea.

The Seoul Cinema Collective, bringing together up-and-coming professionals such as Park Kwang-su, Hong Ki-seok, Kim Eui-suk, Kim Hong-joon, and Jeon Yang-jun, produced several short documentaries. The directors drew inspiration from the New Latin American Cinema to make the docudrama *Water Tax* (1984), in which they asked farmers to re-enact scenes of demonstrations in which they had taken part. For *Blue Bird* (1986), the team spent several months in total immersion alongside the farmers, filming their daily lives as closely as possible. This documentary led to the very first direct state intervention in the film industry under Chun Doo-hwan's regime, with the arrest of producers Hong Ki-seon and Yi Hyo-in for failing to submit their script to the censorship committee before shooting.

The same year, the Yonsei University General Student Council produced the documentary *The Mountains and Rivers Resurrected*, a commented montage of scenes from demonstrations and the Gwangju Uprising. The film

The Jangsangot-mae film collective was on the set of *O Dreamland* (1988), a film that tackles trauma among some of the participants in the many uprisings against the military regime in the 1980s.

Following page spread: Directors Lee Eun, Jang Dong-hong, and Chang Yoon-hyun on the set of *O Dreamland* (1988) and *The Night Before the Strike* (1990).

was quickly censored, accused of violating the National Security Law. This ban, and the arrest of *Blue Bird*'s producers the same year, caused a stir in student circles and stimulated the creation of even more politically committed films.

In 1988, Jangsangot-mae, a collective made up of members of some 40 other associations, produced *O Dreamland* (Lee Eun, Jang Dong-hong, and Chang Yoon-hyun), the very first independent 16mm feature film in Korean cinema, which deals aptly with the trauma of a participant in the Gwangju uprising. Criticized at the time of its release for focusing on a single individual rather than the entire Minjung community, the film nevertheless attracted 100,000 viewers in over 150 independent screening venues, universities, and factories.

Members of the collective were arrested, this time for violating the film law, failing to declare an official production company, and failing to submit the script and final cut to the censorship board for approval before screening. Jangsangot-mae retaliated by suing for violation of freedom of expression. The trial lasted eight years, but in 1996 the collective won, helping to abolish the censorship board amid the Korean film revival of 1999.

The collective followed up with a second feature, *The Night Before the Strike* (Lee Eun, Lee Jae-gu, Chang Yoon-hyun, and Jang Dong-hong, 1990), the first Korean fiction film to directly address workers' rights since the KAPF collective's productions in the 1920s. The team spent more than six months living alongside striking workers in a factory, gathering testimonies and feeding their script. The final cast includes real protesters.

The film also faced censorship, with a copy seized by the authorities at its premiere on April 9, 1990. The team then organized clandestine screenings throughout the country over the following months, once again attracting over 100,000 spectators, mainly students and workers. By contrast, their third feature, *Open-*

ing the Closed School Gate (Lee Chae-gu, 1992), about a teacher's efforts to form a teachers' union against the advice of his superiors, was released to relative indifference at the height of the democratic transition period under the new presidency of Kim Young-sam (1993–1998). The collective was dissolved in 1993.

Jangsangot-mae had a considerable impact on the history of Korean cinema, encouraging other producers to make films on the margins of the system, such as *Mother, I Am Your Son* (Lee Sang-yin, 1991), the story of a mother who accompanies her militant son to protest movements. The collective also fostered the emergence of the first Korean New Wave, with films such as *Chilsu and Mansu* (Park Kwang-su, 1988) and *Kuro Arirang* (Park Jong-won, 1989).

Some members of these collectives went on to join the mainstream film industry: Chang Yoon-hyun directed *The Contact* (1997) and *Tell Me Something* (1999), Oh Ki-min produced *Whispering Corridors* (Park Ki-hyung, 1998) and *A Tale of Two Sisters* (Kim Jee-woon, 2003), and Lee Eun founded Myung Films, the company behind some of the most successful independent films of the 1990s and 2000s.

The Minjung movement also gave birth to the completely new format of the feature-length independent documentary. In 1987, Kim Dong-won directed *Sanggyedong Olympics*, a harrowing account of the forced relocation of disadvantaged populations from the main sites of the future Seoul Olympic Games. He went on to become one of the most celebrated exponents of independent documentary filmmaking, notably with *Repatriation*—awarded the Freedom of Expression prize at the Sundance Film Festival in 2004—which follows the return

A rare flyer from *The Night Before the Strike* (1990), an independent feature film created on the margins of the traditional film industry and smuggled into universities and factories.

to their families of 12 North Korean spies who were imprisoned and tortured for over 30 years in South Korea.

The first feature-length documentary to be released in traditional cinemas is *The Murmuring* (Byun Young-joo, 1995), which, along with *Habitual Sadness* (1997) and *My Own Breathing* (1999), forms a trilogy about "comfort women" during World War II. Their release prompted an official apology from the Japanese authorities.

Independent documentaries enjoy regular successes on the mainstream Korean film circuit, such as *Old Partner* (Lee Chung-ryoul, 2008), a moving story about an old farmer and his cow and the seventh biggest box office hit in 2009 with over 2.9 million viewers, and *My Love, Don't Cross That River* (Jin Mo-young, 2013), the beautiful love story of a couple married for 76 years, and the biggest box office success ever for a Korean documentary with over 4 million viewers.

1. Even though he has always claimed to have been born in 1922.

Old Partner (2008), one of the first successes of a documentary in a traditional cinema circuit, gathered over 2.9 million viewers on its release.

Following page spread: *Chilsu and Mansu* (1988) is considered one of the first fully independent Korean feature films, and one of the jewels in the crown of the 1980s.

재건의 시작

1992
1998

1992–1998
THE DAWN OF RENEWAL

During the 1990s, despite director Im Kwon-taek's surprise successes with *The General's Son* (1990), which attracted 678,000 viewers, and *Sopyonje* (*The Pansori Singer*) (1993), the first Korean film to top the million-view mark, Korean cinema experienced its darkest period since the revival of the 1950s. The number of films fell drastically, from 121 titles in 1991 to just 43 in 1998, reaching its lowest level since 1957. At the same time, the number of imported films, mainly American, increased significantly, rising from 51 in 1986 to 382 in 1994, relegating the market share of Korean films to just 16 percent. Cinema attendance followed the same trend, falling to just 42 million in 1996. It was during this difficult period that the introduction of new political measures completely overturned the film industry, laying the foundations for a future revival.

In 1993, Kim Young-sam became Korea's first democratically elected civilian president (1993–1998). His accession to the presidency represented a fine revenge for him, having been Park Chung-hee's fiercest political opponent in the 1970s. He continued to modernize the country, launching a series of economic reforms, including the decision in 1994 to make Korean cinema a strategic national industry on a par with textiles and metallurgy. This decision was prompted by the international success of *Jurassic Park* (Steven Spielberg, 1993), which brought the American film industry the equivalent, for Korea, of the profit from the sale of 1.5 million Hyundai cars abroad.

In 1995, the Korean parliament passed a tax exemption law for all film productions, the provision of support funds for the training of Korean technicians and directors abroad, and the organization of national writing residencies for scriptwriters. In the same year, a 1960s law limiting films to a maximum of 16 prints was lifted to allow for greater circulation of releases. In 1999, the motion of censure was finally relaxed, and was completely abolished in 2001.

With these new measures, the *chaebol* (conglomerates of companies similar to Western multi-nationals) invested massively in the film industry, thereby accelerating its professionalization. The multinationals set up teams of marketing specialists, accountants, and business school graduates to sketch out the first contours of the new film industry. They also financed the projects of young producers who were more in tune with public tastes and created a vast distribution network by acquiring numerous cinemas to promote the circulation of their own films.

While these interventions did not initially halt the decline of Korean cinema, they did lay the foundations for a future revival, with the repeated success of co-productions such as *Marriage Story* (Kim Eui-suk, 1992), with 526,000 admissions, and *Two Cops 1* and *2* (Kang Woo-suk, 1993 and 1996), with 860,000 and 636,000 spectators, respectively, encouraging new producers to gradually reinvest in this sector and encouraging spectators to return to the cinema.

After the Asian financial crisis of 1997, the 96.5 percent devaluation of the local currency forced the chaebol to withdraw from the film industry and refocus their activities. Ironically, the last film co-produced by Samsung, *Shiri* (Kang Je-gyu, 1999), became the biggest success in the history of Korean cinema, with over 6 million viewers, and marked the definitive revival of the Korean film industry.

Following the chaebol's withdrawal, former co-producers continued their legacy. Oh Jung-wan, behind *Marriage Story*, produced *The Foul King* (Kim Jee-woon, 2000), *A Bittersweet Life* (Kim Jee-woon, 2005), and some Hong Sang-soo films. Shin Chul financed *A Promise* (Kim Yoo-jin, 1998), *Lies* (Jang Sun-woo, 1999), and *My Sassy Girl* (Kwak Jae-young, 2001). Kang Woo-suk, director-producer of the *Two Cops* trilogy (1993–1998), bought the Cinema Service network of cinemas and joined forces with American studios Miramax and New Line Cinema to release their films, notably those by Quentin Tarantino and the *Scream* franchise (1996–2023). He also produced successful domestic blockbusters: *Bichunmoo* (Kim Young-jun, 2000), *Libera Me* (Yang Yun-ho, 2000), and his own trilogy, *Public Enemy* (2001–2008).

The new producers adopted the marketing methods of the chaebol, with their model of vertical integration: from production to the sale of derivative products, via the distribution and sale of films on video. In 1998, CJ Entertainment joined forces with two major Hong Kong and Australian cinema networks, Golden Harvest and Village Roadshow, to build Korea's first multiplex cinema, the CGV. This modern cinema, equipped with the latest sound and image technology, is a huge success with young audiences. The model was quickly imitated by other professionals, such as Lotte, who integrated the construction of cinema complexes with that of their shopping malls. The number of cinema screens multiplied, rising from 497 in 1997 to 1,880 in 2006, while the number of moviegoers grew from 47.5 million to 253.4 million over the same period.

Previous Page: *First Love* (Lee Myung-se, 1993).

Gangster films and comedies become the leading genres of the decade. Melodramas still account for a third of total film production, but begin to migrate to the small screen, before a revival in the late 1990s. Erotic films continued to flood into Korean cinemas at the start of the decade, before shifting to the booming video market. The independent productions that emerged from the Minjung movement gave rise to two Korean New Waves, one in the early 1990s and the other in the mid-90s.

A view of Seoul in the 1980s.

THE FIRST KOREAN NEW WAVE

The Minjung movement and the independent production of fiction and documentary films in the 1980s contributed to the emergence of what Korean critics dubbed "realist" films, and international cinephiles called the Korean New Wave.

Authorization to set up production companies in the mid–1980s led to a boom in new independent companies. Screenplays were no longer subject to revision before shooting, and censors became (somewhat) more tolerant under the presidency of Roh Tae-woo (1988–1993). Some members of the film collectives that had emerged from the Minjung movement then decided to enter the more traditional circuit, with films situated midway between their earlier committed productions and more commercial formats, tackling subjects previously forbidden from representation on the big screen and often tinged with defeatism.

Park Kwang-su was one of the first representatives of this new wave. A former member of the Seoul Cinema Collective, he made his first feature film in 1988: *Chilsu and Mansu*, which follows on from works such as *The March of Fools* (Ha Gil-jong, 1975) and *Declaration of Fools* (Lee Chang-ho, 1984). It portrays two young painters of giant billboards, disoriented in contemporary Korean society; the first dreams of trying his luck abroad, while the second seeks to escape the pressure exerted on his family by the authorities, because of his activist brother's commitment.

Although the film starts out rather cheerfully, its ending is tragic, with the two main characters being arrested by the police when they shout their despair to the world from the roof of a building in downtown Seoul. Park Kwang-su took advantage of the confusion preceding the Seoul Olympics to get his film through without difficulty, in the face of less vigilant censors. Although the film drew only 73,000 spectators,

its relative success encouraged other committed directors to produce independent films.

Park Kwang-su became a veritable spearhead of independent cinema in the early 1990s, thanks to the themes addressed in his films. His magnificent *The Black Republic* (1990) tells the story of an activist forced into hiding in a remote mining village to escape the forces of law and order, and who sets out to improve working conditions there. The film thus continues the tradition of works produced during the Minjung movement.

Kuro Arirang (Park Jong-won, 1989) is another emblematic film of this period. This debut feature tells the story of a young man who infiltrates a textile factory to encourage workers to join the student movement. The director spent several weeks working alongside the workers, again perpetuating the filming style of the 1980s collectives in order to offer a more accurate representation of reality.

Unlike *Chilsu and Mansu*, released a few months earlier, *Kuro Arirang* was severely censored, with around 20 compulsory cuts, including scenes of harassment of female workers by their bosses (although based on real testimonies), and the re-enactment of the forces of law and order's vigorous methods against the demonstrators. The film was a relative box office success, but has since acquired cult status among film buffs, as it marked the debut of future star Choi Min-sik (*Old Boy*, 2003) in the role of the factory boss.

A few years later, Park Kwang-su created another feature film dedicated to the workers' cause, *A Single Spark* (1995), a biographical adaptation of the story of a South Korean activist who set himself on fire in 1970, at the age of 22, to draw attention to the exploitation of workers in the textile industry. This is the first Korean feature film to benefit from participatory financing, while, curiously, being co-produced by a chaebol.

The release of *Berlin Report* (Park Kwang-su,

1991) triggered a series of films dealing with the taboo theme of Korean child adoption, first in the aftermath of the Korean War, then in the 1980s, when President Chun Doo-hwan relaunched the adoption program to "clean up" the streets of Seoul before the opening of the Olympic Games, so as not to tarnish the country's image.

Berlin Report is also inspired by the historical and political upheavals of the time, such as the dismantling of the Soviet Union, the liberation of its satellites, and German reunification. It tells the story of a journalist in Berlin, who helps an adopted Korean girl find her missing brother in the former East Germany (German Democratic Republic). The film combines history, politics, and national identity. *Susanne Brink* (Jang Gil-su, 1991) tells the sad story of a Korean girl adopted by a Swedish couple, who is the victim of racism, bullying, and opportunistic lovers.

To the Starry Island (Park Kwang-su, 1993), for the first time, encourages Koreans to revisit certain obscure pages of their own history, such as the "hunt for communists" in the years 1945–1950. Co-written by Lee Chang-dong,

future director of *Poetry* (2010), the film follows a man's return to his native island to bury his father's ashes. He is confronted by the hostility of the local population and gradually discovers a tragedy that has been hushed up. The theme is taken up again in *The Taebaek Mountains* (1994), a tribute film by Im Kwon-taek to the memory of his father, a leftist accused of pro-communism in his native village in the years 1945–1950.

Song of Resurrection (Lee Jung-gook, 1990) is the first fiction film to tackle the subject of the Gwangju Uprising; the film is surprisingly outspoken in its criticism, which accuses Park Chung-hee's military regime of being responsible for the popular uprisings and the student massacre. Lee Jung-gook refused to cut 20 minutes from his film and finally released it only three years later, with 5 minutes less.

After the commercial films *The Letter* (1997)

Resurrection of the Little Match Girl (2002) was one of the most expensive failures to date in Korean cinema and marked the end of the brilliant career of director Jang Sun-woo, spearhead of the Korean First New Wave.

and *Blue* (2003), the director returned once again to the Gwangju Uprising in *In the Name of the Son* (2021), but this time from the point of view of those responsible for the massacres, portraying a former soldier who had opened fire on the crowd. Still haunted years later by the events, the character decides to punish his former superiors to avenge the victims.

The Korean New Wave of the late 1980s was characterized not only by its willingness to tackle subjects previously forbidden in cinema, but also by its desire to propose new ways of telling stories. Lee Myung-se and Jang Sun-woo are among the most famous filmmakers of this trend.

Lee Myung-se began his career as Bae Chang-ho's assistant. His independent productions laid the foundations for the commercial cinema of the future. His first film, *Gagman* (1989), launched the revival of Korean comedy, while his second, *My Love, My Bride* (1990), foreshadowed the future sub-genre of battles of the sexes, depicting with humor and tenderness the trials and tribulations of newlyweds in Korean society in the 1990s. As his filmography progressed, Lee Myung-se gradually detached himself from screenplays to focus solely on the formal side of his productions. *Nowhere to Hide* (1999) completely reinvents the world of gangster films, while *Duelist* (2005) formally revolutionizes historical and swordplay films.

Jang Sun-woo, a former film critic, made his first feature film, *Seoul Jesus* (1986), which follows in the footsteps of *Declaration of Fools* (Lee Chang-ho, 1984); it recounts the mad odyssey of a man, escaped from an asylum and believing himself to be Jesus, who tries to save Seoul from the Last Judgment. Although this first film was released to general indifference, his second, *The Age of Success* (1988), an incredible satirical comedy that mocks the ultraliberalism of 1980s Korea through the rise and fall of an unscrupulous businessman, was a hit, with 107,000 spectators.

Jang Sun-woo continued to work on projects as the mood took him. With *A Short Love Affair* (1990), he blends the erotic productions of the 1980s with auteur films and explores the deep feelings that drive two lovers in a destructive relationship of passion. *The Road to the Race Track* (1991), with its series of long sequences of discussions between different characters, heralds the cinema of Hong Sang-soo.

In 2002, producers curiously entrusted him with the direction of one of the first blockbusters with the revival of *Resurrection of the Little Match Girl* (2002), a futuristic adaptation of Hans Christian Andersen's fairy tale *The Little Match Girl*. The film became the most expensive failure in the history of Korean cinema and put an end to Jang Sun-woo's career; at the same time, the world was witnessing the second Korean New Wave, led by a new generation of directors such as Kim Ki-duk, Hong Sang-soo, and Lee Chang-dong.

My Love, My Bride (1990) marks the perfect transition from the Korean New Wave to the planned films of the chaebol. Lee Myung-se's second feature film, once again independently produced, adopts the American model of romantic comedies of the period to dissect the ups and downs of daily life for a newly married Korean couple.

THE PLANNED FILMS OF THE CHAEBOL

In 1992, *Marriage Story* (Kim Eui-suk), a romantic comedy inspired by American battle-of-the-sexes films of the 1960s and more contemporary comedies such as *When Harry Met Sally* (Rob Reiner, 1989), was a huge success, attracting 526,000 spectators. This film marks a turning point in the history of Korean cinema, being the first in a series of productions meticulously planned by the chaebol, which was playing a key role in the revival of Korean cinema.

Chaebol are family-owned conglomerates, based on the Japanese *zaibatsu* (now *keiretsu*) model, with cross-holdings in a wide range of economic sectors. Among the 30 most famous Korean multinationals worldwide are Samsung, Hyundai, and LG. In the 1980s, they expanded their activities from heavy industry into the electronics sector, manufacturing VCRs in particular. The presence of video players in Korean homes rose from 10 percent in 1985 to 80 percent in 1995, generating higher revenues than the film industry in that year.

When the Korean market opened up to foreign distributors in 1987, the three leaders in the electronics industry—Samsung, Sunkyung Group (renamed SK Group in 1997), and Daewoo—quickly concluded agreements with the major American studios to produce and distribute videocassettes, not only of their theatrically released films, but also of unreleased titles sold directly on video. However, in 1988, the arrival on the market of the American distributor United International Pictures, representing the catalogs of Universal, Paramount, and MGM studios and producing its own videocassettes, forced the chaebol to rethink their local policy.

The multinationals decided to enter the production business to compete with foreign films and make a profit from both theatrical and video releases. The arrival of cable TV in 1995 and the creation of the first pay-TV channels, such as the Daewoo Cinema Network and Samsung's Catch on Channels, provided additional opportunities. To maximize their chances of success, the chaebol opted for an approach aimed at bypassing the older generation of studios by recruiting young producers who were more in tune with public tastes and more transparent in managing their budgets.

Shin Chul, former head of the Piccadilly cinema in Seoul in the 1980s and director of his own production company, Shincine, was one of the first to collaborate with the chaebol. He is known for his avant-garde methods, designed to better meet audience expectations. For his

233

first production, *Happiness Has Nothing to Do with Student Records* (Kang Woo-suk, 1989), which tells the story of a model student's suicide under the pressure of her school results, he interviewed hundreds of students over a period of more than a year and a half, in order to get as close to reality as possible.

For his next project, *Marriage Story* (Kim Eui-suk, 1992), co-financed by Samsung, a total of eight people worked on 16 screenplays, gathering testimonies from hundreds of young couples to tell the story of a newly married man's existential crisis, which faded into the background as his wife began her meteoric rise up the social ladder.

For the female lead, Shin Chul hired Shim Hye-jin, nicknamed Coca-Cola Girl because of her many popular appearances in advertisements for the famous American soda brand. The incredible success of *Marriage Story* launched the fashion for romantic comedies and battles of the sexes, such as *That Woman, That Man* (Kim Eui-suk, 1993), *How to Top My Wife* (Kang Woo-suk, 1994), *Doctor Bong* (Lee Kwang-hoon, 1995), and *Mister Condom* (Yang Yun-ho, 1997).

Their success prompted other chaebol to take up co-production. Daewoo approached Kang Woo-suk, young producer and director of the hit *Mister Mama* (1992), to co-produce *Two Cops* (Kang Woo-suk, 1993), which blends the French film *Les Ripoux* (*My New Partner*) (Claude Zidi, 1984) with the American buddy movie genre, in vogue following *Lethal Weapon*

The main set of the romantic comedy *First Love* (1993) was built 12 times before shooting began.

Following page spread: *My Love, My Bride* (1990) had a profound influence on the chaebol-planned films.

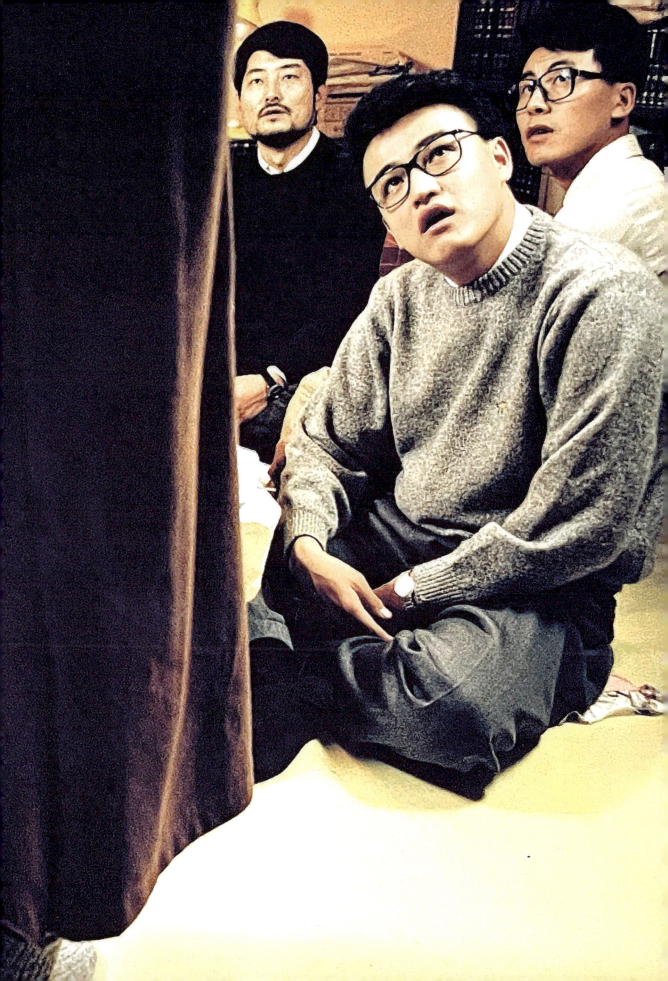

(Richard Donner, 1987) and *Tango & Cash* (Andrei Kontchalovski, 1989). The film tells the story of an energetic rookie cop paired with a jaded, dirty detective. *Two Cops* attracted over 860,000 viewers and led to two sequels, *Two Cops 2 and 3* (Kang Woo-suk and Kim Sang-jin, 1996 and 1998).

The financial backing of multinationals gave independent producers the opportunity to consolidate their status and spearhead the revival of Korean cinema in 1997. It also enabled them to experiment with new technologies, as in the first special-effects films *The Fox with Nine Tails* (Park Heon-soo, 1994) and *The Gingko Bed* (Kang Je-gyu, 1996).

The chaebol consolidated their vertical integration by controlling all phases in the development of a film project. Not only did they work with independent production companies, but they also started making their own films. Samsung released *A Hot Roof* (Lee Min-yong, 1995), *Money in My Account* (Kim Sang-jin, 1995), and *Three Friends* (Yim Soon-rye, 1996); Daewoo released *A Single Spark* (Park Kwang-su, 1995) and *Their Last Love Affair* (Lee Myung-se, 1996); SKC released *The Adventures of Mrs. Park* (Kim Tae-gyun, 1996) and *Farewell My Darling* (Park Cheol-su, 1996). By 1994, the chaebol accounted for over 30 percent of film production, and topped the box office charts in 1995 and 1996.

They increased their influence by acquiring shares in American studios, such as Samsung's stake in New Regency and CJ's in Dreamworks, to distribute their films directly in Korea. They also expanded their distribution network by building their own theatres. At the same time, they were multiplying their derivative products, adding sales of music albums, video games, and board games.

By 1997, Korean cinema had regained a 25 percent market share, but this success also led to inflation in the fees paid to famous actors such as Shim Eun-ha and Han Seok-gyu, as well as in production costs. This situation led to a concentration of production. The chaebol decided to produce fewer films, but at higher costs, thus reducing the number of titles from 121 in 1991 to around 60 between 1993 and 1997. The commercial failures of the blockbusters *Firebird* (Kim Young-bin, 1997), *Ivan the Mercenary* (Lee Hyun-seok, 1997), and *Inshallah* (Lee Min-yong, 1997) made the chaebol reluctant to continue investing for the first time.

In 1996, LG was the first company to pull out. The Asian financial crisis of 1997 dealt the final blow. The won suddenly plummeted by 96.5 percent and 11 of the 30 most powerful chaebol went bankrupt, forcing the multinationals to refocus their activities. SKC withdrew from the film industry in 1998, and Daewoo was dismantled in 1999. Ironically, the last film co-produced by Samsung, *Shiri* (Kang Je-gyu, 1999), became the biggest hit in cinema history, with 2 million more spectators than *Titanic* (James Cameron, 1998). It paved the way for the revival of Korean cinema and the golden age of domestic blockbusters.

Im Kwon-taek's *The Pansori Singer* (1993) was the first film in the history of Korean cinema to top 1 million admissions.

THE PANSORI SINGER:
THE CINEMA OF IM KWON-TAEK

Between 1990 and 1997, director Im Kwon-taek scored several of the biggest hits of the decade, and indeed of the entire history of Korean cinema: *The General's Son* (1990), *Sopyonje* (*The Pansori Singer*) (1993), and *Downfall* (1997). With 102 films made in 50 years, he embodies both the Korean cinema of the past and the present and has earned a reputation as the most famous Korean filmmaker in the world.

Born in 1934 in South Jeolla province, Im Kwon-taek was raised by a mother and grandfather deeply steeped in Confucian culture. The father's vague activities in Manchuria earned the family accusations of pro-communism from their neighbors and relatives at the start of the Korean War (1950–1953). Im Kwon-taek was forced to flee to Busan, selling military boots to survive. He soon joined the team of Chung Chang-wha, future director of the famous martial arts film *Five Fingers of Death* (*Tian xia di yi quan*) (1972), and had his first opportunity with *The Story of Jang-hwa and Hong-ryeon* (Kim Yeong-hwan, 1956) before becoming assistant

director on *A Sunny Field* (1960) and *Horizon* (1961), two films by Chung Chang-wha that were at the origin of Korean Westerns.

Im Kwon-taek's first feature, *Farewell Duman River* (1962), is often mistakenly cited as the origin of Manchurian action films, even though the entire plot takes place in the vicinity of Manchuria. The film is deeply influenced by the style of his mentor, Chung Chang-wha; attracted over 100,000 viewers on its release; and features an impressive battle scene on skis. The film's success launched the career of Im Kwon-taek, who made 80 films in the first 20 years of his career, with a peak of 25 between 1968 and 1972.

Im Kwon-taek specialized in historical epics such as *A Wife Turned to Stone* (1963) and *The Ten-Year Rule* (1964), martial arts films such as *Return of the Left-Handed Man* (1968) and *The Night of Full Moon* (1969), and anti-communist films such as *Lady in Dream* (1968), the first feature film in Korean cinema history to be recorded in four-track stereo sound and the second in 3D. During the first period of his career, between 1962 and 1973, Im Kwon-taek distinguished himself for his dynamic mise-en-scène female characters sacrificed in the name of Confucian values, and flashback montages, with most of his films beginning with the final shot before unfolding what had gone before.

In the 1970s, Im Kwon-taek was forced by his producers to make mainly anti-communist epics, reminding him of his father's "leftist" past if he refused. These productions at least ensured him relative "artistic freedom," and he benefited from comfortable budgets that enabled him to experiment with the CinemaScope format, directing and editing his films. He also took advantage of shooting in natural settings, far from the capital, Seoul, to escape the control of his producers. These feature-length propaganda films were astonishing above all for their impressive formal mastery.

The success of Im Kwon-taek's anti-communist war films, such as *Testimony* (1974), *Wives on Parade* (1974), and *I Won't Cry* (1974), remains relative, however, as their admissions came mainly from compulsory school screenings designed to "educate" young viewers. Im Kwon-taek was not particularly proud of this, and accompanying *Testimony* at its screening at the Taiwan Film Festival in 1974, he speculated for the first time: "What defines a Korean as a Korean?"

On his return, Im Kwon-taek made the only self-production of his long career, a fiftieth film entitled *The Deserted Wife* (also known as *Weeds*, 1973), which he now regards as the real start of his career as a filmmaker, conveying a real message behind a seemingly simple story. This now-lost feature film was both a critical and public failure, dashing Im Kwon-taek's hopes of making films with a more personal message. Nevertheless, in the second half of the 1970s and after the assassination of President Park Chung-hee, he managed to choose his projects more carefully. This period saw the release of his first masterpieces, such as *Wangsimni* (1976), *Genealogy* (1979), and *Jjagko (Pursuit of Death)* (1980).

Im Kwon-taek achieved his first worldwide recognition in the 1980s, unlike his former colleagues such as Kim Soo-yong, Kim Ki-young, and Yu Hyun-mok, who could no longer find their place in a Korean film industry in a state of upheaval. His films *Mandala* (1981), *The Surrogate Woman* (1986), and *Come, Come, Come Upward* (1989) were selected for and rewarded at various international festivals, confirming his more personal artistic choices; but while these films won international acclaim, they were not really successful in Korea.

Amid doubts, Im Kwon-taek received a proposal from Lee Tae-won, his producer since 1989, to take a "creative break" and return to the action films that had brought him fame in his early days, but which he had not attempted since *The Big Chase* in 1973. The result was *The General's Son* (1990), a fictionalized biography of gangster and future politician Kim Du-han, set during the Japanese occupation. Im Kwon-taek included a number of sequences paying tribute to Korean cinema, and in particular to the work of the byeonsa, the famous hucksters of early cinema. *The General's Son* became the most successful film in the history of Korean cinema at the time, with 678,000 admissions.

Against his will, Im Kwon-taek was obliged to direct two sequels, *The General's Son 2* and *3* (1991–1992), but the success of these films enabled him to return to more personal projects: the first, *Sopyonje (The Pansori Singer)* (1993), tells the story of a couple from the 1960s who recall their years learning the traditional art of sung storytelling in the 1930s.

The film broke all records, becoming the very first Korean film to attract over 1 million viewers in Seoul. It also rekindled public interest in pansori, striking a chord with audiences with its nostalgic and patriotic evocation. Im Kwon-taek finally fulfilled his own wish to explore the nature of Korean identity.

Im Kwon-taek followed up with several personally ambitious projects: *The Taebaek Mountains* (1994) is a tribute to his father, recounting the years of leftist struggle between 1945 and 1950. *Festival* (1996), dedicated to his mother, deals with traditional Korean funerals. *Chunhyang* (2000), the eighteenth film adaptation of the famous pansori, was the first Korean film in official competition at the Cannes Film Festival, where two years later the director won the Best Director prize for *Painted Fire* (*Chihwaseon* or *Drunk on Women and Poetry*) (2002), a biography of the painter Jang Seung-Ub, known as Owon (1843–1897).

Im Kwon-taek ended his career as a director after the release of his 102nd film, *Revivre* (*Hwajang*) (2014), in which he tells the story of a middle-aged man torn between his love for his wife, who has cancer, and his love for a much younger colleague. Numerous tributes, honorary awards, and retrospectives have established Im Kwon-taek as the world's most recognized "classic" Korean director.

The success of *The Pansori Singer* (1993) rekindled Korean interest in pansori and prompted Im Kwontaek to direct the eighteenth adaptation of *Chunhyang* (2000), selected in the official competition at the Cannes Film Festival that same year.

GANGSTER FILMS

The gangster film, which originated in the 1920s and 1930s, enjoyed several periods of popularity in the 1960s and 1970s, before reaching its peak in the 1990s and 2000s. It is one of the most internationally recognized genres of Korean cinema, with its origins in American, Japanese, and Hong Kong cinema.

It made its debut with Na Un-gyu's films *Field Mouse* (1927) and *Incident of the 7th Bamboo Flute* (1936), inspired by American action films of the same period, starring Douglas Fairbanks and Errol Flynn. The end of the Japanese occupation saw the fleeting emergence of crime films financed by the salaries of officers affiliated with the Korean police union, who wished to raise public awareness of the evils of crime in a poverty-stricken society. *The Sun of Night* (Park Gi-chae, 1948) recounts the arrest of a smuggling ring. In *Su-u* (Ahn Jong-hwa, 1948), a lawyer tries to clear a wife who has accidentally killed her thug husband. *The Dawn* (An Jin-sang, 1948) features a "dirty cop" overcome with remorse. All these films exploit the image of the gangster as a threat to the fragile equilibrium of a nation in the throes of reconstruction.

A Flower in Hell (1958) is at the origins of the genre. The only crime film directed by Shin Sang-ok, it is now considered one of the best films in the history of Korean cinema. It follows the tragic destiny of a woman in love with a man who turns out to be a gangster wanted for mur-

The Man from Nowhere (2010), a Korean noir film, surpassed the box office takings of the American blockbuster *Inception* (Christopher Nolan, 2010). It also marked Won Bin's last appearance on the big screen.

der. *Black Hair* (Lee Man-hee, 1964), an absolute masterpiece of the genre in the 1960s, tells the unhappy love story of a man in love with a bar singer who is the partner of a gangster. The film is famous as much for its visual style as for its many scenes of violence and sexuality, which earned it numerous censorship cuts.

While Korean gangster films had until then been deeply influenced by American film noir, the genre underwent a profound evolution in the late 1960s, taking its inspiration from Japanese *yakuza* (gangster) films. Although Nipponese films were still banned in Korea, the producers and directors of the period belonged to a generation in which some of them had been trained in Japan during the occupation, and they continued to keep abreast of Nipponese film news through illegally imported magazines. Korean films are therefore vague remakes born of the filmmakers' imagination alone. Dealing with internal conflicts within a gang or external conflicts between rival clans, these film noirs emphasize loyalty.

One of the most famous examples is Kim Hyo-cheon's *Eight Gallant Men* series (8 films, 1969–1991), in which gangsters from all regions of Korea, each with their own particularities and dialect, join forces to fight a common enemy. The release of these films coincided with the inauguration of the Gyeongbu highway, which connects Seoul to Busan, improving links between the various provinces and accelerating the country's industrialization. The message of these films is obviously one of national unity (made even easier by the new road infrastructure under Park Chung-hee) in the collective fight against evil.

In the same vein, *King Yong-pal of Namdaemun* (8 films, 1970–1986), directed by action movie specialist Sul Tai-ho, established actor-director Park Nou-sik as the star of 1970s action films. He plays a cabdriver who battles the local mafia in the Gwangju district. Another area of Seoul known for housing the city's biggest gang,

Myeong-dong, became the main setting for numerous gangster movies, such as the famous franchise, simply entitled *Myeong-dong* (6 films, Collective, 1969–1973).

The *Faldo* series (Collective, 1970–1973) systematically features a Japanese in the role of the villain. It triggered a wave of gangster films under Japanese occupation, including the famous *Kim Du-han* quadrilogy (Kim Hyo-cheon, 1974–1975), which served as the main inspiration for the future *General's Son* trilogy (Im Kwon-taek, 1990–1992), and the gangster film revival of the 1990s. In 1971, the South Korean government stepped up its censorship, banning all films that glorified violence and sex. This measure obviously hindered the development of gangster films—which tended toward ever more spectacular sequences, with the aim of outdoing competing products—but it helped to create one of the main characteristics of Korean films: fist-fighting rather than gun-fighting, as in American films of the period. This practice continued into more contemporary productions and was accentuated by Korea's ban on weapons for military use. Most confrontations are therefore settled with fists and sometimes include techniques from the national martial art, taekwondo, not to mention a whole arsenal of objects such as baseball bats, knives, or hammers.

The 1970s also saw the advent of group fighting, i.e., the confrontation of one man against many opponents. This practice derives from the anti-communist war films and historical epics of the same period, which often featured scenes in which one individual faced down hordes of enemies. The gangster film takes its inspiration from this to heighten both the fragility and invincibility of the main characters. One of the most impressive sequences in more contemporary Korean cinema is the long sequence in *Old Boy* (Park Chan-wook, 2003), in which actor Choi Min-sik punches (and hammers) numerous opponents in a tunnel. Audi-

ences were abandoning the gangster films of the 1970s, often shot on the cheap simply to meet compulsory quotas, in favor of martial arts films. The genre produced no more than a dozen titles until the early 1990s. The revival of the genre came in the form of Hong Kong productions, which enjoyed great success with martial arts films in cinemas and television series on the small screen in the 1970s and 1980s. In 1986, the opening up of the film industry to imports of American productions put small and medium-sized cinemas at a disadvantage, as they were unable to afford the licenses for the most eagerly awaited film releases. They then turned to less-expensive Hong Kong productions, which were in their golden age at the time, with over 250 films shot each year for a population of 5 million! Among the most popular genres in the archipelago: crime films.

The absolute masterpieces of the genre, *A Better Tomorrow 1* and *A Better Tomorrow 2* (1986–1987) and *The Killer* (1989), all three by John Woo, were a huge success in Korea, with over 250,000 admissions, and boosted imports of this type of film from 17 in 1987 to over 90 in 1989. Korean producers were quick to copy the phenomenon, producing a dozen films of the same genre every year. The action sequences were directed by one of the first choreographers, Jung Doo-hong, who surrounded himself with a team of stuntmen made up of former martial artists who had retired since the end of the genre. Among the biggest hits were *Terrorist* (Kim Young-bin, 1995), with over 350,000 viewers, *Come to Me* (Kim Young-bin, 1996), and *Underground* (Kang Yong-kyu, 1996).

While the gangster films of the first half of the 1990s were inspired by the productions of John Woo, Ringo Lam, and Kirk Wong, those of the second half of the decade adopted the more formal approach of the new generation of Hong Kong filmmakers, such as Wong Kar-wai, through a series of stylized film noirs such as *Born to Kill* (Jang Hyun-soo, 1996) and *Green Fish* (Lee Chang-dong, 1997). These films also introduce the figure of the solitary, taciturn hero who must at some point choose between loyalty to his gang and love for a woman. *A Bittersweet Life* (Kim Jee-woon, 2005) is a perfect homage to the Hong Kong–influenced Korean gangster films of the time.

Kim Jee-woon's *A Bittersweet Life* (2005) is a tribute to 1990s Hong Kong noir films and introduces Lee Byung-hun, one of the few Korean actors to have made a career in the United States.

The real revival of the Korean gangster film, however, is marked by *The General's Son* (Im Kwon-taek, 1990–1992), a trilogy that re-adapts the four *Kim Du-han* films released in the 1970s. The first movie shattered the record of 585,000 admissions held since 1977 by *Winter Woman* (Kim Ho-sun), with 678,000 admissions, and helped launch the wave of gangster films, along with the success of the previously mentioned Hong Kong–inspired productions, but also that of American buddy movies, often involving pairs of policemen, which gave rise to hits such as *Two Cops 1* and *2* (Kang Woo-suk, 1993 and 1996). At the same time, on television, the historic gangster series *Sandglass* (24 episodes, Kim Jong-hak, 1995) became the biggest hit on the small screen, with ratings reaching 65 percent.

The decline of Hong Kong cinema in the second half of the 1990s prompted Korean filmmakers to perpetuate the genre, first to satisfy Korean demand and then, in the 2000s and 2010s, global demand. The emergence of new production companies during this period encouraged the diversification of the genre, with the birth, in particular, of gangster films for young people, such as *Run Away* (Kim Sung-soo, 1995), with future superstar Lee Byung-hun in one of his first roles on the big screen, the adaptation of the manwha *Beat* (Kim Sung-soo, 1997), and the cult film *No. 3* (Song Neung-han, 1997). Kim Sang-jin's trilogy *Attack the Gas Station* (1999), *Kick the Moon* (2001), and *Jail Breakers* (2002) gave birth to the sub-genre of parody gangster films for young people.

The early 2000s saw the emergence of a talented young director, Ryoo Seung-wan, who directed *Die Bad* (2000), a first independent production influenced by the cinema of British director Guy Ritchie, before moving on to *No Blood, No Tears* (2002), a female gangster film. The director was also the author of some of the most successful action and gangster films, *The City of Violence* (2006), *The Agent* (2013), and *Veteran* (2015).

His feature film *The Unjust* (2010) brought a new era to gangster films. Since the 1970s, the genre had been characterized by loyalty, considered in Korea as an essential moral virtue and an obligation to family, friends, community, business, the state, and even one's enemies. This quality, which demands loyalty, honesty, solidarity, and commitment, is linked to jeong, a deep Korean feeling of affection, connection, and empathy toward others. Korean gangster films of the 1970s and 1990s often feature a main character torn between his sense of loyalty to his "adopted family," the gang, and a more personal feeling of individual drive, such as love for a woman from outside this world.

With its tale of corrupt cops, crooked prosecutors, and corrupt politicians, *The Unjust* opens the genre to a series of films in which this loyalty is betrayed by people or institutions that should, in principle, be trustworthy. The Korean gangster film of the 2010s is therefore not only a film of pure entertainment, it is also an expression of the Korean population's growing distrust of its political representatives, who were increasingly being convicted of corruption, and of its multinationals, whose sprawling structures exert a growing hold on the country's socioeconomic life.

In 2023, five of the top ten Korean box office hits of all time were gangster films (or their sub-genres): *Extreme Job* (Lee Byeong-heon, 2019), *Veteran* (Ryoo Seung-wan, 2015), *The Thieves* (Choi Dong-hoon, 2012), *Assassination* (Choi Dong-hoon, 2015), and *The Roundup* (Lee Sang-yong, 2022). Numerous other productions have been international successes over the last 20 years, making a major contribution to the worldwide visibility of Korean cinema, including *A Dirty Carnival* (Yoo Ha, 2006), *Breathless* (Yang Ik-jun, 2008), *The Man from Nowhere* (Lee Jeong-beom, 2010), *New World* (Park Hoon-jung, 2013), *The Outlaws* (Kang Yoon-sung, 2017), *The Gangster, the Cop, the Devil* (Lee Won-tae, 2019), and *Deliver Us from Evil* (Hong Won-chan, 2020).

Previous page spread: *The City of Violence*
(Ryoo Seung-wan, 2006).

Choi Min-sik in *Old Boy* (Park Chan-wook, 2003) is
undoubtedly one of the most famous images in Korean
cinema. This sequence from the film also contributed
significantly to the fashionable use of hammers as weapons
in many future Korean action films.

REVIVAL OF THE COMEDIES

After an initial golden age in the 1960s, comedy gradually disappeared under the military regimes of Park Chung-hee and Chun Doo-hwan, moving to the small screen, where comedy variety shows were commonplace. A resurgent success during Korea's democratization and economic boom of the late 1980s, it enjoyed a new golden age in the early 2000s.

Comedy did not totally disappear during the 1970s and 1980s, as it infiltrated other popular genres, such as martial arts and anti-communist and children's films. Actor Shim Hyung-rae, later world-famous for his films *Yonggari* (1999) and *Dragon Wars: D-War* (2007), became a cult actor for the young Korean generation of the 1980s with his character Young-gu in parodies of well-known films such as *Young-gu Rambo* (1990) and *Young-gu and Count Dracula* (1992); but these films were scorned by adults and did little to revive the genre.

Comedy was reborn, thanks to one of the pillars of the Korean New Wave in the late 1980s, Lee Myung-se, whose first film, *Gagman* (1989), pays homage to burlesque cinema with the character of a hapless filmmaker, vaguely reminiscent of Charlie Chaplin, desperate to make his first feature film. This joyously extravagant comedy was a flop on release but has since gained a cult following. Lee Myung-se followed up with *My Love, My Bride* (1990), about the misadventures of a young married couple. This film was at the origins of the Korean comedy revival, and more specifically of battle-of-the-sexes comedies in the tradition of *When Harry Met Sally* (Rob Reiner, 1989).

Battle-of-the-sexes films are all about creating comic situations by featuring male and female characters with different perspectives, expectations, and behaviors. The jokes rely on their absurd challenges, piquant dialogue, comic misunderstandings, physical gags,

and unexpected twists, which eventually lead to their mutual understanding and respect, emphasizing that gender differences can be overcome.

Many of the comedies of the early 1990s were inspired by the sudden rise of women to important positions in Korea's rapidly expanding economy. The character of the outmoded husband is reminiscent of 1960s comedies that challenged the patriarchal status of Confucian society at the time.

After *My Love, My Bride*, the triumph of *Marriage Story* (Kim Eui-suk, 1992)—a film "planned" by the chaebol—definitively consolidated the battle-of-the-sexes genre with a series

of similar titles flooding the market, such as *Marriage Story 2* (Kim Kang-no, 1994), *The Man Who Cannot Kiss* (Cho Kum-hwan, 1994), *How to Top My Wife* (Kang Woo-suk, 1994), and *Bellybutton Bus* (Park Kwang-woo, 1995).

These films gave rise to another sub-genre, that of "emasculated men." *Mister Mama* (Kang Woo-suk, 1992), *Love-Pro, Marriage-Amateur* (Kim Do-gyeong and Lee Doo-yong, 1993), *Baby Sale* (Bon Kim, 1997), and *Baby and Me* (Kim Jin-young, 2008) all feature a carefree young man who suddenly finds himself caring for a baby or toddler in the mother's absence.

In the years that followed, producers retained the "antagonistic couple" concept of battle-of-the-sexes comedies and applied it to stories of first love for a younger audience. *My Sassy Girl* (Kwak Jae-young, 2001) became the archetype of the genre. Inspired by an authentic romance, posted in the form of blog entries in the early days of the internet, the film recounts the misadventures of a shy high-school student falling in love with a mischievous young woman,

---

Famous Korean comedy *My Sassy Girl* (2001) has been remade numerous times as films and TV series in countries as diverse as Nepal, Lithuania, the Philippines, India, and the United States.

Blending crime, action, and drama, Lee Byeong-heon's *Extreme Job* (2019) is to date the second biggest hit in the history of Korean cinema, with over 16 million spectators.

who puts him through a series of trials to prove his love.[1]

The film was a huge success in Korea on its release, becoming the most popular comedy and one of the top five hits of all time, with 4.8 million viewers. It also triumphed throughout Asia, topping the box office charts in Japan, Taiwan, and Hong Kong. Although not officially distributed in China, it sold over 150 million pirated copies and inspired numerous film and TV remakes around the world.

Director Kwak Jae-young tried to exploit the vein of antagonistic couples in his subsequent productions. In *Windstruck* (2004), he pitted an energetic policewoman against a poised professor; in *My Mighty Princess* (2008), a girl with superpowers falls in love with a harassed young man; and in the Japanese co-production *Cyborg She* (2008), the girlfriend turns out to be an android.

Comedy also infiltrated other popular genres, such as gangster films. *No. 3* (Song Neung-han, 1997), which has gained a cult following over the years, launched the sub-genre of parody gangster films, telling the story of a loser who tries at all costs to become the godfather of Seoul. This feature film brings together for the first-time future stars Choi Min-sik (*Old Boy*, 2003) and Song Kang-ho (*Parasite*, 2019) in the lead roles. *No. 3* triggered a series of young thug comedies, such as Kim Sang-jin's *Attack the Gas Station* (1999), *Kick the Moon* (2001), and *Jail Breakers* (2002), and the trilogy comprising *My Boss, My Hero* (JK Youn, 2001), *My Boss, My Teacher* (Kim Dong-won, 2006), and *The Mafia, The Salesman* (Shim Seung-bo, 2007), in which a young gangster must successively infiltrate a high school, a university, and a multinational corporation. In *Hi! Dharma!* (Park Cheol-kwan, 2001), a gang of thugs take refuge in a temple run by monks who are experts in martial arts.

My Sassy Girl (Kwak Jae-young, 2001) created the archetypal character of the emanci-

pated young woman in the early 2000s, an era marked by a gradual rise of feminist causes, notably with the creation of the Ministry of Gender Equality and Family in 2001 under President Kim Dae-jung, which helped to free the press on the subject of domestic violence. These factors, combined with the success of parody gangster films, led to a new sub-genre, female gangster comedies, including the franchises *My Wife Is a Gangster* (3 films, 2001–2006) and *Marrying the Mafia* (5 films, 2002–2012), both of which tell an unlikely love story between a shy young man and the daughter of a mafia godfather.

The early 2000s also saw the advent of erotic comedies: While, unlike in the rest of the world, *American Pie* (Paul and Chris Weitz, 1999) was a relative flop when released in Korea, the American film nonetheless gave rise to an avalanche of saucy comedies aimed at a young adult audience. These included *Sex Is Zero 1* and *2* (JK Youn, 2002 and 2007), *Sex of Magic* (Bang Sung-woong, 2002), *Wet Dreams 1* and *2* (Zeong Cho-sin, 2002 and 2005), and one of the first adaptations of a webtoon, *Dasepo Naughty Girls* (Lee Je-yong, 2006).

Pirates: The Last Royal Treasure (Kim Joung-hoon, 2022), the thriller *Veteran* (Ryoo Seung-wan, 2015), the disaster film *Exit* (Lee Sang-geun, 2019), and the film noir *Extreme Job* (Lee Byeong-heon, 2019).

1. The damsel's impertinence is put into perspective at the end of the film by a typically Confucian ending in the tradition of Han Hyung-mo's *Madame Freedom* from 1956, in keeping with the patriarchal Korean sensibilities still reigning supreme in Korea in the early 2000s.

The golden age of comedies in the 1990s and 2000s curiously declined at the same time as the recession in Korean cinema, between 2007 and 2011, with far fewer film releases each year. Yet audiences remain fond of the genre, as evidenced by the repeated success of titles such as *The Scandal Maker* (Kang Hyoung-chul, 2008), *My Girlfriend Is an Agent* (Terra Shin, 2009), and *Cyrano Agency* (Kim Hyun-suk, 2010).

Miss Granny (Hwang Dong-hyuk, 2014) was one of the most successful comedies, with over 8 million admissions; it belongs to the body-swap sub-genre, inspired by American successes such as *Freaky Friday* (Mark Waters, 2003). The story of a 74-year-old woman who suddenly regains the body she had in her twenties is a resounding success, making the film one of the prototypes for co-productions that will help the Koreans in their conquest of new Asian markets, through remakes—in this case, Chinese, Vietnamese, and Indonesian.

During the 2010s, comedy infiltrated new, sometimes unexpected genres, such as *The Pirates* (Lee Seok-hoon, 2014) and its sequel, *The*

My Wife Is a Gangster (2001) made a major contribution to the success of the Korean comedy sub-genre of female gangster films in the 2000s.

재건

1998
2012

재건

1998–2012
THE RENAISSANCE OF KOREAN CINEMA

The 1990s saw the emergence of a new generation of producers and directors, the creation of a genuine film industry and a solid distribution network. Toward the end of the 1990s, this revival was confirmed by a new series of political measures, among the most important for the economic and ideological liberalization of Korean cinema.

In 1999, President Kim Dae-jung (1998–2003) transformed the Korean Film Council into a self-regulating body, so that it could fully manage Korean film policy and promotion. Distributors could now sell Korean films on international film markets, thus promoting their worldwide distribution. In 2001, Kim Dae-jung also abolished the Motion Picture Law and the Censorship Board once and for all, in favor of the Korea Media Rating Board, an institution responsible for authorizing the release of films according to age group.

Added to the visibility of these films is the hallyu phenomenon, i.e., the remarkable spread of South Korean pop culture, such as k-pop (music), k-drama (TV series), fashion, and cuisine. The phenomenal success of several k-dramas, such as *First Love* (268 episodes, Lee Eung-jin, 1996–1997), *Winter Sonata* (20 episodes, Yoon Seok-ho, 2002), and *Jewel in the Palace* (54 episodes, Kim Geun-hong, 2003–2004), first in Asia and then in the rest of the world, drew attention to stars Bae Yong-jun, Rain, Choi Ji-woo, and Lee Young-ae, and then to the film offering in general, supporting the export of titles such as *Shiri* (Kang Je-gyu, 1999), *JSA—Joint Security Area* (Park Chan-wook, 2000), and *My Sassy Girl* (Kwak Jae-young, 2001).

February 13, 1999, the release date of *Shiri*, can be considered the starting point of the "official revival" of Korean cinema. The biggest hit in Korean cinema history, with over 6 million admissions nationwide, it paved the way for domestic blockbusters and the repeated success of *Friend* (Kwak Kyung-taek, 2001), *Brotherhood* (Kang Je-gyu, 2004), and *The Host* (Bong Joon-ho, 2006), which gave producers the confidence to reinvest in cinema.

The local success of Korean films was also reflected worldwide, with a series of titles released in many countries throughout the 2000s, including *Old Boy* (Park Chan-wook, 2003), *The Host* (Bong Joon-ho, 2006), *The Good, the Bad, the Weird* (Kim Jee-woon, 2008), *The Chaser* (Na Hong-jin, 2008), *I Saw the Devil* (Kim Jee-woon, 2010) in the commercial circuit, and *Painted Fire* (Im Kwon-taek, 2002), *Spring, Summer, Fall, Winter . . . and Spring* (Kim Ki-duk, 2003), *3-Iron* (Kim Ki-duk, 2004), and *Poetry* (Lee Chang-dong, 2010) in a network of independent cinemas. In Europe, this reputation was amplified by the release and success of numerous Korean films on DVD, then VOD, in the 2000 and 2010 decades.

In 2006, Korean cinema reached its peak, taking 63.8 percent of the market share against American competition with the incredible success of *The Host* (Bong Joon-ho) and its 13 million viewers. Between 2007 and 2012, however, it experienced its first period of recession, following a series of failures of several costly blockbusters. In 2008, market share fell back to 42 percent, its lowest level since 2001.

The overly rapid growth in the number of productions also explains this recession: from 43 titles in 1998, the number rose to 112 in 2007, the average budget for blockbusters quintupled, while average profitability fell from 41.5 percent in 2001 to -45 percent (!) in 2007. Of the 36 films released by CJ Entertainment in 2008, only 5 were financially profitable. The concentration of the 3 main producer-broadcasters—Cinema Service, CJ, and Showbox—who monopolized 87 percent of screens with their own titles, left their competitors' productions virtually no chance. Many independent structures were going bankrupt, and private investors were beginning to withdraw.

The measures taken by the government also played an important role in the poor health of the film industry. After the positive measures put in place under Kim Dae-jung, the new president, Roh Moo-hyun (2003–2008), decided to halve the quota of 146 days of compulsory screening of Korean films as part of a free-trade agreement, under pressure from the United States and despite numerous demonstrations by film professionals in 2006.

Korean society was changing. Young cinema-goers, who had made a major contribution to the success of national cinema in the early 2000s to "beat" the eternal American competitor, were gradually deserting cinemas in favor of small screens and illegal downloading. The first VOD platforms appeared in 2009, leading to the rapid collapse of the DVD market and depriving Korean studios of high revenues. By 2010, over 80 percent of Korean households were equipped with internet access, and surveys revealed that the average Korean illegally downloads 54 films a year. The advent of the smartphone and a sharp rise in cinema ticket prices are precipitating a decline in cinema attendance.

Previous page: *Old Boy* (Park Chan-wook, 2003).

Following page spread: Neon signs in the streets of Seoul.

The first sign of the future revival of Korean cinema came in 2011 with the double success of *War of the Arrows* (Kim Han-min) and *Sunny: Our Hearts Beat Together* (Kang Hyoung-chul), with over 7 million admissions each, taking market share back above 50 percent for the first time since 2006. Alas, the political turmoil of the 2010s and the Covid-19 pandemic once again put Korean cinema to the test.

Poetry (2010) was selected for the Cannes Film Festival, where it won the Screenplay Prize.

THE HALLYU PHENOMENON

At the end of the 1990s, a Korean cultural wave dubbed hallyu spread first across Asia, then around the world, making a major contribution to the dissemination of Korean films and other cultural products.

This hallyu wave emerged thanks to a series of economic measures taken by the State, which first elevated cinema to the status of a national industry in 1994, before adopting a series of tax exemption measures and subsidies in 1995. After the financial crisis of 1997, the government of Kim Dae-jung (1998–2003) introduced a law to promote the cultural industry. This policy was continued under the presidency of Lee Myung-bak (2008–2013), with new measures aimed at exporting the "Korean success model" and encouraging the establishment of national companies abroad to promote and sell domestic cultural products.

The export of k-dramas (Korean series) is the first major success of this policy. With the proliferation of television channels in the 1990s, producers competed to attract audiences with high-quality programs. In 1995, *Sandglass* (24 episodes, Kim Jong-hak) changed the usual series format from hundreds of episodes to a season of only 12 to 24 episodes. At the same time, due to the financial crisis of 1997, many Asian countries were looking for new, less-expensive entertainment products than those usually supplied by Japan and Hong Kong. China turned to k-dramas.

Thus, *First Love* (268 episodes, Lee Eung-jin, 1996–1997), broadcast in 1997 on the Chinese state channel China Central Television (CCTV), recorded the second-highest audience in its history and caused a veritable craze for South Korean series. In 2006, these programs alone accounted for more than all foreign productions combined. As a result, China, in order to protect its local production, adopted quotas limiting foreign programs to 50 episodes per year and broadcasting them outside prime time.

The popularity of Korean products quickly spread throughout Southeast Asia, then to more distant countries such as Sri Lanka and even Nepal. The hallyu wave triumphed in Japan, thanks to the success of series such as *Winter Sonata* (20 episodes, Yoon Seok-ho, 2002) and *Jewel in the Palace* (54 episodes, Kim Geun-hong, 2003–2004), and then conquered the Middle East and Africa. The popularity of these programs can be explained, in part, by the authors' ability to adopt the American style of narration to tell stories deeply rooted in Asian culture and Confucianism.

Unlike their Western counterparts, most Korean series at the time were also characterized by an absence of sexuality and violence, and an emphasis on moral values, such as *Three Guys and Three Girls* (157 episodes, Eun Kyung-pyo and Song Chang-ui, 1996–1997), a toned-down version of the American sitcom *Friends* (236 episodes, NBC, 1994–2004), which was less subject to censorship in certain countries, notably the Muslim countries.

The popularity of Korean soap stars in Asian countries, where the star system is much more established than in the West, was also driving the acquisition of feature films in which they appear. The presence of Lee Young-ae, the actress in *Jewel in the Palace*, benefited the export of *One Fine Spring Day* (Hur Jin-ho, 2001), in which she plays the lead role. Similarly, Choi Ji-woo and Bae Yong-jun, the star couple of the k-dramas *First Love* and *Winter Sonata*, boosted the circulation of *Everybody Has Secrets* (Jang Hyun-soo, 2004) and *April Snow* (Hur Jin-ho, 2005).

Asian countries were also beginning to take an interest in other Korean films. *Shiri* (Kang Je-gyu, 1999) was exported to Japan, Taiwan, and Hong Kong, where it topped the box office for two consecutive weeks, a first for a Korean film. *My Sassy Girl* (Kwak Jae-young, 2001) became a

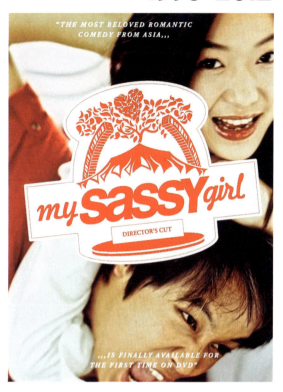

phenomenon, topping the Japanese, Taiwanese, and Hong Kong box office charts with record box office receipts—at the time $35 million. It was re-released in numerous official and unofficial remakes, notably in India, Nepal, the Philippines, and Indonesia, and was one of the best-selling illegal DVDs in China, where the pirate copy sold over 150 million copies.

To avoid prohibitive acquisition costs in the event of unexpectedly successful releases, some Asian countries were starting to pre-purchase future titles simply by reading the script, or on the basis of the names of the stars involved. This was the case for films such as *Duelist* (Lee Myung-se, 2005) or *Running Wild* (Kim Sung-soo, 2006), with the presence in the cast of another k-drama star of this era, Kwon Sang-woo from *Stairway to Heaven* (20 episodes, Lee Jang-soo, 2003–2004).

In the West, and especially in France, the success of Korean cinema had less to do with the rise of k-dramas than with the visibility gained through festivals, DVD releases, and the internet in the early 2000s. In the following decade, k-dramas and k-pop music remained largely absent from TV screens and radio stations, due to the dominance of French and American cultures; only Psy's hit song "Gangnam Style" was a success in 2012, as it was elsewhere in the world.

The media had clearly underestimated the power of the hallyu wave, which has been spreading since the early 2000s by means of websites, blogs, and social networks, and which has already made several Western generations aware of Korean culture. And if the triumph of *Parasite* (Bong Joon-ho) at the 2019 Cannes Film Festival and then at the 2020 Oscars still felt like a surprise to many professionals, it seemed a simple logical outcome for millions of fans.

Hallyu phenom *My Sassy Girl* (2001) became one of the most exported Korean feature films in the world. In China, the unofficial DVD bootleg is said to have sold over 100 million copies.

NATIONAL BLOCKBUSTERS

Blockbusters in Korean cinema are not a recent phenomenon: Na Un-gyu's blockbusters *Across Tuman River* (1928) and *Deaf Sam-ryong* (1928), for example, already involved the construction of gigantic sets and the participation of thousands of extras, while the historical epics and anti-communist war films of the 1950s and 1960s increasingly emphasized the spectacular, with their many battle scenes designed to seduce the crowds. At the same time, producers were particularly careful with their budgets, given the relatively limited Korean market and the absence of international sales.

To win back audiences, the chaebol's involvement in Korean cinema in the 1990s saw the emergence of the first blockbusters that had higher budgets, such as *Marriage Story* (Kim Eui-suk, 1992) and *Two Cops* (Kang Woo-suk, 1993). This period also saw the first productions with digital special effects, including the fantasy films *The Fox with Nine Tails* (Park Heon-soo, 1994) and *The Gingko Bed* (Kang Je-gyu, 1996), which required large budgets but were also highly successful.

In 1999, *Shiri* (Kang Je-gyu) marked the official start of the Korean film revival and the beginning of the golden age of blockbusters, with the repeated success of *JSA—Joint Security Area* (Park Chan-wook, 2000) and its over 5 million admissions, *Friend* (Kwak Kyung-taek, 2001) with 8 million, *Silmido* (Kang Woo-suk, 2003) with 11 million, and *The Host* (Bong Joon-ho, 2006) with 13 million viewers, films that have definitively shaped the Korean film industry and contributed to its worldwide recognition.

Shot on a budget of $3 million (including $1 million for marketing alone), *Shiri* sold 2.4 million tickets in Seoul and 6 million nationwide. The story of a secret agent's race against time to defuse a bomb in the heart of Seoul, the detonation of which would reignite the war between the two Koreas, is both Korean and universal.

Shiri and the Korean blockbusters to follow are fundamentally inspired by the Hollywood model, in that they tighten scriptwriting and energize direction. At the same time, they infuse their stories with a touch of nationalism to strike a chord with Korean patriots.

Their triumph was also aided by the consolidation of the network of the 3 biggest broadcasters of the time and the multiplication of multiplexes. Audience numbers soared from 47.5 million in 1997 to 253.4 million in 2006. Un-

Previous page spread: Successful TV series *Jewel in the Palace* (2003–2004) was exported to more than 90 countries worldwide, grossing over $100 million.

The biggest hit of all time at its release, *JSA—Joint Security Area* (2000) was Park Chan-wook's first public and critical success after the failures of *The Moon Is… the Sun's Dream* (1992) and *Trio* (1997).

(Korean music). *Shiri* (Kang Je-gyu, 1999), *My Sassy Girl* (Kwak Jae-young, 2001), *One Fine Spring Day* (Hur Jin-ho, 2001), and *Everybody Has Secrets* (Jang Hyun-soo, 2004) were released in many Asian countries. Pan-Asian co-productions such as *The Warrior* (Kim Sung-soo, 2001) and *Shadowless Sword* (Kim Young-jun, 2005) were on the increase.

American distributors such as Warner Bros., MGM, and Dreamworks began buying the rights to remake these films. *Il Mare* [*The Sea*] (Lee Hyun-seung, 2000) was adapted by Alejandro Agresti into *The Lake House* (2006); *A Tale of Two Sisters* (Kim Jee-woon, 2003) by Charles and Thomas Guard into *The Uninvited* (2009); and *Into the Mirror* (Kim Sung-ho, 2003) by Alexandre Aja into *Mirrors* (2008).

But the resounding failure of a number of blockbusters, such as *Resurrection of the Little Match Girl* (Jang Sun-woo, 2002), *Yesterday* (Jeon Yun-su, 2002), *2009: Lost Memories* (Lee Si-myung, 2002), *Natural City* (Min Byung-chun, 2003), and *Tube* (Baek Woon-hak, 2003), led to a retreat on the part of investors, despite the subsequent success of *Band of Brothers* and *The Host* (Bong Joon-ho, 2006). Between 2007 and 2011, Korean cinema experienced its first recession.

Korean blockbusters became successful once more in 2012, thanks to *The Thieves* (Choi Dong-hoon) and *Masquerade* (Choo Chang-min), which each attracted over 12 million viewers. Henceforth, the 10 million spectator mark—in a country of 51 million inhabitants—became the new milestone as a film worthy of the blockbuster designation, and almost every new year saw its new champion: *Miracle in Cell No.7* (Lee Hwan-kyung) in 2013, with 12.8 million admissions; *Ode to My Father* (JK Youn) in 2014, with 14.2 million; *Along with the Gods: The Two Worlds* (Kim Yong-hwa) in 2017, with 14.4 million; and *Extreme Job* (Lee Byeong-heon) in 2019, with 16.2 million spectators.

In 2023, the undisputed champion re-

like the United States, where a law passed in 1948 forced the major studios to sell off their network of cinemas to avoid monopolizing the market for their films, in South Korea, production companies are allowed to operate their own screens. *Silmido* (Kang Woo-suk, 2003) and *Brotherhood* (Kang Je-gyu, 2004) were screened on 30 percent and 40 percent, respectively, of the 1,100 cinema screens in existence at the time, thus benefiting from broad national coverage that left little chance for competing productions.

National blockbusters soon dominated the market. The share of Korean films exceeded 50 percent for the first time in 2001, making Korea one of the few countries, alongside China and India, to supplant the American film industry.

The creation, in 2000, of dedicated sales units within the major studios led to the first international exports and contributed to the emergence of the hallyu wave, marked by the success of k-dramas (Korean series) and k-pop mained the historical epic *The Admiral: Roaring Currents* (Kim Han-min, 2014), a re-enactment of the Battle of Myong-yang (1597), against the Japanese invaders, with 17.6 million viewers, a third of the total Korean population. The Covid-19 pandemic put a temporary end to this run of successes. Titles such as *Steel Rain 2* (Yang Woo-suk, 2020) and *Escape from Mogadishu* (Ryoo Seung-wan, 2021) achieved box office figures of 1.8 and 3.6 million, where 5 and 10 million, respectively, were expected; and only the triumph of *The Roundup* (Lee Sang-yong, 2022), with 12 million spectators, suggested a possible "return to normal" in the years to come. The movie *12.12: The Day* (Kim Sung-su, 2023) attracted 13.1 million people at the of 2023 and beginning of 2024.

The dominance of blockbusters produced by the major studios, which also controlled the distribution networks, left little room for competition. But the versatility of audience tastes can lead to surprises and unexpected successes for films with much more modest budgets, such as *Dongju: Portrait of a Poet* (Lee Joon-ik, 2016), *Gonjiam: Haunted Asylum* (Jung Bum-shik, 2018), or *Kim Ji-young, Born 1982* (Kim Do-young, 2019).

The Admiral: Roaring Currents (Kim Han-min, 2014) is the biggest Korean success to date, with over 17 million admissions (potentially one in three Koreans). It revived the trend for big-budget historical epics.

우리는 결코
두려움에 질

감독

봉

제작 (주)빅스톤 픽쳐스 제공/배급 CJ엔터테인먼트   조진웅 김명곤 진구 이정현 권율 노민우 김태훈

GENERATION 386

The revival of Korean cinema led to the emergence of many new talents in the decade 2000–2010, three of whom stood out both in Korea and internationally: Park Chan-wook, Kim Jee-woon, and Bong Joon-ho. They are the finest proof of the incredible ability of Korean artists to adapt foreign influences to create their own unique style. Their films are not mere copies or homages, but deeply Korean cinematic works.

Park Chan-wook, Kim Jee-woon, and Bong Joon-ho belong to the first generation of filmmakers to emerge from the old studio assistantship, and are genuine cinephiles who were drawn to the cinema due to a pure passion for the art. They grew up during the 1980s boom in university film clubs and the video market, which gave them access to a multitude of films from all over the world. They rented VHS cassettes by the hundreds and recorded feature films that were broadcast without subtitles on the US Army's Armed Forces Korea Network (AFKN), or in censored versions on the national channels MBC (Weekend Movie Classic) and KBS 1 (Classic Movie Theater).

Bong Joon-ho and Park Chan-wook set up their own film clubs while studying sociology and philosophy, respectively, to exchange ideas and debate with other film enthusiasts. The discovery of *Vertigo* (Alfred Hitchcock, 1958) sparked Park Chan-wook's desire to become a director. He worked for a production company to earn a living, while making a name for himself as a film critic and author of cinema reference books.

Kim Jee-woon, an actor and director of acclaimed plays, wrote screenplays in his spare time. In 1998, he directed his first feature film, *The Quiet Family*, which blends different genres, from satirical comedy to horror. The film was a success, ranking sixth at the box office that year, with 343,000 admissions. His second feature, the social sports drama *The Foul King* (2000), star-

ring actor Song Kang-ho (*Parasite*) in a leading role for the first time, was the second success of the year, with 817,000 admissions.

Park Chan-wook and Bong Joon-ho were less fortunate. The former suffered bitter failures with his first two films, *The Moon Is…the Sun's Dream* (1992) and *Trio* (1997), before achieving success with *JSA—Joint Security Area* (2000), the biggest hit of all time at the time of its release. As for *Barking Dogs Never Bite* (2000), Bong Joon-ho's first feature film, it went completely unnoticed on its release.

All three had a particular affection for B movies and genre films. Their careers began at the height of the Korean film revival, when producers encouraged the diversification of genres to attract large audiences. The cinema of these three directors thus reflects both their personal passion and the market trends of their time: Park Chan-wook explored the film noir genres with his "revenge trilogy"—consisting of *Sympathy for Mr. Vengeance* (2002), *Lady Vengeance* (2005), and above all *Old Boy* (2003), fantasy comedy with *I'm a Cyborg, But That's OK* (2006), the vampire film with *Thirst* (2009), and the thriller with *The Handmaiden* (2016) and *Decision to Leave* (2022).

Bong Joon-ho successively created an investigative film, *Memories of Murder* (2003), a monster movie, *The Host* (2006), and a futuristic film, *Snowpiercer* (2013), often blending different genres within the same film. *Okja* (2017), for example, skillfully combines comedy, social drama, science fiction, and environmental fable.

Kim Jee-woon's filmography is undoubtedly the most diverse. Each of his works explores a new genre to test its codes and limits. He directed a sports comedy with *The Foul King* (2000), a horror film with *A Tale of Two Sisters* (2003), an homage to Hong Kong film noir with *A Bittersweet Life* (2005), a Manchurian Western with *The Good, the Bad, the Weird* (2008), a historical espionage thriller with *The Age of Shad-*

ows (2016), and a futuristic film adapted from anime with *Illang: The Wolf Brigade* (2018).

All three directors come from the "386 generation" (named after the Intel 386 computer produced at that time), those born in the 1960s, who lived through the many protests, notably the Gwangju Uprising of the 1980s, and who were in their thirties in the 1990s–2000s. Their careers have been shaped by the country's profound upheavals, from military regimes to democracy and the incredible economic boom of recent decades. Their films combine their passion for cinema, their own personal experience, and the evolution of Korean society.

Kim Jee-woon's *A Tale of Two Sisters*, the fifth remake of the traditional folk tale *The Story of Jang-hwa and Hong-ryeon* (Kim Yeong-hwan, 1924), is set in an imposing Japanese-style building with Western interior decoration, which immediately takes the Koreans back to their own past, marked by the successive historical periods of Japanese and American occupation. The characters were placed in a context that is already highly metaphorical, but also charged with a terrible drama. Like the Korean people, these characters are prisoners of an onerous and turbulent past in a setting that blends different cultural influences.

Park Chan-wook took up aspects of this idea of metaphorical location in *The Handmaiden* adapted from Sarah Waters's 2002 Welsh novel *Fingersmith*. The original plot, set in 1860s London, is transposed to 1930s Korea under Japanese occupation. The setting for the film is the real-life Rokkaen, a villa built by a British architect in 1913 in Kuwana, Japan. The building also blends Western and Japanese styles, once again reminding Korean viewers of their country's different historical periods.

Bong Joon-ho is perhaps the filmmaker who best tells the story of his country through typically Western genres. In *Memories of Murder*, his investigative film, the focus is less on the misdeeds of the country's first proven serial

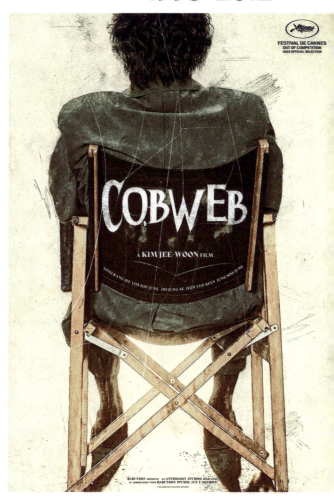

killer than on the hidden page of Korean history in the 1980s. Western viewers may only see the main characters as slightly "dumb" police officers overwhelmed by the situation, but they send Koreans straight back to the memory of the soldiers of the former Park Chung-hee regime, "promoted" to law enforcement overnight under President Chun Doo-hwan in the early 1980s, with no training and a complete lack of equipment and infrastructure.

Their superiors, equally incapable of carrying out the investigation in the film, are even

---

Kim Jee-woon's tenth feature, *Cobweb* (2023), is both a satirical comedy about the 1970s Korean film industry and a violent denunciation of the Park Chung-hee regime. The film also pays tribute to Shin Sang-ok and Kim Ki-young, who spearheaded the revival of Korean cinema in the 1950s.

responsible for another murder after making the wrong decision. Above all, Bong Joon-ho depicts a dismal period in Korean society, where death and confusion reigned under a regime incapable of handling crisis situations.

The Host, while ostensibly a "simple" monster movie, is also a sharp underlying critique of both the West and Korea. The birth of the creature at the beginning of the film is inspired by the McFarland Incident, a real-life story of an ecological disaster caused by the American military in Korea in the early 2000s. The final confrontation, involving Molotov cocktails, recalls the many popular uprisings in Korea, particularly the one in Gwangju. In this way, the "monster" becomes a metaphor for the many domestic and foreign threats to the Korean family.

Similarly, *Parasite*, while seemingly telling the universal story of class struggle, also highlights the growing socioeconomic disparities in the ultraliberal system. The film even dares to make a number of strong "local" references, such as the scene, seemingly innocuous to non-Korean viewers, of the forging of a diploma, which refers directly to a political scandal that occurred during the filming, when a minister falsified documents to facilitate his children's admission to a famous university. The father's final gesture refers directly to the typically Korean emotion *hwabyeong* ("anger disease" or "fire disease"), which results in sudden outbursts of violence after an accumulation of different angers. So, with films that seem to address universal themes, Bong Joon-ho succeeds above all in telling the story of his own country.

While contemporary Korean cinema is full of many fine but less internationally renowned filmmakers, Park Chan-wook, Kim Jee-woon, and Bong Joon-ho are the perfect representatives of a whole new generation of directors who have succeeded in perfectly incorporating Western film genres into their own culture. The recent success of Korean cinema can therefore,

in part, be explained by the fact that it shows things that are immediately identifiable by a global audience—but with subtly unique Korean particularities—visible or otherwise—that make all the difference.

Sympathy for Mr. Vengeance (2002) is the first film in the "vengeance trilogy" with *Old Boy* (2003) and *Lady Vengeance* (2005).

THE SECOND KOREAN NEW WAVE

Kim Ki-duk, Hong Sang-soo, and Lee Chang-dong, spotted at the Busan International Film Festival, are the first directors whose films, following in the footsteps of the independent filmmakers of previous decades, were selected and rewarded in the most prestigious competitions.

Born into a modest family in Daegu in 1954, Lee Chang-dong, who lived through military regimes and the transition to democracy, is a direct descendant of the Korean New Wave of the early 1990s, having worked as Park Kwang-su's assistant and screenwriter on the films *To the Starry Island* (1993) and *A Single Spark* (1995).

Before embarking on a career in film, he worked as a theater director and writer of socially engaged novels. His first work, *The Booty* (1983), deals with the bloody riots in Gwangju in 1980. His second, *Nokcheon* (1992), contains two short stories: The first tells the story of a young man expelled from university for his political activism, who eventually fractures his own family unit; the second recounts the violent interrogation of a young woman falsely accused of having an affair with an activist.

Lee Chang-dong made his directorial debut with *Green Fish* (1997), which turns the fashionable gangster film on its head, subtly portraying the political evolution of Korean society from the 1970s to the 1990s. He followed this up with the drama *Peppermint Candy* (2000), which earned him his first selection at the Cannes Film Festival's Quinzaine des cinéastes in 2000, before winning the Best Actress prize for Jeon Do-youn in *Secret Sunshine* in 2007, and the Screenplay prize for *Poetry* in 2010. *Oasis* won Best Director and Best Actress for Moon Soo-ri at the Venice Film Festival in 2002. His latest film to date, *Burning* (2018), is inspired by a short story by the famous Japanese writer Haruki Murakami.

After his first two films dealing with political subjects, Lee Chang-dong then refocused exclusively on the human condition. For the director, nothing is more artistic than people's lives. He believes that mankind often makes irrational choices that open the way to new possibilities, so he seeks to create films that are as realistic as possible, showing life without artifice while exploring emotions and feelings that are usually considered invisible or imperceptible.

Lee Chang-dong often depicts characters who aspire to beauty and joy, but encounter suffering and adversity. In *Oasis*, for example, the two main characters, a mentally retarded man and a motor-impaired woman, find pure, sincere love, but are ostracized by society because of their "difference." In *Poetry*, an Alzheimer's sufferer clings to the words of poetry to forestall the disease that is eating away at her. In *Secret Sunshine*, a mother seeks refuge and answers in religion to mourn the loss of a child, only to encounter a far more real human wickedness.

In these films, the Korean family unit is systematically fractured, with characters desperately searching for their parents and family. This portrayal reflects the filmmaker's consideration of his own past, with an unemployed leftist father, an overworked mother supporting the family, and a sister suffering from cerebral palsy. For him, the family is the first environment with which human beings are confronted. Instead of being a protective cocoon, family can be a reflection of societal problems—and therefore a (Korean) reflection of itself, necessarily fractured due to its political past. In this, his cinema perpetuates the approach of the independent directors of the late 1980s and early 1990s.

Kim Ki-duk, regarded as an emblematic figure of independent cinema in transition, also uses cinema as a means of expressing his anger at Korean society, but unlike Lee Chang-dong, he does so more head-on.

Also from a modest background, he had to leave school at 17 and work as a laborer. He enlisted in the Korean army for five years and was so traumatized by the experience that he

became an ordained priest to care for blind people. Once again disappointed by the hypocrisy of the Church and his superiors, he left on a whim for France two years later, where he improvised as a painter and sold his paintings in Montpellier and Paris. He discovered cinema for the first time in 1991, when by chance he saw Jonathan Demme's *The Silence of the Lambs* and Leos Carax's *Les Amants du Pont-Neuf* [*The Lovers on the Bridge*], both released that year.

After his return to Korea, Kim Ki-duk began writing screenplays, several of which won awards, enabling him to direct his first two feature-length films, *Crocodile* (1996) and *Wild Animals* (1997), which are largely autobiographical. *Birdcage Inn* (1998), selected in the Panorama section of the 1999 Berlin International Film Festival, marked the start of a long series of international festival awards, including *Samaria* (2004), which won the Silver Bear in Berlin, and *3-Iron* (2004) and *Pieta* (2012), both winners of the Golden Lion in Venice. He achieved international recognition with the success of *The Isle* (2000), *Spring, Summer, Fall, Winter . . . and Spring* (2003), and *The Bow* (2005).

His films are very different from one another, but they share a common theme: solitary characters living on the fringes of Korean society. According to the director, their behavior and silence are the consequence of the deep scars that Koreans carry within them, a lack of trust since the occupation and successive military regimes.

Kim Ki-duk also deals directly with Korean history in several of his films: *Address Unknown* (2001) depicts the social marginalization of a young man of mixed race, the product of the union of a Korean mother and an African-American soldier, who has since returned to the United States. *The Coast Guard* (2002) recounts the descent into hell of a young Coast Guard officer who shoots a man he believes to be a North Korean spy, when in fact the man was simply a lover joining his fiancée on a beach at night. *The*

Net (2016) follows the violent interrogation of an innocent North Korean fisherman by South Korean authorities, after his boat capsizes due to a breakdown.

Hong Sang-soo is, of the three, the director who seems to stand out most from the earlier Korean New Wave, or rather, the one who best illustrates its evolution by taking entirely new paths. With 31 films made in 27 years—at the time of writing—he is the most prolific Korean

Filmmaker Kim Ki-duk, leader of the Korean Second Wave with such world-renowned titles as *Spring, Summer, Fall, Winter . . . and Spring* (2003), *3-Iron* (2004), and *The Bow* (2005), died of Covid-19 on December 11, 2020, in Riga, Latvia.

Following page spread: *Peppermint Candy* (Lee Chang-dong, 2000).

director of the last two decades, and the one who has received the most international distribution and awards. His work, which may be difficult to grasp, might arouse either immediate passion or eternal rejection, or curiosity, which makes the viewer try again and again, over the years, eventually to appreciate its particular flavor. Taken as a whole, his work is an absolutely logical and fascinating cinematic canvas.

The Best Film award at the 1997 Rotterdam International Film Festival for *The Day a Pig Fell into the Well* (1996) was the first in a long line of awards crowning his career. Fascinated by the directors Yasujiro Ozu and Robert Bresson, Hong Sang-soo focuses more on substance than form in his relatively austere films. He focuses entirely on the acting and dialogue of his actors, with long sequence shots sometimes lasting ten minutes, interrupted only on rare occasions by slight camera movements within the frame or zooms in on certain details.

Hong Sang-soo, fascinated by dual narratives, constantly has the same challenging ideas repeated, either within the same film or from one to the next. In *Like You Know It All* (2009), the filmmaker recounts a man's successive encounters with two of his friends, whose wives each attempt to seduce him over meals, with fundamentally different outcomes. *Right Now, Wrong Then* (2015), for its part, is divided into two distinct parts, recounting the same attempt by a director to seduce a woman, the first time aggressively, the second more reservedly.

Hong Sang-soo often explores triangular relationships in love, as in *Woman Is the Future of Man* (2004), *Woman on the Beach* (2006), *Like You Know It All* (2009), and *Our Sunhi* (2013). Each film tells the story of the same meal between a woman and two men, during which tongues are loosened under the influence of alcohol, leading to a different ending every time.

Hong Sang-soo finds fascinating potential in the infinity of possibilities, where every word, action, or gesture can trigger multiple variations.

In the end, his universe is not so different from the Marvel Multiverse, with ordinary people in the role of superheroes and human feelings in place of special effects.

While Lee Chang-dong enjoys a certain degree of recognition, Kim Ki-duk and Hong Sang-soo are completely unknown in Korea. Their films only exist through festival selections and foreign funding; and they are only marginally successful in terms of box office in their own country. As is often the case with independent productions—particularly from Asia—while they are considered representative of their country by Westerners, they are often not even shown there.

HORROR FILMS

Horror films are one of the key genres to emerge from the Korean film revival of the late 1990s. *The Hole* (Kim Sung-hong, 1997) marked the origins of the phenomenon, while *A Tale of Two Sisters* (Kim Jee-won, 2003) was the first world-wide success.

The Story of Jang-hwa and Hong-ryeon (Kim Yeong-hwan, 1924) is the first feature-length horror film in the history of Korean cinema. Adapted from a traditional tale, it recounts the revenge of twin sisters murdered by their

---

A Tale of Two Sisters (2003) is a subtle retelling of the Korean horror classic *The Story of Jang-hwa and Hong-ryeon* (1924), which refers to the traumas of the Japanese occupation.

wicked stepmother. It was remade several times, as historical rather than truly fantastic films, in 1936, 1956, 1962, and 1972, before Kim Jee-woon's famous 2003 version, *A Tale of Two Sisters*.

Mok-Dan Ghost Story (Kim So-dong, 1947) and *Madam White Snake* (Shin Sang-ok, 1960) initiated a series of adaptations of traditional Chinese tales. The latter tells the story of a snake spirit who takes on the appearance of an attractive young woman to deceive humans. The film's success led to the remake of *The Snake Woman* (Shin Sang-ok, 1969) and its sequel, *Revenge of the Snake Woman* (Lee Yong-min, 1970), as well as a new version, *Legend of the White Snake* (Choi Dong-joon, 1978).

Madam White Snake also triggered a wave of films featuring demonic folk creatures, including *A Thousand-Year-Old Fox* (Shin Sang-ok,

1969), with the figure of the *kumiho*, a vixen who takes on human appearance to deceive her wary victims and feed on their livers. This creature also appears in *Saho Martial Arts* (Choi Dong-joon, 1979), *Daughter of a Ghost* (Park Yun-gyo, 1983), *A Fairy Mandarin's Duck* (An Seung-ho, 1990), and—above all—in the very first Korean blockbuster with digital special effects, *The Fox with Nine Tails* (Park Heon-soo, 1994).

In *Mok-Dan Ghost Story,* the director portrays the *Cheonyeo Gwisin* (ghost of a young virgin), a spirit who returns to haunt those who have wronged her. The phantom usually appears in the form of a woman dressed in a white *sobok* (traditional mourning garment), with long black hair covering her face to protest against the traditional Korean women's ritual of tying their hair back. Yet the victim was quite respectful of Confucian codes during her lifetime, and might have even taken her own life to avoid undermining Confucian values, for example, after a rape or wrong committed by a higher-class person.

The Cheonyeo Gwisin returns from the dead to try to find the peace she needs to reach the afterlife. She usually has a destiny to fulfill, such as looking after a relative or punishing her tormentors. She generally does not harm people outside the conflict, but rather seeks their attention so that justice can be served. Park Yun-gyo, nicknamed the Master of Horror, is the specialist of the *Cheonyeo Gwisin* sub-genre with his film series consisting of *Ok-nyeo's Resentment* (1972), *Resentment of Daughter-in-Law* (1972), *Resented Spirit of Baby Bride Groom* (1973), and *A Young Lady's Resentment* (1974). These films all tell stories of young women unjustly killed by their employers, lovers, or mothers-in-law, and whose spirits return to seek revenge.

The numerous British Hammer and American Universal Studios "monster" productions of the 1950s were a notable source of inspiration for Korean directors. Lee Yong-min, in particular, made a series of films based on the Western vampire myth. In *A Flower of Evil* (1961), a bot-

anist feeds the blood of his victims to a flower that harbors the soul of his beloved, who had died 20 years earlier. In *Bride from the Grave* (1963), a young married man discovers that his wife is actually a vampire, who digs up corpses at night to drink their blood. In *A Bloodthirsty Killer* (also known as *Devilish Homicide*, 1965), the spirit of a murdered young woman reincarnates as a cat to suck the blood of her killer's family members.

Other mythical creatures appeared in Korean cinema in the 1960s, such as the "invisible man" in *The End of an Invisible Man* (Lee Kang-cheon, 1960) and *Invisible Man* (Lee Kyu-woong, 1969), or Godzilla in the monster films *Space Monster Wangmagwi* (Gwon Hyeok-jin, 1967) and *Yongary, Monster from the Deep* (Kim Kee-duk, 1967). The latter two films were aimed at young audiences, at a time when television was beginning to turn children away from the big screen.

The 1970s saw the hardening of the Misin tapa political movement, which sought to eradicate shamanism and ancient beliefs in the name of progress. Korean horror cinema reflects this trend in the sudden upsurge of shaman characters, often portrayed as impostors or vile characters. Thus, in *Woman with Half a Soul* (Shin Sang-ok, 1973), a man haunted by a ghost is given a shamanistic amulet that proves totally ineffective. In *Every River and Mountain* (Choe In-hyeon, 1969), a shaman claims to have vanquished the vengeful spirit of a *Cheonyeo Gwisin* but is in fact possessed by her. In *Human Affairs Are Nothing* (Gwon Yeong-sun, 1975), a malevolent shaman takes possession of a young man's

Memento Mori (1999) is the second installment in the Japanese-style *Whispering Corridors* horror franchise, created in 1998.

spirit in order to manipulate him. All these infamous characters were systematically eliminated at the end of the film by official representatives of the regime at the time.

The second half of the 1970s saw a proliferation of international co-productions featuring wild animals, following the success of films such as *Jaws* (Steven Spielberg, 1975) and *Eaten Alive* (Tobe Hooper, 1976). Korea was no exception, with the release of *A*P*E* (*Kingkongui Daeyeokseub* [*King Kong's Great Counterattack*]) (Paul Leder, 1976), an unofficial Korean-American sequel to the classic, featuring the famous giant gorilla escaping from a ship and wreaking havoc in Seoul, before succumbing to the charms of an actress, and the deadly fire of Korean pilots. *Crocodile* (Lee Won-se, 1977) is a Korean-Thai collaboration, in which a Korean unit lends a hand to a small Thai community to rid it of a giant crocodile.

At the beginning of the 1980s, horror films made on the cheap, just to fill production quotas, were gradually tiring audiences, who preferred the cult series *Korean Ghost Stories*, broadcast every summer on television between 1977 and 1989. After quotas were abolished in 1984, the number of horror films fell to just 15 or so between 1985 and 1996.

The revival of Korean horror cinema began with the surprise success, in 1997, of *The Hole*, with 141,000 spectators. Directed by Kim Sung-hong, screenwriter of *Two Cops 1* and *2* (Kang Woo-suk, 1993 and 1996), the film revived the character of the wicked stepmother or mother-in-law, emblematic figures in horror cinema since 1924's *The Story of Jang-hwa and Hong-ryeon*. While women were often portrayed as sacrificial characters or the "whipping boys" of patriarchal society, the stepmother or mother-in-law was generally presented as a source of conflict and evil. *The Hole* is no exception, with its terrifying tale of a young wife sequestered and abused in her apartment by her mother-in-law. A cult film in Korea, it unfortunately remains little known abroad.

Korean horror cinema enjoyed a second golden age during the Korean film revival, with the confirmed success of *The Gingko Bed* (Kang Je-gyu, 1996) and *The Quiet Family* (Kim Jee-woon, 1998). Producers encouraged directors to diversify genres and emulate international successes. At the time, Korean filmmakers were drawing inspiration from the slasher genre, which was dominating the American box office with horror franchises such as *Scream*, and *I Know What You Did Last Summer*, for a series of plagiarized films such as *Bloody Beach* (Kim In-soo, 2000), *Nightmare* (An Byung-ki, 2000), and *The Record* (Kim Ki-hun and Jong-seok, 2000).

In 1998, the gradual lifting of the ban on importing Japanese cultural products, imposed since 1945, led to a massive influx of Japanese films, manga, and TV series into Korea. The world became enthusiastic about Japanese horror productions labeled J-Horror (Japanese-Horror) and following the success of the *Ring* and *Ju-On / The Grudge* franchises, this genre became a new source of inspiration for Korean horror cinema.

The Ring Virus (Kim Dong-bin, 1999) took advantage of the lack of release of the original Japanese film, *Ring* (Hideo Nakata, 1998), to remake the famous story of the curse of a mysterious videotape that causes the death within seven days of anyone who dares to watch it. The film's success triggered a wave of similar films, including: *Unborn but Forgotten* (Lim Chang-jae, 2002) and its cursed website; *Phone* (An Byung-ki, 2002) and its killer phone number; *Into the Mirror* (Kim Sung-ho, 2003) and its deadly mirrors; *The Red Shoes* (Kim Yong-gyun, 2005) and its killer (pink) shoes; *The Wig* (Won Shin-yeon, 2005) and its suffocating wig; *White: Melody of Death* (Kim Gok and Sun, 2011) and its fatal song, as well as *Don't Click* (Kim Tae-kyoung, 2012) and its fatal online video.

Another popular Japanese horror sub-genre of the late 1990s was the haunted school

film, which followed the successful publication of several collections of Japanese urban legends in the late 1980s. Korea re-adapted this concept with the *Whispering Corridors* franchise (6 films, 1998–2021), whose first episode, by Park Ki-hyung, surprised everyone by ranking second at the box office in 1998, with 621,000 admissions. The second episode, *Memento Mori* (Kim Tae-yong and Min Kyu-dong, 1999), was released in several other countries. *Death Bell* (Chang, 2008) blends the genre with the American *Saw* franchise for a *Squid Game* before its time, featuring a series of deadly ordeals for kidnapped students.

The failure of several horror films in the early 2010s marked the end of low budgets and the emergence of more ambitious Korean productions: *A Werewolf Boy* (Jo Sung-hee, 2012),

Hide and Seek (Huh Jung, 2013), *The Priests* (Jang Jae-hyun, 2015), *The Strangers* (Na Hong-jin, 2016), *Along with the Gods 1* and *2* (Kim Yong-hwa, 2017 and 2018), and *The Witch 1* and *2* (Park Hoon-jung, 2018 and 2022). But the film that definitively establishes Korean horror cinema internationally is *Train to Busan* (Yeon Sang-ho, 2016).

The zombie film genre was historically not very popular in South Korea, as in most Asian

---

To attract children back to cinemas in the 1960s, *Space Monster Wangmagwi* (1967) is a vague remake of the 1954 Japanese classic *Godzilla*.

countries. This typically Western genre has its origins in Haitian voodoo folklore and was popularized by American cinema with classics such as *White Zombie* (Victor Halperin, 1932) and *I Walked with a Zombie* (Jacques Tourneur, 1943), followed by George A. Romero's *Night of the Living Dead* (1968), *Dawn of the Dead* (1978), and *Day of the Dead* (1985).

The worldwide success of the Japanese video games *Resident Evil* and *The House of the Dead*, introduced in Korea in 1998, and that of the *Walking Dead* comic book (and future TV adaptation) first popularized the zombie figure in Asia in the 2000s, and may explain, in part, the success of *Train to Busan* (2016). Its director, Yeon Sang-ho, noted for a series of animated shorts that won awards at international festivals in the 2000s, made his first feature-length animated film for adults, *The King of Pigs* (2011), directly selected for the Quinzaine des Cinéastes at the 2012 Cannes Film Festival.

In 2016, Yeon Sang-ho directed two films in quick succession: *Train to Busan*, and its animated prequel, *Seoul Station*. Although on the surface these two films appear to be simple zombie movies inspired by the Western model, they in fact depict profound realities of Korean society. In *Seoul Station*, the famous train station, the capital's rail and subway hub, becomes a symbol of the galloping and increasingly visible impoverishment of a section of the population, as it tells the story of homeless people who turn into human flesh-eaters—symbolically "contaminating" the rest of the population with their own misery. The film also includes a key sequence with the military opening fire on their own people, evoking the many popular protests, particularly that of the Gwangju massacre.

Train to Busan features a train speeding from Seoul to Busan with a horde of zombies on board. The story's central characters, who are drawn from different categories of Korean society, essentially serve to embody the possible threats to the Korean family unit: a careerist

divorced businessman is (literally) on the verge of losing his daughter; a blended couple, whose wife is pregnant, might never give birth to either life or a new family unit. Two middle-aged ladies find themselves symbolically "separated" by a sliding door, which obviously evokes the division of Korea in 1948. And finally, a young couple in love and full of illusions find themselves among the first victims. Furthermore, their lives are threatened by a wealthy businessman, who, to ensure his own survival, does everything he can to get rid of the "working classes," including trying to detach the other carriages.

Train to Busan was a huge success, not only in Korea, with over 11 million viewers, but also throughout Asia and the rest of the world. Yeon Sang-ho has since directed a sequel, *Peninsula* (2020), which mixes the heist film with the post-apocalyptic film, a genre hitherto unseen in Korea. He is also one of the first Korean filmmakers to have completed several projects for streaming platforms, including the adaptation of his own horrific webtoon *Hellbound* (6 episodes, 2021) and the sci-fi film *Jung_E* (2023).

Previous page spread: *Yongary, Monster from the Deep* (Kim Kee-duk, 1967).

Zombie film *Train to Busan* (2016) was a worldwide success and even spawned an American remake, *The Last Train to New York* (Timo Tjahjanto, 2024). Beyond its simple horror formula, the film is also a profound metaphor for the breakdown of today's Korean family unit.

새로운 시대

2012
2023

2012-2023

A NEW ERA

After a period of recession that began in 2007, Korean cinema made a strong comeback in 2012, with the surprise success of *The Thieves* (Choi Dong-hoon) and *Masquerade* (Choo Chang-min), attracting over 12 million viewers. The strong performances of *Architecture 101* (Lee Yong-ju), *Dancing Queen* (Lee Seok-hoon), and *Unbowed* (Chung Ji-young) enabled the sector to regain a 58.8 percent market share, ushering in a new era of smaller-scale productions that are regularly topping the domestic box office due to more original, less predictable subjects and the discovery of new talent.

The 2010s were marked by the arrival in power of Park Geun-hye (2013–2017), daughter of former president Park Chung-hee (1962–1979), whose ambitious plan to revive the creative economy, after the worldwide success of Psy's song "Gangnam Style" (2012), above all benefitted, curiously enough, nationalist productions, such as the patriotic, anti-Japanese blockbusters *The Admiral: Roaring Currents* (Kim Han-min, 2014), *Northern Limit Line* (Kim Hak-soon, 2015), and *Memories of War* (John H. Lee, 2016).

When Park Chung-hee was deposed in 2017, a blacklist of 9,743 artists from all cultural backgrounds was revealed, including directors Im Sang-soo, Park Chan-wook, Kim Jee-woon, and actor Song Kang-ho, who had publicly criticized her policies. These personalities could no longer receive any support, even financial, and some had even been prevented from working. The new president, Moon Jae-in (2017–2022), restored support for culture, with the rehabilitation of artists and the restoration of subsidies for cultural institutions.

Korean cinema's market share remained above 50 percent throughout the decade, making it one of the few countries in the world, alongside China and India, to dominate the American film industry. The diversity of the biggest hits testifies to the eclectic taste of audiences and the studios' desire to continue promoting different genres: melodramas (*Miracle in Cell No.7*, Lee Hwan-kyung, 2013); historical films about ordinary people who made history (*The Face Reader*, Han Jae-rim, 2013), or, on the contrary, about great figures of the past (*The Admiral: Roaring Currents*, Kim Han-min, 2014); spy thrillers revisiting the occupation (*Assassination*, Choi Dong-hoon, 2015); the action film denouncing elite impunity (*Veteran*, Ryoo Seung-wan, 2015); the zombie film (*Train to Busan*, Yeon Sang-ho, 2016); and webtoon adaptations (*Along with the Gods 1* and *2*, Kim Yong-hwa, 2017 and 2018).

Some directors tried to conquer Hollywood without much success. After the ill-fated release of the Korean monster movie *Dragon Wars: D-War* (Shim Hyung-rae), in 2007, the "American" productions *The Last Stand* and *Stoker*, directed, respectively, by Kim Jee-woon and Park Chan-wook in 2013, were failures. On the other hand, some producers and distributors were starting to weave their web in Southeast Asia (Vietnam, Indonesia) and Turkey to promote Korean films and co-productions.

The repeated failure of a new series of blockbusters at the end of the decade, including *Illang: The Wolf Brigade* (Kim Jee-won, 2018), *Swing Kids* (Kang Hyoung-chul, 2018), *The Divine Fury* (Kim Joo-hwan, 2019), and *Jo Pil-ho: The Dawning Rage* (Lee Jeong-beom, 2019), once again threatened the film industry's fragile economic system.

This didn't account for the Covid-19 pandemic, which had the same devastating impact on the Korean film industry as in the rest of the world. Despite the absence of shutdowns imposed on cinemas, cinema attendance was expected to fall by more than 70 percent between 2019 and 2021, due to the various outbreaks of the virus. In 2023, cinema attendance reached 125 million ticket sales, an 11 percent increase from 2022 but a decrease of nearly half of 2019's 227 million. The shooting of many films was interrupted, and the releases of several blockbusters were postponed. Market share for Korean cinema fell to 30 percent by 2021, reaching its lowest level since 1998.

Exhibitors sought to encourage producers to continue releasing their blockbusters by offering to temporarily pay back all ticket sales revenue up to the level of their investments, rather than sharing revenue equally, as is usually the case. The attempt proved futile, as evidenced by the failure of one of the most eagerly awaited films of 2021, *Escape from Mogadishu* (Ryoo Seung-wan), which attracted just 3 million viewers instead of the hoped-for 10 million.

And yet many Korean films continued to win awards at major international film festivals, such as the Director's Prize for *The Handmaiden* and for *Decision to Leave* (Park Chan-wook, 2016 and 2022) at the Cannes Film Festival; the Golden Lion for *Pieta* (Kim Ki-duk, 2012) at the Venice Film Festival; the Golden Leopard for *Right Now, Wrong Then* (Hong Sang-soo, 2015) at the Locarno Film Festival; and the Silver Bear for *The Novelist's Film* (Hong Sang-soo, 2022) at Berlin.

Korean cinema continued to attract international audiences: *Snowpiercer* (Bong Joon-ho, 2013), *The Handmaiden* (Park Chan-wook, 2016), *Burning* (Lee Chang-dong, 2018), and *Train to Busan* (Yeon Sang-ho, 2016). And of course, the first Korean feature to win a Palme d'Or at Cannes and the first Asian film to win four Oscars (Best Picture, Best International Film, Best Director, and Best Original Screenplay), *Parasite* was an utter triumph.

Major distributors, such as CJ, Lotte, and Megabox, tried to revive the film industry by modernizing their aging multiplexes to bring back moviegoers. They equipped some theaters with the world's largest screens, such as the CGV Yeongdeungpo ScreenX Theater or the Super Plex G, which had installed screens measuring 72 x 13.9 meters and 34 x 13.8 meters, respectively.

Previous page: With over 12 million viewers, *Miracle in Cell No.7* (2013) was one of the biggest Korean hits of all time, and a feature film with one of the highest number of international remakes, including in Turkey and the Philippines.

The 4 DX technology, invented in Korea in 2009, became more widespread; it offers moving seats synchronized to the action on screen, with light, smell, and atmospheric effects such as wind, rain, or fake snow during projections of 3D films. ScreenX, another Korean invention, enables certain films to be viewed in 270 degrees, with the use of side panels.

New theaters also offered virtual reality (VR) screenings, where viewers wear headsets for an even more immersive experience. The 38-minute romantic comedy *Stay with Me* (Bryan Ku, 2018) is known for being the very first VR film in the world to be screened in a 4 DX room for total immersion with its ambient effects.

Despite the Covid-19 pandemic, the global craze for Korean audiovisual productions is not waning, but it is shifting from the big to the small screen. The k-drama *Squid Game* became one of the most viewed Korean series in the world, and its success stimulated the release of other productions in its wake, such as *All of Us Are Dead* (12 episodes, Lee Jae-kyoo, 2022) and *The Glory* (16 episodes, Ahn Gil-ho, 2022). The pandemic also favored the transfer of worldwide distribution rights for certain Korean titles originally intended for theatrical release to streaming platforms, such as *Space Sweepers* (Jo Sung-hee, 2021), *#Alive* (Cho Il-hyeong, 2020), and *The Pirates: The Last Royal Treasure* (Kim Joung-hoon, 2022).

Although they may not have recouped their investments, these productions have benefited from exceptional worldwide visibility, helping to maintain international public interest in Korean cinema. Further, the major streaming platforms—Netflix, Disney+, and Apple TV+—announced record new investments in 2023 to produce original content, thus contributing more or less directly to the current evolution of the Korean film industry.

The successes, in 2023 of *12.12: The Day* (Kim Sung-su) with over 13 million spectators and in 2024 of *Exhuma* (Sang Jae-hyun) with over 10 million viewers, seems to herald the re-conquest of the Korean box office, while the growing popularity of the hallyu wave continues to drive the export of cultural products, including webtoons, which are also a new source of Korean cinematic success.

Could Korean cinema in the 2020s be the dawn of a new era?

Previous page spread: The Buddha statue at the Bongeunsa temple in Seoul's Gangnam district.

The Handmaiden is one of the most successful Korean films of the late 2010s. It was selected for the 2016 Cannes Film Festival and won Best Foreign Language Film at the 2018 British Academy of Film and Television Arts (BAFTA) awards.

WOMEN FILMMAKERS

In 1955, *The Widow* went out of circulation after just three days. Few people in the cinema audiences at the time were aware that this release was the very first feature film in the history of Korean cinema by a female director, Park Nam-ok. Over the next four decades, only five other women became filmmakers, before a tentative change in this situation in the 2000s.

Park Nam-ok (1923–2017) is an emblematic example of the condition of women in Korea in her day. Despite her initial desire to become an athlete or artist, she was forced to abandon her ambitions following a marriage arranged by her parents with her first husband. During the Korean War, after joining the Ministry of Defense, she worked on various documentary reports. In 1954, she borrowed money from her sister to make her first—and only—feature film, *The Widow*. In the absence of any support from her family, she had to fight constantly to bring the project to fruition, preparing meals for her crew herself and carrying her baby on her back during filming, as no one had agreed to look after the child.

The Widow tells the story of a war widow who abandons her daughter and takes off with a lover. While this may still seem shocking today, the story must of course be seen in the context of the immediate post-war period, when such cases were relatively common but never openly discussed in public, and especially not in the cinema. The film's main character is all the more astonishing in that she fits neither the usual melodramatic stereotype of the "woman sacrificed" for the well-being of men, nor that of the vile temptress; she is a person who thinks above all of her own happiness. Unfortunately, the film's commercial failure put an end to Park Nam-ok's career and also to the possibility of similar realistic female characters in Korean cinema for several decades to come.

Hong Eun-won (1922–1999) began her career at almost the same time as Park Nam-ok. She started out as a scriptwriter on *Affection and Apathy* (Shin Kyeong-gyun, 1959) and *Bawigogae* (Jo Jeong-ho, 1960), while working as assistant director to Jeon Chang-keun and Yu Du-yeon. In 1962, she directed her first feature film, *A Woman Judge*, an adaptation of a true story about a judge's suicide under public pressure. She made two more features, *A Single Mom* (1964) and *What Misunderstanding Left Behind* (1965), before leaving the film industry, deeming it far too difficult for women of her time.

Choi Eun-hee received more support than her creative sisters Park Nam-ok and Hong Eun-won. Urged on by her husband, director and producer Shin Sang-ok, who wanted to demonstrate that his legendary Shin Films studio encouraged diversity, she directed and starred in the historical comedy *The Girl Raised as a Future Daughter-in-law* (1965). This film was adapted from one of the first TV series of the period, which promoted the virtues of marriage. She followed this up with a historical epic, *One-Sided Love of Princess* (1967) and the youth film *An Unmarried Teacher* (1973), both of which are simple entertainments and above all testament to Choi Eun-hee's desire to demonstrate the multiplicity of her talents. She made her last film, *The Promise* in 1984, in collaboration with Shin Sang-ok, during their captivity in North Korea.

Hwang Hye-mi forged a reputation as a producer with the success of the literary adaptation *Mist* (Kim Soo-yong, 1967), but also with the failure of the melodrama *Potato* (Kim Seung-ok, 1968), a victim of censorship for its overly bleak depiction of Korea. She made her first erotic film, *First Experience* (1970), which foreshadowed the wave of productions in the same genre that hit Korean screens in the second half of the 1970s. The film was a success, earning her the Best Director prize at the Baeksang Arts Awards ceremony, the first ever cinematic award for a woman in Korea.

She followed this up with two more feature-length films, *When Flowers Sadly Fade Away* (1972) and *Relationship* (1972), which continued to tackle issues surrounding female sexuality—specifically, the notion that women had to preserve their virginity until marriage. These two films were accused of plagiarizing the American productions *The Sound of Music* (Robert Wise, 1965) and *The Graduate* (Mike Nichols, 1967), bringing Hwang's career to an abrupt end.

Lee Mi-rye, the only female director of the 1980s, was the first to direct six films. Trained by the renowned filmmaker Yu Hyun-mok, she began with the young offenders' film *My Daughter Rescued from a Swamp*, the fifth biggest hit of 1984, with 118,000 admissions. She went on to make other films in this genre, choosing projects close to her heart, *A Cabbage in a Pepper Field* (1985), *School Days* (1987), and *Forget-Me-Nots* (1987), then by obligation, as producers limited her to youth films, with *Young Shim* (1990) and *Beginning of Love* (1991). Disappointed by a fragmented and declining film industry, she changed careers, becoming the manager of several restaurants.

The 1990s saw the emergence of a veritable first generation of female directors. Changes in the film industry finally gave women access to key positions, and the upsurge in the number of female students at film schools encouraged the production and distribution of short films by female directors, notably as programmed at the Seoul International Women's Film Festival, an event created in 1997. Early female filmmakers include Lee Jeong-hyang (*Art Museum by the Zoo*, 1998; *Jiburo*, 2002), Jeong Jae-eun (*Take Care of My Cat*, 2001; *The Aggressives*, 2005) and Pang Eun-jin (*Princess Aurora*, 2005; *Way Back Home*, 2013).

Yim Soon-rye, who spearheaded this movement with *Three Friends* in 1996, is one of the few women of this generation to make several feature films, including *Waikiki Brothers* (2001) and *South Bound* (2013). Her biggest success to date, *Forever the Moment* (2008), ranked fifth at the box office in 2008, with over 4 million admissions. Despite this achievement, she continued to struggle with each of her subsequent projects, including *Little Forest* (2018) and *The Point Men* (2023).

July Jung had the same experience. Her first film, *A Girl at My Door*, was selected for the Directors' Fortnight at the 2014 Cannes Festival; her second, *Next Sohee*, was released eight years later, this time programmed for Critics' Week in 2022.

Shin Su-won also experienced difficulties: despite being selected with *Pluto* (2012) at the 2013 Berlin festival and with *Madonna* at the 2015

Shin Su-won, director of *Pluto* (2012) and *Madonna* (2015), at the 2015 Cannes Film Festival.

Following page spread: Director Yoon Dan-bi on the set of her graduation film, *Moving On* (2019).

Cannes Festival, she struggled to finance her next projects, *Glass Garden* (2017) and *Hommage* (2021).

Shin Su-won refers to the unspoken rule that producers are reluctant to entrust high budgets to women filmmakers, considering them incapable of imposing themselves within predominantly male teams or directing action films with male heroes.

Lee Eon-hee remains the only female director to date to have directed a genuine blockbuster, *The Accidental Detective 2: In Action*, ninth at the 2018 box office, with over 3 million admissions. Lack of funding therefore relegated female filmmakers to making low-budget films with the expectation of distribution in a limited network of cinemas.

The second half of the 2010s saw the emergence of a second generation of female directors: Yoon Ga-eun (*The World of U*, 2016; *The House of Us*, 2019), Jeon Go-woon (*Microhabitat*, 2017), Kim Bo-ram (*The House of Hummingbird*, 2018), Kim Se-in (*The Apartment with Two Women*, 2021), and Yoon Dan-bi (*Moving On*, 2019). Their films often address the lives of 30-somethings in present-day Korea, with a strong focus on female characters. They also focus on the problems associated with family and professional pressures, and the growing sense of loneliness.

Most of these women directors are graduates of film schools, where they now account for 60 percent of students. However, they remain a minority in the various film professions, with 20.2 percent of directors, 31.4 percent of producers, 28.6 percent of screenwriters, and 11.4 percent of cinematographers in 2021. These figures are partly distorted, as they coincide with the Covid-19 pandemic, which led to a sharp decline in the number of blockbusters, in favor of productions with more modest budgets, and therefore more easily entrusted to female directors. It is not certain, therefore, that these figures will continue to be as representative once the film industry picks up again in the coming years.

The situation is also likely to deteriorate since President Yoon Seok-yul came to power on May 10, 2022. After an election campaign largely based on anti-feminist positions and his declaration of his intention to abolish the Ministry of Gender Equality and Family, he announced future budget cuts to independent cinema—in which women therefore predominate.

CONQUERING THE UNITED STATES

Since opening up to the world at the end of the nineteenth century, Korea has enjoyed a privileged relationship with the United States, a relationship that was further strengthened by American intervention in World War II and the Korean War. There have been several waves of Korean emigration: during the failed attempt at political reform in 1884, in the run-up to Japan's annexation of Korea in 1910, after the Korean War in 1953, following the Immigration and Nationality Act of 1965, and during the economic boom of the 1990s, which saw a large exodus of thousands of young Korean investors and entrepreneurs. The ethnic Korean population in the United States is currently estimated at 1.8 million, or 0.56 percent of the total population, making it the largest Korean community in the world outside of Korea.

The arrival of Koreans in the United States has also been helped by the "rainbow kids phenomenon," i.e., the adoption of Korean children. At the end of the Korean War, over 2 million chil-

dren were without parents. In 1955, the couple Bertha and Harry Holt succeeded in changing a law in the US Congress, enabling them to take in 8 orphans. Their action led to the adoption of over 200,000 Koreans abroad between 1953 and the 2000s.

The presence of Americans in Korean films was seen as "prestigious," not least in the anti-communist war films of the 1950s and 1960s. *Arirang* (Lee Kang-cheon, 1954) was falsely promoted as the "first Korean-American production," simply because of the presence of American extras in the roles of soldiers. The low-budget fantasy comedy *Dracula in a Coffin* (Lee Hyung-pyo, 1982) featured "American star Ken Christopher" in the role of the famous vampire; but in reality, the actor was an ordinary resident of Korea at the time of filming and could

Dragon Wars: D-War (2007) was the first Korean film to attempt to conquer the American box office directly, opening on 2,275 screens—a record at the time. Profits were less than $10 million.

not claim any fame after his participation in this film.

The first official co-production between Korea and the United States was *Northeast of Seoul*, directed jointly by David Lowell Rich, an American director specializing in B movies, and Jang Il-ho, a Korean filmmaker. This vague remake of John Huston's *Maltese Falcon* (1941), starring John Ireland and Anita Ekberg, with Korean actors Shin Young-kyun and Choi Ji-hee in supporting roles, was released unsuccessfully in Korea in 1974 under the title *Katherine's Escape* (also known as *The Seoul Affair*).

The Koreans' first attempt to conquer Hollywood was *Inchon* (1981), infamous as one of the "worst films in the history of cinema" and one of its greatest economic failures. Originally, billionaire Moon Sun-myung, founder of the Moon sect, planned to produce a film about the life of Jesus or Elvis Presley, but astrologer Jeane Dixon suggested instead a re-enactment of the famous Battle of Incheon, after "the spirit of General MacArthur" had spoken to her.

Following this advice, the billionaire embarked on a "pharaonic" blockbuster, directed by American filmmaker Terence Young in Korea, the United States, Italy, Ireland, and Japan, and starring renowned actors Laurence Olivier, Jacqueline Bisset, Ben Gazzara, and Toshiro Mifune. Shooting was marked by the death of actor David Janssen and a series of devastating typhoons, which destroyed many of the sets. The battle scenes awkwardly mix archival footage from the Korean War with studio re-enactments using over 1,500 American army soldiers.

The film was a resounding failure, grossing just $2 million against an initial budget of $46 million. It eventually disappeared without a trace, except for a single broadcast on a cable channel, Good Life Television Network, owned by the Moon sect.

The first Korean-American co-productions officially got underway in the 2000s, at the height of the Korean film revival, with *Love House* (Kim Pan-soo, 2005), a film now forgotten in favor of *Never Forever* (Gina Kim, 2007), selected for the Sundance Film Festival and released in several countries around the world, including France. The latter paved the way for a series of art-house co-productions, including the Korean-made feature *Make Yourself at Home* (Sohn Soo-pum, 2008), as well as *August Rush* (Kirsten Sheridan, 2007), *West 32nd* (Michael Kang, 2007), and *American Zombie* (Grace Lee, 2007), made in the United States.

Dragon Wars: D-War (2007) was Korea's first real attempt to break into the Hollywood market. Its director, Shim Hyung-rae, is best known for his comic character Young Gu in low-budget comedies and children's sci-fi films in the 1980s. In 1999, he surprised the industry with his ambitious self-production *Yonggari*, a distant remake of the 1967 monster movie of the same name, directed by Kim Kee-duk, and with a record budget at the time of $13 million. The film was designed to capitalize on the monster movie trend initiated by *Godzilla* (Roland Emmerich, 1998), and featured a cast of relatively unknown American actors.

Yonggari turned out to be a costly failure, largely due to mediocre special effects, poor acting, and a muddled script. Despite this, Shim Hyung-rae persisted and managed to raise a total of $75 million for a new project, *Dragon Wars: D-War* (2007), the story of a giant snake that attacks Los Angeles, this time with a cast of better-known American actors, including Robert Forster, Jason Behr, and Amanda Brooks. The film was released in the United States on an impressive 2,275 screens but for a disastrous result of $10 million.

In Korea, however, the film was a success, topping the box office in 2007 with 8.4 million admissions. Shim Hyung-rae made clear his ambition to conquer Hollywood by including an intertitle at the end of the film: "We can all win together against America!" set to the popular song *Arirang*, which appeals directly to the

patriotic feelings of Korean viewers. This strategy paid off, mobilizing thousands of young adults, who set up websites and support forums to encourage as many people as possible to go and see the film in order to beat the number of American releases.

Shim Hyung-rae did it again with *The Last Godfather* (2010), in which he transposed his famous Young Gu comic character to the United States, playing the illegitimate son of a fearsome New York mafia godfather (Harvey Keitel) charged with taking over his father's criminal business. This mediocre comedy was another commercial failure, this time being released in a limited number of cinemas. Since then, Shim Hyung-rae, heavily in debt, made himself scarce, appearing sporadically in Korean TV series and variety shows, and having definitively abandoned the idea of a sequel to his film *Dragon Wars: D-War*.

The conquest of Hollywood proved difficult, as the difference in budget between Korean blockbusters and American blockbusters was too great. No Korean star was as yet able to gather a worldwide audience on his or her name alone, and the absence of a real distribu-

tion network hindered the distribution of Korean films. Despite this, recent decades have seen the regular release of Korean films in a small combination of American cinemas: *Chunhyang* (Im Kwon-taek, 2000) led the way, grossing nearly $800,000, *Spring, Summer, Fall, Winter . . . and Spring* (Kim Ki-duk, 2003) sprang a surprise with $2.38 million, surpassed only by *The Admiral: Roaring Currents* (Kim Han-min, 2014) and its $2.59 million; then, of course, *Parasite* (Bong Joon-ho, 2019), the second biggest success for a foreign film at the US box office after *Crouching Tiger, Hidden Dragon* (Ang Lee, 2000), with $53 million recorded.

In 2013, Kim Jee-woon and Park Chan-wook tried their luck in Hollywood. Despite the presence of Arnold Schwarzenegger in the former's *The Last Stand* and Nicole Kidman in the

---

Previous page spread: Director Kim Jee-woon on the set of his American film, *The Last Stand*, in 2012.

Dracula in a Coffin (1982) tried to win over Korean audiences by featuring an (amateur) American actor in the lead role.

latter's *Stoker*, these films were relative failures. Several Korean stars have also tried to break into Hollywood, such as Bae Doo-na, who appeared in the series *Sense8* (2015–2018) and the feature film *Jupiter Ascending* (2015) by Lana and Lilly Wachowski. Actor-singer Rain appears in *Speed Racer* (Lana and Lilly Wachowski, 2008) and *Ninja Assassin* (James McTeigue, 2009), and Lee Byung-hun featured in both *G.I. Joe* (Stephen Sommers, 2009, and Jon M. Chu, 2013) and *Terminator Genisys* (Alan Taylor, 2015).

In recent years, Korean cinema's American and international conquest no longer seems to be via the "traditional circuit," but rather through astute partnerships with streaming platforms. Bong Joon-ho was one of the first to succeed in this challenge with his film *Okja* (2017), followed by other successful directors such as Kim Seong-hun with his series *Kingdom* (13 episodes, 2019–2020), Hwang Dong-hyuk with *Squid Game* (2021), Kim Jee-woon with *Dr. Brain* (6 episodes, 2021), and Yeon Sang-ho with *Hellbound* (6 episodes, 2021) and his feature *Jung_E* (2023).

CONQUERING ASIA

The boom in the Korean film industry in the 2000s has led to a growing interest in conquering new markets, particularly in Asia. Although Korea has been collaborating with Hong Kong since the 1950s, it is only in the last two decades that the country has embarked on a truly ambitious expansion, albeit not without challenges of its own.

The first co-productions between Korea and Hong Kong began in the 1950s, with the collaboration between Hong Kong's Shaw & Sons studios (later renamed Shaw Brothers) and the pioneers of the Korean film industry. They made a series of films, including *Love with an Alien* (Jeon Chang-keun, Tu Kuang-Chi, Mitsuo Wakasugi, 1958), *The Affection of the World* (Kim Hwarang, 1957), and *Nostalgia* (Chung Chang-wha, 1958).

This association continued in the 1960s under the impetus of Shin Sang-ok, who established close ties with the influential Shaw Brothers studios with a view to shooting a series of films in two versions in Hong Kong, swapping lead roles for principal photography. These included *The Last Woman of Shang* (Choe In-hyeon, 1964), *The Goddess of Mercy* (Lim Won-sick and Shin Sang-ok, 1966), *That Man in Chang-a* (Yan Jun and Choe Gyeong-ok, 1966), and *The King with My Face* (Ho Meng-Hua, 1967). They consolidated their relationship with numerous collaborations on martial arts films in the 1970s, but Korea failed to secure recognition for its cinema or to establish a lasting presence on the international scene.

It was not until the success of the hallyu wave and k-dramas of the late 1990s that Korean cinema finally gained worldwide recognition. China was the first stage in this conquest of the Asian market. Successful Korean TV series such as *First Love* (268 episodes, Lee Eung-jin, 1996–1997) and *Star in My Heart* (16 episodes, Lee Jinseok and Lee Chang-hoon, 2002) led to several

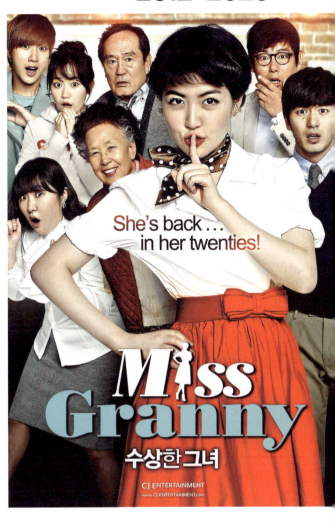

stages of co-production. The first consisted of producing Korean films in China, such as *The Warrior* (also known as *The Ultimate Warrior*) (Kim Sung-soo, 2001) and *Shadowless Sword* (Kim Young-jun, 2005), in order to benefit from local expertise and lower production costs. The second continued with investment in pan-Asian blockbusters, notably the then-fashionable *wu xia pian* (Chinese swordplay) films, such as *Seven Swords* (Tsui Hark, 2004), *Red Cliff* (John Woo, 2008), and *Reign of Assassins* (Su Chao-Bin, 2010).

The final step was the creation of subsidiaries to produce and distribute films directly in China. CJ opened several branches in China in the 2010s to launch titles specifically aimed at the Chinese market, such as *Late Autumn* (Kim Tae-yong, 2010), *Bunshinsaba* (An Byung-ki, 2012), *A Wedding Invitation* (Oh Ki-hwan, 2013), and *Mr. Go* (Kim Yong-hwa, 2013). The Chinese-Korean Film Co-Production Agreement, signed in 2014 to strengthen exchanges between the two countries, led to two notable early Korean successes: *The Third Way of Love* (John H. Lee, 2015), with $11 million, and *20 Once Again* (Leste Chen, 2015), a remake of *Miss Granny* (Hwang Dong-hyuk, 2014), with $60 million. At the same time, CJ expanded its network to over 500 cinemas.

This Sino-Korean collaboration came to an abrupt halt in 2016, when China banned all imports of Korean cultural products, in response to South Korea's decision to deploy the US THAAD (Terminal High Altitude Area Defense) system on its territory. These bans have been partially lifted with the first authorization for the online release of *Hotel by the River* (Hong Sang-soo, 2018) on streaming platforms, and the cinema release of *Oh! My Gran* (Jung Se-kyo, 2020). This hasn't stopped Chinese producers from remaking some 15 Korean films during this period, including *Scandal Maker* (An Byung-ki, 2016), adapted from *The Scandal Makers* (Kang Hyoung-chul, 2008).

Korean professionals were also targeting Japan, especially after the lifting of restrictions on imports of Japanese cultural products into Korea in 1998. The two countries signed two first official co-productions, *Asako in Ruby Shoes* (Lee Je-yong, 2000) and *KT* (Junji Sakamoto, 2002), which were flops. But the hallyu tidal wave and the wave of k-drama exports changed the situation with the series *Winter Sonata* (20 episodes, Yoon Seok-ho, 2002), which propelled its lead actor, Bae Yong-jun, to idol status and paved the way for the feature film *April Snow* (Hur Jin-ho, 2005), in which he plays the lead

---

Previous page spread: *Mr. Go* (2013), the first Korean-Chinese co-production to be shot entirely in 3D.

Miss Granny (2014) is the Korean movie with the highest number of remakes worldwide (8 by 2024).

role, to become the biggest Korean success of all time in Japan.

In 2004, the market share of Korean feature films at the Japanese box office reached 10 percent, and Japan accounted for $60 million of Korea's total exports of $76 million that year. However, this period of success was short-lived. Former Japanese Prime Minister Junichiro Koizumi's visit to the Yasukuni Shrine to honor the soldiers who died (including those from Korea) in the name of the Japanese Emperor, Prime Minister Shinzo Abe's refusal to recognize the "Korean comfort women" under occupation, and Japan's claim to the Liancourt Rocks (islets in the Sea of Japan) rekindled tensions between the two countries. Since then, South Korea has never managed to repeat the record sales figures of 2004 in the Japanese market.

After this latest relative failure, the Koreans turned their attention to other emerging markets in Southeast Asia, notably Vietnam and Indonesia. Vietnam currently has a population of 100 million, 70 percent of whom are under the age of 35. Since opening up its cinemas to the private sector in the early 2000s, the network of cinemas has expanded considerably, and the country has been producing an average of 40 films a year since 2015. The Koreans therefore saw Vietnam as an ideal partner for the expansion of its film industry.

The CJ Group set up its first subsidiary in Vietnam in 1998 and co-produced the very first horror film in Vietnamese cinema history, *Muoi: The Legend of a Portrait* (Kim Tae-kyoung), in 2007. In 2011, the group bought MegaStar, the country's leading cinema operator, with a commitment in 2014 to modernize the cinema network, invest in Vietnamese film production, and promote Vietnamese culture abroad. In less than 10 years, Group CJ expanded its network to 76 cinemas and currently holds a 60 percent share of the Vietnamese box office market.

As distributor of American and Korean films, such as *Parasite* (Bong Joon-ho, 2019) and *Peninsula* (Yeon Sang-Ho, 2020), CJ was involved in several co-productions that have become the biggest successes in Vietnamese cinema history, including *Let Hoi Decide* (Charlie Nguyen, 2014), *Sweet 20* (Phan Gia Nhat Linh, 2015), and, above all, *The House of No Man* (Tran Thanh, 2023), the best-selling film of all time (at the time of writing), with a revenue of $19 million.

Lotte Entertainment, the second Korean company to establish itself, in 2008 became the first group to build a multiplex in a shopping mall. Lotte Entertainment and CJ currently own 26 of the country's 40 multiplexes. After an initial failure, with *Saigon Cinderella* (Kim Gok-jin, 2013), Lotte eventually produced several big hits at the Vietnamese box office, such as *Furie* (Le-Van Kiet, 2019), *The Royal Bride* (Namcito, 2020), and *Blood Moon Party* (Nguyen Quang Dung, 2020), one of 18(!) remakes of the Italian film *Perfect Strangers* (Paolo Genovese, 2016), with an American feature currently in the works, with Italian filmmaker Carlo Carlei set to direct. Which generated over $6.7 million in box office takings.

Lotte and CJ did not limit their investments to the cinema alone; they also developed other activities from their respective groups. Lotte, for example, is taking advantage of the construction of its huge shopping malls to erect new multiplexes on the top floor, reserving 30 percent of the mall space for its cosmetics, food, and clothing products, which are often featured in its film productions. For its part, CJ serves its own food products in restaurants set up in or near their multiplexes.

Indonesia is another cinematic Eldorado, with a population of 270 million, 65 percent of whom are under 40. Between 2015 and 2020, the number of cinemas doubled, reaching 2,000 screens, mainly concentrated in the Java region; and with 81 cities of over 100,000 inhabitants, this number should reach

10,000 in the coming years. In 2013, after the country opened up to foreign producers and distributors under President Joko Widodo, CJ acquired the local Blitz Megaplex network. The number of its screens has risen from 76 in 9 multiplexes in 2013 to 233 in 35 multiplexes in 2018. The goal of 100 multiplexes by 2022 was hampered by the Covid-19 pandemic but is well on track.

CJ's early co-productions were relative failures, including remakes of *Miss Granny* titled *Sweet 20* (Ody Harahap, 2017); *Whispering Corridors* titled *Death Whisper* (Awi Suryadi, 2019), and *Sunny* titled *Glorious Days* (Riri Riza, 2019). But the triumph of *Miracle in Cell No.7* (Hanung Bramantyo, 2022), third at the box office in 2022, with 5 million admissions, shows a better understanding of the market and augurs great success in the future.

CJ also made a great discovery by supporting Joko Anwar, a former film critic and promising young director. After awarding him a grant in 2014 at the Busan International Film Festival to complete his fifth feature, *A Copy of My Mind* (2015), CJ is funding several of his projects: *Satan's Slaves 1* and *2* (2017–2022) are hugely

successful, becoming the highest-grossing Indonesian films of all time on release.

Korea is currently investing heavily in the Turkish film industry. The two countries have been linked since Turkish troops were sent to support South Korea during the Korean War in 1950. With the advent of the hallyu wave, Korean cultural products enjoyed immense popularity, and many successful k-dramas were remade, such as *Can Love Become Money?* (20 episodes, Han Cheol-soo, 2012), adapted as *Kiralik Ask* (69 episodes, Collective, 2015), and *Boys Over Flowers* (25 episodes, Jeon Ki-sang, 2009), adapted as *Waiting for the Sun* (54 episodes, Altan Dönmez, 2013).

In 2016, CJ acquired Mars Cinema, Turkey's leading network with 710 screens. In addition

---

Miracle in Cell No. 7 (2019) is the Turkish remake of the 2013 Korean hit of the same name. The film was also one of Netflix's biggest hits when it was released in 2020.

Following page spread: In China, shooting *The Warrior* (2001).

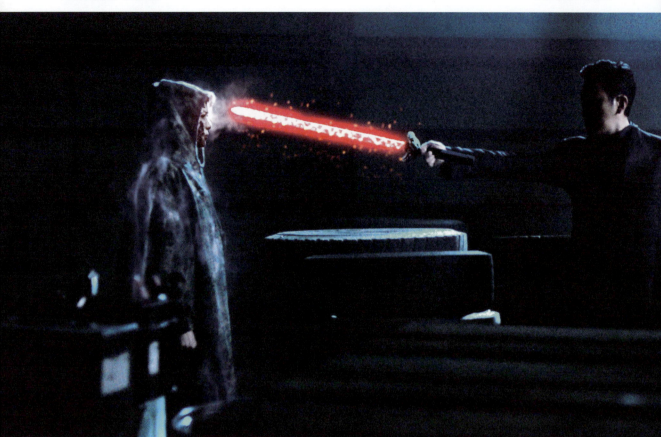

to distributing Turkish, Korean, and American films, the group also ventured into production with a remake of its own Chinese hit *The Wedding Invitation* under the title *Hot Sweet Sour* (Andac Haznedaroglu, 2017), followed by *Miracle in Cell No. 7* (Mehmet Ada Öztekin, 2019), which became Turkish cinema's biggest-ever hit on release, with 5.3 million admissions.

This latest success is real proof of Korea's success in conquering Asian markets: remaking homegrown productions. A new version of an existing film not only saves on scriptwriting costs, but also multiplies the chances of future success for having proven itself in other countries and, sometimes, being identified by a section of the public. The remakes of *Miracle in Cell No.7* are among the biggest hits of all time in Turkey and Indonesia, and *Miss Granny* has also made good money with its Vietnamese version *Sweet 20*, its Japanese version *Sing My Life* (Nobuo Mizuta, 2016), its Thai version *Suddenly Twenty* (Araya Suriharn, 2016), and its Filipino version *Miss Granny* (Joyce E. Bernal, 2018).

Along with the Gods (2017), the first large-scale manwha adaptation with a colossal budget, featured impressive special effects.

WEBTOON ADAPTATIONS

Since their inception, Korean films have drawn inspiration from a variety of cultural sources. In recent decades, the growing success of manhwa (Korean comics) has led to numerous film transpositions. A new trend is the emergence of webtoon adaptations, a veritable national peculiarity.

In the early days of Korean cinema, many early feature films were based on pansori, folk legends, and shinpa plays. This approach enabled producers to capitalize on the already established reputation of these materials. Subsequently, literature, both Korean and foreign, became a major source of film adaptations, giving rise to the specific genre of literary films during the golden age of Korean cinema in the 1960s. The advent of radio in the 1940s and 1950s, followed by television in the 1960s, contributed to the development of transpositions of radio plays and television series.

Manhwa have become an increasingly important source of inspiration for Korean films over the last four decades. This art form, which has its origins in the earliest Buddhist engravings dating back to the tenth century, developed in the form of illustrations and satirical drawings known as *daehanminbo*, published in newspapers from 1909 onward. With the relaxation of censorship in 1919, manhwa became a discreet means of criticizing the Japanese occupiers.

Their popularity grew after the Korean War, with *takji manhwa*, a series of low-cost publications printed on poor-quality paper, aimed at the underprivileged classes in search of escape. These collections of around 20 pages adopted the Western format of boxes and speech bubbles. The appearance of *manhwaban*, bookshops specializing in the loan and sale of comics in the 1950s, finally helped to institutionalize manhwa. However, under the Park Chung-hee regime in 1966, the Habdong Munhwa Sa publishing house acquired a monopoly by buying out all its competitors, and published mainly comic adventures for children, as well as historical stories for adults.

The 1980s marked a turning point for manwha. With the relaxation of censorship following the June 10, 1987, demonstration, the release of numerous new magazines made genre diversification possible. Korean comics withstood the opening of the market to manga imported from Japan and the financial crisis of the 1990s, thanks to the creation of a growing number of new publishing houses, independent magazines and collectives, and the sustained popularity of manhwaban.

As manwhas evolved, so did film adaptations. *Fool* (Lee Phil-woo, 1926) is an adaptation of the five-frame comic strip published daily in the *Chosun Ilbo* newspaper entitled *The Vain Efforts of an Idiot* by Noh Soo-hyun, itself inspired by the American comic strip *Bringing Up Father* (1913–2000) by George McManus. The comedy *Gobau* (Jo Jeong-ho, 1959) is a transposition of Kim Sung-hwan's comic strip of the same name, the longest in Korean history, with

14,139 four-panel strips published daily between 1950 and 2000 in various newspapers. Both films were flops.

The first successes came in the form of animated science-fiction films for children in the 1970s, and feature-length sports films at the time of the Seoul Olympic Games in 1988. *Lee Chang-ho's Baseball Team 1* and *2* (Lee Chang-ho, 1986, and Jo Min-hee, 1988) and *Poem of the Chameleon* (No Se-han, 1988) eventually paved the way for further successes, such as *Memories of Balbariou* (Kang Cheol-su, 1989) and *Money, Money, Money* (You Jin-sun, 1991), while the adaptations *Terrorist* (Kim Young-bin, 1995) and *Beat* (Kim Sung-soo, 1997) accompanied the revival of gangster films.

Huh Young-man, a famous *manhwaga* (Korean comic book artist), inspired the first big Korean box office hits in the 2000s. With over 150,000 drawings in 215 albums, he is considered the Korean Tezuka, in homage to Japan's most famous *mangaka* (manga artist), Osamu Tezuka. He launched a wave of masked vigilantes with his manhwa *Bridal Mask* in 1974, adapted for the cinema with the title *Blood of Dragon Peril* (Kim Seon-gyeong, 1978). After the box office success of the 1997 adaptation of *Beat* (Kim Sung-soo), *Tazza: The High Rollers* (Choi Dong-hoon, 2006) topped the box office in 2006, leading to two sequels and a popular TV series; the following year, the transposition of *Grand Chef* (Jeon Yun-su, 2007), whose 3 million viewers led to a sequel and a k-drama, *Gourmet* (24 episodes, Choi Jong-soo, 2008), also topped the box office.

But the biggest successes to date, *Along with the Gods 1* and *2* (Kim Yong-hwa, 2017 and 2018) are adaptations of manhwas from a new generation, the webtoons.

The webtoon (a logical contraction of the words *web* and *cartoon*), a Korean invention, is the digital transcription of the traditional manhwa. To make a name for themselves, in the late 1990s the first webtoons authors offered scans of original comic strips, downloaded free of charge from the internet. With the development of computer technology, some creators added flash animations, before adapting their layout to smartphones and tablets with a single vertically scrolled box to offer a more dynamic reading experience.

The webtoon reinvents the traditional comic strip by breaking established norms. Authors can exploit elements such as sound effects, animation, shot size, and color, without being limited by the rigid structure of a page. The first webtoons were published in 2003 on the Korean websites Daum and Naver and have been growing in popularity ever since. During the Covid-19 pandemic, these webtoons had over 17 million regular users in Korea and over 85 million worldwide. This model has also been adopted by other countries, such as the French webtoon *Lastman* (12 volumes, Michaël Sanlaville, 2013–2019).

After the failure, in 2006, of the first two webtoon adaptations, *Dasepo Naughty Girls* (Lee Je-yong) and *APT* (An Byung-ki), the success of *Secretly, Greatly* (Jang Cheol-soo, 2013) finally triggered a wave of transpositions, including *Inside Men* (Woo Min-ho, 2015), *Steel Rain* (Yang Woo-suk, 2017), and above all *Along with the Gods 1* and *2*. The first Korean blockbusters to have been conceived from the outset for a two-part release, they drew 14 million and 12 million viewers, respectively, ranking as the 2nd and 10th biggest hits of all time in Korea on their release.

The webtoon also inspired numerous animated series—*Tower of God* (13 episodes, Takashi Sano and Hirokazu Hanai, 2020), *Noblesse* (13 episodes, Collective, 2020), and *Lookism* (8 episodes, Collective, 2022), as well as the

The first major success of a manhwa adaptation: *Tazza: The High Rollers* (2006), with over 6.8 million viewers on its release.

k-drama series *Sweet Home* (10 episodes, Collective, 2020), *Itaewon Class* (16 episodes, Kim Sung-yoon, 2020), and *Kingdom* (13 episodes, Kim Seong-hun, 2019–2020). Between 2022 and 2023, more than 30 TV series were webtoon adaptations. The TV series *Extraordinary Attorney Woo* (16 episodes, Yoo In-sik, 2022) and films like *Hard Day* (Kim Seong-hun, 2014) were adapted into webtoons.

The specific formatting of webtoons can pose problems for screenwriters, who sometimes confess to spending months finding the right way to adapt them to the big screen. So far, only *Moss* (Kang Woo-suk, 2010) has attempted to respect its particular form. However, this situation could change in the future: manwhaga Cho Seok has just made an adaptation of his own webtoon *Moon You* (2023) in the form of a medium-length film, around 50 minutes long, specially designed for cinemas equipped with 4 DX, offering viewers greater immersion. The ticket price is also half that of a traditional cinema ticket, with the aim of attracting new audiences and experimenting with new narrative forms on the big screen.

In addition to the future success of so-called "classic" adaptations, the webtoon could also be at the origins of a new revolution in the way we consume cinema.

THE STREAMING REVOLUTION

In 2021, during the Covid-19 pandemic, the k-drama *Squid Game* (9 episodes, Hwang Dong-hyuk, 2021) became a global phenomenon, highlighting the ability of streaming platforms to promote Korean culture through their own productions, such as *Kill Bok-soon* (Byun Sung-hyun, 2023) and *Jung_E* (Yeon Sang-ho, 2023), or titles acquired for international distribution, such as *Space Sweepers* (Jo Sung-hee, 2021) and *#Alive* (Cho Il-hyeong, 2020), and available on the same day in 190 countries. A great opportunity, but also a real challenge for the future of the Korean film industry.

In 1997, two Americans created a start-up called Netflix (a contraction of the terms *internet* and *flicks*), without knowing that it would one day revolutionize the world. Initially, the company offered only an online service for renting and buying DVDs delivered to your home. In 2002, its listing on the New York NASDAQ stock exchange enabled it to raise the funds needed to develop an online video-on-demand feature. Due to the digital revolution, this service launched in 2010 in Canada, then expanded to South America in 2011, Western Europe in 2015, and the rest of the world (excluding China) from 2016. The number of subscribers continues to grow, reaching 250 million paying subscribers by 2023.

Korea is one of the most advanced countries when it comes to the internet: in 2013, 93 percent of the Korean population had access to the internet, 5G has been available since 2019 and the launch of 6G is scheduled for 2028. In 2004, the first bypass services finally gave users satisfactory access to the first audio and video media and enabled Korean hosting site Pandora TV to beat YouTube by a year. The first video-on-demand sites, such as POOQ and Tving, appeared in 2009.

When it arrived on the Korean market in 2016, Netflix was the first online service to offer a

monthly subscription to watch unlimited audio-visual content, while its competitors still offered either pay-TV channels or only the purchase of single movies. Even so, Netflix has struggled to establish itself, as Korean production companies initially refused to collaborate, reducing its catalog to just 40 Korean titles. The first direct competitor, WatchaPlay, quickly retaliated, offering 20,000 domestic programs at a third of the price of Netflix's subscription.

The streaming platform also faces copyright issues in Korea, as only 600 of its 14,400 titles are royalty-free in the country. Some of the platform's flagship series at the time, such as *House of Cards* and *The Walking Dead*, are still contractually bound to rival channels. In addition, each program must be systematically submitted to the Korean age rating committee, delaying the launch of certain programs, such as *Better Call Saul*, by several weeks. To remain

competitive, Netflix Korea therefore decided to invest rapidly in the creation of original content, successively producing two global hits, the drama film *Okja* (Bong Joon-ho, 2017) and the drama series *Kingdom* (13 episodes, Kim Seong-hun and Park In-jae, 2019–2020).

Bong Joon-ho had already proven his ability to handle high budgets, with the success of his previous worldwide co-production, *Snow-piercer* (2013), which earned $86.7 million on an initial outlay of $40 million. Even so, Netflix was taking a risk by allocating to him the hefty sum of $50 million, especially as the streaming

---

Kingdom (2019–2020), released by Netflix, is the first Korean TV series to attain worldwide success. Besides its two seasons, there is a 93-minute special episode, "Kingdom: Ashin of the North" (2021).

platform's most expensive original production to date, *Beasts of Nation* (Cary Joji Fukunaga, 2015), had cost a mere $6 million.

Without a traditional theatrical release, it is difficult to assess *Okja*'s true profitability. However, in addition to being of fine quality, the film provides an extraordinary showcase for Netflix, notably generating a strong reaction (and therefore great publicity) as the first film produced by a streaming platform to compete in official competition at the Cannes Film Festival, in 2017. But *Okja* triggered a wave of indignation in Korea, where major cinema exhibitors refused to release the film simultaneously in cinemas and on Netflix.

Following the success of *Okja*, the platform once again created a buzz by producing the historical zombie series *Kingdom*. Screenwriter Kim Eun-hee, known for her hit k-dramas *Ghost* (20 episodes, Kim Hyung-shik, 2012) and *Signal* (16 episodes, Kim Won-seok, 2016), had been trying to get her new creation produced since 2011 without success and eventually released the project as a webtoon in an attempt to continue attracting the attention of potential investors. The Netflix production caused a sensation, with its colossal (for the Korean TV industry) $30 million budget, its unusual format of 6 episodes of 36 to 56 minutes each and the involvement of a renowned filmmaker, Kim Seong-hun (*Tunnel*, 2016). The series was a resounding national and international success.

But it was *Squid Game* that hit the jackpot. Here again, no Korean producer had been willing to finance the project, born in 2009, despite the notoriety of its creator, director Hwang Dong-hyuk, known for his feature films *The Fortress* (2017) and *Miss Granny* (2014). Released during the Covid-19 pandemic, this story of 456 people taking part in a series of deadly trials in an attempt to win a large sum of money struck a chord with international audiences, who saw it as a metaphor for a certain social reality, both Korean and global. *Squid Game* became the

most-watched series of all time on Netflix, racking up 1.65 billion viewing hours in 28 days.

Netflix finally became the market leader for video-on-demand in Korea in 2023, with a market share of 35 percent, ahead of local rivals Wavve with 21 percent, and Tving with 16 percent. The platform continued to co-produce other successful k-dramas, such as *Sweet Home* (10 episodes, Collective, 2020), *All of Us Are Dead* (12 episodes, Lee Jae-kyoo, 2022), and *Extraordinary Attorney Woo* (16 episodes, Yoo In-sik, 2022). After an initial investment of $750 million

between 2015 and 2021, followed by a 2nd investment of $700 million in 2022 alone, in 2023 Netflix unveiled an ambitious four-year, $2.5 billion plan to develop South Korean content.

The competition was not idle, however. Tving co-produced the horror film *Seo Bok* (Lee Yong-ju, 2021) and *A Year-End Medley* (2021) by director Kwak Jae-young (*My Sassy Girl*, 2001), whose success in cinemas prompted them to release a longer version as a series on their platform. Disney+, which launched its service in November 2021, also announced consider-

able investments, including the production of 12 k-dramas in 2023, in addition to numerous documentaries dedicated to the biggest k-pop groups such as BTS, Super Junior, and NCT 127. The latest arrival on the market, Apple TV+, launched its service on November 4, 2022, with

---

To date, *Squid Game* (2021) is the most viewed Korean series in the world on the Netflix streaming platform, with over 1.65 billion viewing hours in 28 days.

the broadcast of the never-before-seen adaptation of the webtoon *Dr. Brain*, directed by filmmaker Kim Jee-woon.

Korean production studios are greeting this new disruption with mixed feelings, as they are unable to compete with high American production costs, leading to a notable migration of actors and filmmakers to the platforms and a rise in average film budgets, due to the new, higher salary expectations. Some professionals are also concerned about the poor image being projected of Korea, with the development of screenplays on streaming platforms that are often darker, more violent, and more erotic than those usually promoted by Confucian culture.

Rising budgets and the expectations of an audience that is now global, not just Korean, are also detrimental to artistic creativity, with a reduction in risk-taking and a certain standardization of productions. The success of *Kingdom*, for example, has led to a wave of fantasy and horror series, such as *All of Us Are Dead*, *Sweet Home*, and *Hellbound* (6 episodes, Yeon Sang-ho, 2021). *Money Heist: Korea—Joint Economic Area* (12 episodes, Kim Hong-sun, 2022) is a copy-paste of the Spanish series *La Casa de Papel* (41 episodes, Jesús Colmenar, 2017–2021), simply transposed to Korea. *Narco-Saints* (6 episodes, Yoon Jong-bin, 2022) taps into the current trend for series revolving around major drug lords, such as the similarly titled American franchise *Narcos* (30 episodes, Collective, 2015–2017).

Some directors also express frustration at the artistic limits dictated by streaming platforms, such as the obligation to favor tight shots for "better viewing" by audiences "on their phone screens." Kim Jee-woon, for his part, said he was disconcerted by the countless meetings with his American producers on the set of *Dr. Brain*, which forced him to make changes to the script, better suited, according to them, to Western audiences, but totally inappropriate to Korean culture, even though the entire plot takes place in Korea.

The quest for worldwide recognition therefore also imposes some tough challenges on the Korean industry, starting with the erasure of some of their singularities, which have nonetheless been essential to their success over the last two decades.

Netflix produced feature film *Kill Bok-soon* (2023) for worldwide distribution exclusively on its platform. The title cleverly plays on the promise of a revisited *Kill Bill* (Quentin Tarantino, 2003) and a bloody thriller, a genre for which contemporary Korean cinema is world renowned.

ACKNOWLEDGMENTS

I would like to extend my warmest thanks to the de Paris Korean Cultural Center (Centre culturel coréen) in Paris, its current director, Mr. Lee Il-Yul, and his predecessor, John Hae-oung, for all their attention and kindness toward the project; but also to the formidable Woo Ji-young and her colleagues, Kim Ji-in and Ahn Hye-shin.

And above all, Mr. Georges Arsenijevic, who was there from the beginning of this book and without whom it would not exist.

I would like to thank the Korean Film Archive for being so receptive and making the images available—and especially Mr. Shin Jaeyeong and Ms. Lee Jiyoung, associates of the Acquisition & Cataloging team.

I would like to thank the staff of the Seoul History Museum, Oh Soo-mi, Seung Ha-hoon, Cho Young-gak, Kwak Yong-soo, Bae Chang-ho, Lee Myung-se, Bansuk Wolf, Shin Su-won, Yoon Dan-bi, Im Sang-soo, Laurent Koffel, Frédéric Ambroisine, Goran Topalovic, and Daniel Martin for their kindness, invaluable help, and making photographs from their personal collections available. And many thanks to Charlotte Sivrière for her layout work.

I have no words to express my gratitude to the many people who have read and re-read my work: Fabien Schneider, who has sacrificed many a night's sleep to proofread and discuss the form and content of the project with me; the incredible Georges Vandalle, who is so efficient at all hours of the day and night; and also Françoise Le Maux, Sophie Robert, Jean "Eagle Eyes" Marchal, Virginie Forestier, Janice Yip, and—of course—Katia de Azevedo and Sandrine Decroix.

I would like to express my utmost respect for my Korean "soul brother," Park Suk-young, for moving mountains to finalize this project; and also to Park Sung-ho, for believing in me.

I would like to sincerely apologize to all those who have made enormous sacrifices to enable me to see this project through to the end: my parents; my daughter and her mother; Corinne Benoit; and Pierre Convers; but also to all my friends and family, who have had to put up with my absences, doubts, and questions.

A special thought for my editor, Boris Guilbert, and his assistant, the incredible Rocco Dimondo, for carrying me through to the end. They were my rejuvenating cure.

Thanks to Shin Ha-young (Acemaker), Christina Suk (Contents Panda), Kwak Sae-jeong and Jenny Kim (Finecut), Kim Jeong-yeon (Indiestory), Hahn Se-jeong (Kofic), Chun Sung-ho (KT Alpha), Leah Choi (Lotte), Michelle Son, Alice Chang (M Line), and Amy Jo (Showbox).

I dedicate this book to my parents, who, even if they do not always understand what I do (or why), support all my crazy quests in the pursuit of my dreams with a great deal of kindness. I am very lucky.

And I dedicate this book to my daughter, Emmy Meiresonne, in modest compensation for all the hours she spent watching me write. I will always be on the lookout for your own dreams, my daughter, rest assured.

The publisher would like to thank the Korean Cultural Center (Centre culturel coréen) in Paris, particularly its director, Mr. Lee Il-Yul, for his unfailing support in this complicated project.

The publisher also thanks Mr. Georges Arsenijevic, whose mediatory assistance made this book possible.

WORKS CITED

Ahn Soo-jeong, *The Pusan International Film Festival, South Korean Cinema and Globalization,* Hong Kong University Press, 2011.

An Jin-soo, *Parameters of Disavowal. Colonial Representation in South Korean Cinema,* University of California Press, 2018.

An Pyong-sup and Aprà Adriano, *Le Cinéma coréen,* Centre Georges-Pompidou, 1990.

Justin Bowyer, *The Cinema of Japan and Korea,* Wallflower Press, 2004.

Steve Choe, *Sovereign Violence. Ethics and South Korean Cinema in the New Millennium,* Amsterdam University Press, 2018.

Choe Young-min, *Tourist Distractions. Traveling and Feeling in Transnational Hallyu Cinema,* Duke University Press, 2016.

Choi Jin-hee, *The South Korean Film Renaissance. Local Hitmakers, Global Provocateurs,* Wesleyan University Press, 2020.

Choi Jin-hee and Mitsuyo Wada-Marciano, *Horror to the Extreme. Changing Boundaries in Asian Cinema,* Hong Kong University Press, 2009.

Chung Hye-seung, *Hollywood Asian,* Temple University Press, 2006.

Chung Hye-seung, *Kim Ki-duk,* University of Illinois Press, 2012.

Chung Hye-seung and David Scott Diffrient, *Movie Migrations. Transnational Genre Flows and South Korean Cinema,* Rutgers University Press, 2015.

Chung Steven, *Split Screen Korea. Shin Sang-ok and Postwar Cinema,* University of Minnesota Press, 2014.

Chung Sung-ill, *Im Kwon-taek,* Seoul Selection, in partnership with KOFIC, 2006.

Collective, *A History of Korean Cinema,* Korean Film Archive (Kofa), 2005.

Collective, *A History of Korean Cinema—from 1970s through 1990s,* Korean Film Archive (Kofa), 2006.

Collective, *Empire of the Cinema— Shin Film,* Korean Film Archive (Kofa), 2009.

Collective, *Exploiting East Asian Cinemas. Genre, Circulation, Reception,* Bloomsbury Academic, 2018.

Collective, *Film Censorship During the Colonial Rule Period (1910–1934),* Korean Film Archive (Kofa), 2009.

Collective, *Film Prodigy Lee Man-hee,* Korean Film Archive (Kofa), 2005.

Collective, *Han Hyung-mo. The Alchemist of Popular Genres,* Korean Film Archive (Kofa), 2008.

Collective, *Joseon Films in Japanese Magazine (7 vol.),* Korean Film Archive (Kofa), 2010–2016.

Collective, *Joseon Films in Newspaper Articles 1918–1928 (8 vol.),* Korean Film Archive (Kofa), 2008–2017.

Collective, *Kim Kee-duk, On the Front Line of Korean Genre Films,* Korean Film Archive (Kofa), 2011.

Collective, *Kim Ki-duk,* Dis voir, 2006.

Collective, *Kim Seung-ho: Face of Father, Portrait of Korean Cinema,* Korean Film Archive (Kofa), 2007.

Collective, *Korean Film Directors (2007–2009),* Seoul Selection, in partnership with KOFIC, 2008.

Collective, *Korean Film. History, Resistance, and Democratic Imagination,* Bloomsbury Academic, 2003.

Collective, *Korean Film Studies 1960 to 1979,* Korean Film Archive (Kofa), 2004.

Collective, *Korean Film Studies 1980 to 1997,* Korean Film Archive (Kofa), 2005.

Collective, *Korean Films and 4.19 Revolution,* Korean Film Archive (Kofa), 2009.

Collective, *Lee Chang-dong,* Dis voir, 2019.

Collective, *Reflections on 1950s Korean Cinema,* Korean Film Archive (Kofa), 2004.

Collective, *Shin Young-kyun, the Male Icon of Korean Cinema,* Korean Film Archive (Kofa), 2012.

Collective, *The Korean Cinema in Newspapers: 1945–1969 (6 vol.),* Korean Film Archive (Kofa), 2004–2010.

Antoine Coppola, *Dictionnaire du cinéma coréen,* Nouveau Monde Éditions, 2021.

Antoine Coppola, *Le Cinéma asiatique. Chine, Corée, Japon, Hong-Kong, Taïwan,* L'Harmattan, 2004.

Antoine Coppola, *Le Cinéma sud-coréen: Du confucianisme à l'avant-garde,* L'Harmattan, 1997.

Paul Fischer, *A Kim Jong-Il Production. The Extraordinary True Story of a Kidnapped Filmmaker, His Star Actress, and a Young Dictator's Rise to Power,* Penguin Books Limited, 2015.

Frances Gateward, *Seoul Searching. Culture and Identity in Contemporary Korean Cinema,* State University of New York Press, 2007.

Adrien Gombeaud, *Séoul cinéma. Les origines du nouveau cinéma coréen,* L'Harmattan, 2006.

Theodore Hughes, *Literature and Film in Cold War South Korea,* Columbia University Press, 2014.

Huh Moon-yung, *Hong Sang-soo,* Seoul Selection, in partnership with KOFIC, 2007.

David E. James and Kim Kyung-hyun, *Im Kwon-taek. The Making of a Korean National Cinema,* Wayne State University Press, 2002.

Jeong Jong-wha, *A History of Korean Cinema—100 Years of Korean Movies in One Book,* Korean Film Archive (Kofa), 2007.

Jin Dal Yong, *Transnational Korean Cinema. Cultural Politics, Film Genres, and Digital Technologies,* Rutgers University Press, 2019.

Jung Ji-youn, *Bong Joon-ho,* Seoul Selection, in partnership with KOFIC, 2009.

Jung Ji-youn and Hun Mun-yong, *Im Sang-soo,* Seoul Selection, in partnership with KOFIC, 2011.

Kang Cang-il, *Les Débuts du cinéma en Corée,* Éditions Ocrée, 2020.

Kiaer Jieun and Kim Loli, *Understanding Korean Film. A Cross-Cultural Perspective,* Taylor & Francis, 2021.

Kim Dong-hoon, *Eclipsed Cinema. The Film Culture of Colonial Korea,* Edinburgh University Press, 2018.

Kim Hong-joon, *Kim Ki-young,* Seoul Selection, in partnership with KOFIC, 2006.

Kim Kyoung-wook, *Yu Hyun-mok,* Seoul Selection, in partnership with KOFIC, 2008.

Kim Kyung-hyun, *The Remasculinization of Korean Cinema,* Duke University Press, 2004.

Kim Kyung-hyun, *Virtual Hallyu. Korean Cinema of the Global Era,* Duke University Press, 2011.

Kim Lyeo-sil, *Manchuria Movie Association and Chosun Movies,* Korean Film Archive (Kofa), 2011.

Kim Yeong-jin, *Lee Jang-ho vs. Bae Chang-ho. The Front Line of Korean Cinema,* Korean Film Archive (Kofa), 2007.

Kim Young-jin, *Lee Chang-Dong,* Seoul Selection, in partnership with KOFIC, 2007.

Christina Klein, *Cold War Cosmopolitanism. Period Style in 1950s Korean Cinema,* University of California Press, 2020.

Kwon Na-young, Aimee Odagiri Takushi and Baek Moonim, *Theorizing Colonial Cinema. Reframing Production, Circulation, and Consumption of Film in Asia,* Indiana University Press, 2022.

Lee Hyang-jin, *Contemporary Korean Cinema. Culture, Identity and Politics,* Manchester University Press, 2001.

Lee Nam, *The Films of Bong Joon-ho,* Rutgers University Press, 2020.

Lee Sang-joon, *Cinema and the Cultural Cold War. US Diplomacy and the Origins of the Asian Cinema Network,* Cornell University Press, 2020.

Lee Sang-joon, *Rediscovering Korean Cinema,* University of Michigan Press, 2019.

Lee Young-il and Choe Young-chol, *The History of Korean Cinema,* Jimoondang Publishing Company, 1988.

Anthony C. Y. Leong, *Korean Cinema: The New Hong Kong. A Guidebook for the Latest Korean New Wave,* Trafford Publishing, 2002.

Kathleen McHugh and Nancy Abelmann, *South Korean Golden Age Melodrama. Gender, Genre, and National Cinema,* Wayne State University Press, 2005.

Darcy Paquet, *New Korean Cinema. Breaking the Waves,* Columbia University Press, 2010.

Jimmyn Parc and Patrick A. Messerlin, *The Untold Story of the Korean Film Industry,* Springer International Publishing, 2021.

Park Young-a, *Unexpected Alliances. Independent Filmmakers, the State, and the Film Industry in Postauthoritarian South Korea,* Stanford University Press, 2014.

Alison Peirse and Daniel Martin, *Korean Horror Cinema,* Edinburgh University Press, 2013.

Tony Rayns, *Seoul Stirring. 5 Korean Directors,* British Film Institute, 1995.

Shin Chi-yun and Julian Stringer, *New Korean Cinema,* Edinburgh University Press, 2005.

Stephen Teo, *Eastern Westerns. Film and Genre Outside and Inside Hollywood,* Taylor & Francis, 2017.

Simon Ward, *Okja. The Art and Making of the Film,* Titan Books, 2018.

Simon Ward, *Snowpiercer. The Art and Making of the Film,* Titan Books, 2021.

Brian Yecies and Shim Ae-gyung, *Korea's Occupied Cinemas, 1893–1948. The Untold History of the Film Industry,* Taylor & Francis, 2011.

Brian Yecies and Shim Ae-gyung, *The Changing Face of Korean Cinema. 1960 to 2015,* Taylor & Francis, 2016.

Yi Hyo-in, *Shin Sang-ok,* Seoul Selection, in partnership with KOFIC, 2008.

ONLINE SOURCES

• *KOFA YouTube Channel*: https://www.youtube.com/koreanfilm, free, legal viewing platform for over 100 Korean films from before the 2000s, renewed regularly.

• *HanCinema*: https://www.hancinema.net, independent database of Korean films.

• *Kobiz*: http://www.koreanfilm.or.kr, Korean Film Council database (Kofic).

• *Kofa Webzine* (80 volumes, 2008–2023): https://www.kmdb.or.kr/story/webzine, a free digital magazine published online by the Korean Film Archive, with in-depth features on Korean (and world) cinema.

• *Kofic Newsletters* (437 volumes, 2011–2023): https://www.koreanfilm.or.kr/eng/publications/NewsltViewer.jsp, a newsletter published once a week by the Korean Film Council (KOFIC), with Korean film news and, occasionally, more in-depth articles.

• *Korean Film*: https://www.koreanfilm.org/, one of the oldest amateur websites dedicated to Korean cinema (1999), with intelligent, in-depth reviews of films released during the year.

• *Korean Movie DataBase*: https://www.kmdb.or.kr, Korean film database.

SELECTED FILM TITLES

3-Iron (2004)

5 Pattern Dragon Claws (1983)

The Battle of the 38th Parallel (1974)

Chunhyang (2000)

Come, Come, Come Upward (1989)

Come Drink with Me (1966)

The Deep Blue Night (1985)

Downfall (1997)

Dragon Fist (1979)

Drunken Master (1978)

Er Woo Dong: The Entertainer (1985)

Farewell Duman River (1962)

Five Fingers of Death (1972)

The Flower in Hell (1958)

The Gangster, the Cop, the Devil (2019)

Genealogy (1979)

Gilsodum (1986)

The Good the Bad the Weird (2008)

Korean Burial (1963)

The Hut (1981)

I Saw the Devil (2010)

I Won't Cry (1974)

Left Foot of Wrath (1974)

Mandala (1981)

My Love, My Bride (1990)

My Mother and Her Guest (1961)

My New Partner (1984)

My Wife Is a Gangster (2001)

The Ball Shot by a Midget (1981)

The Net (2016)

The Night of Full Moon (1969)

The Novelist's Film (2022)

Nowhere to Hide (1999)

Painted Fire (2002)

The Pansori Singer (1993)

The Pirates: The Last Royal Treasure (2022)

Jjagko / Broken Nose (1980)

Revivre / Hwajang (2014)

Spiritual Kung Fu (1978)

Spring, Summer, Fall, Winter . . . and Spring (2003)

The Surrogate Woman (1986)

Tae Guk Gi: The Brotherhood of War (2004)

The Taebaek Mountains (1994)

Tell Me Something (1999)

The Ten-Year Rule (1964)

The Thieves (2012)

To Kill with Intrigue (1977)

The Wedding Day (1956)

A Wife Turned to Stone (1963)

Wives on Parade (1974)

A Woman Chasing the Butterfly of Death (1978)

Spinning the Tales of Cruelty Toward Women / Yeoinjanhoksa Mulreya Mulreya (1984)

INDEX

Images are indicated in **bold**.

Kim, Seung-ho, 110, 120, **121**, 122
Kim, Si-hyun, 190
Kim, So-bong, 60
Kim, So-dong, 80, 120
Kim, Soo-yong, **58–59**, 97, 109, 114, 126, 128, 129, 134–35, 178, 196, 240, 298
Kim, Su-hyeong, 206
Kim, Su-nam, 214
Kim, Sung-ho, 269, 284
Kim, Sung-hong, 281, 284
Kim, Sung-hoon, 90
Kim, Sung-su, 90, 248, 265, 296, 311, 318
Kim, Sung-yoon, 320
Kim, Tae-gyun, 238
Kim, Tae-jin, 50, 70
Kim, Tae-kyoung, 284, 312
Kim, Tae-yong, 285, 311
Kim, Won-seok, 322
Kim, Yeong-hwan, 60, 132, 281
Kim, Yong-gyun, 284
Kim, Yong-hwa, 269, 285, 292, 311, 318
Kim, Yong-hwan, 177
Kim, Yoo-jin, 97, 227
Kim, Young-bin, 238, 318
Kim, Young-jun, 90, 227
Kim, Young-sam, 218, 226
Kim, Yu-jin, 214
kimchi Western. *See* Westerns
King and the Clown, The, 90, **91**
King Gojong and Martyr An Jung-geun, 84, 88
King Jin-shi and the Great Wall of China, 89
King of Pigs, The, 179, **180–81**, 288
King Yong-pal of Namdaemun, 244
King, Henry, 80
King's Secret Agent, 150
Kingdom, 310, 320, **321**
kino drama, 13, 45–47, 50, 54, 61, 80
Kitayama, Seitaro, 177
Kochi, Junichi, 177
Koizumi, Junichiro, 312
Kontchalovski, Andrei, 238
Koo, Bong-seo, **125**, 126
Korea, 116
Korea Electric Power Corporation, 38–39
Korean Artist Proletarian Federation (KAPF), 18, 51, 70
Korean cinema, 11
  beginnings of, 50–77
  crisis years, 190–223
  dawn of renewal of, 226–55
  decline of, 146–81
  emotions in, 21–24
  first creative interlude, 102–7
  first impression of, 12
  foundations of, 80–99
  global path of, 25–26
  golden age of, 110–43
  influences, 13–15
  local color, 19–20

new era, 292–325
  origins of, 38–47
  renaissance of, 258–89
  second creative interlude, 184–87
  unique voice of, 18–19
Korean New Wave
  First Korean New Wave, 230–32
  Second Korean New Wave, 276–80
Korean Short Film Association, 214
Korean Small-Scale Film Club, 214
Korean War, 18, 21, 61, 66, 81, 84, 89, 92, 96, 102, 116, 129, 132, 140, 231, 239, 303, 306, 313
Koshu, Hayakawa, 57
Kundo, 92
Kwak, Jae-young, 226, 254, 258, 264, **265**, 269, 323
Kwak, Kyung-taek, 268

L

Lady Vengeance, **15**
Land of Love, 96
Last Godfather, The, 307
Last Stand, The, **304–5**
Late Autumn, 141
Laughable Sweeping, 126
Lee Chang-ho's Baseball Team, 208
Lee, Ang, 90, 307
Lee, Bong-rae, 121–22
Lee, Bruce, 152–53
Lee, Byeong-heon, 248, **252–53**, 269
Lee, Byoung-joo, 44
Lee, Byung-hun, 90, 248, 310
Lee, Byung-il, 80, 88, 92, 120, 123, 196
Lee, Chang-dong, 202, 232, 245, 258, 276–80, 293
Lee, Chang-ho, 162, 168, 169, 184, 190, 191, 206, 207–10, 214, 215, 230, 318
Lee, Chang-hoon, 310
Lee, Choon-yun, 214
Lee, Chung-ryoul, 220
Lee, Doo-yong, 66, 152–53, 191–92, 198, 206
Lee, Eon-hee, 302
Lee, Eun, 186, 215, 218
Lee, Eung-jin, 258, 264, 310
Lee, Gu-yeong, 51, 61, 70, 80, 81, 84
Lee, Gyeong-son, 51, 55, 60, 61, 63, 70, 84, 132
Lee, Gyeong-tae, 164, 202
Lee, Gyu-hwan, 66, 71, 81, 83, 92, 132–33
Lee, Gyu-seol, 63
Lee, Hak-bin, 179
Lee, Hwan-kyung, 98, 269, 292
Lee, Hwang-lim, 169
Lee, Hyun-seok, 238
Lee, Hyun-seung, 269
Lee, Hyung-pyo, 60, 103, 121, 129, 132, 190, 303
Lee, Jae-gu, 186, 218

Lee, Jae-kyoo, 296, 322
Lee, Jang-hui, 162
Lee, Jang-soo, 265
Lee, Je-yong, 90, 254, 318
Lee, Jeong-beom, 248, 293
Lee, Jin-seok, 310
Lee, John H., 98, 176, 311
Lee, Joon-ik, 90
Lee, Jung-gook, 97, 231
Lee, Kang-cheon, 88, 150, 170–71, 303
Lee, Ki-se, 46
Lee, Kwang-hoon, 235
Lee, Kyeong-chun, 123
Lee, Kyoung-hee, 62
Lee, Kyu-woong, 90
Lee, Man-hee, 111, 139–43, 140, 141, 143, 160, 171, 196, 243
Lee, Mi-rye, 299
Lee, Min-yong, 238
Lee, Myeong-u, 56, 60, 72, 81
Lee, Myung-bak, 264
Lee, Myung-se, 232, 238, 250, 265
Lee, Phil-woo, 51, 71–72, 81, 123, 317
Lee, Sang-ho, 177
Lee, Sang-yong, 248
Lee, Say-mean, 168
Lee, Seok-hoon, 255
Lee, Seok-ki, 206
Lee, Seong-gu, 88, 114, 147–48, 196
Lee, Suck-ki, 141
Lee, Sung-gang, 179, 202
Lee, Tae-won, 240
Lee, Won-se, 168, 184–85, 284
Lee, Won-tae, 248
Lee, Yong-ju, 292, 323
Lee, Yong-min, 96, 281, 282
Lee, Young-ae, 258
Lee, Yu-hwan, 56
Legend of Gingko, The, 90
Legend of Hong Gildong, The, 60
Les Vampires, **47**
Let's Meet at Walkerhill, 94
Letter, The, 97
liberation films, 84–88
Life, 88
Life of Hong Cha-gi, The, 139
Light of Hometown, 88
Like You Know It All, 280
Lim Kkeok-jeong, 139
Lim, Chang-jae, 284
Lim, Jung-kyu, 179
Lim, Won-sick, 310
Linh, Phan Gia Nhat, 312
literary films, 132–38
Locarno International Film Festival, 194, 198, 202, 293
Lookism, 318
Lost Youth, 103
Lotte Entertainment, 312
Love and Pledge, 74, 92
Love House, 306
Love Me Once Again, 62, 147, 191

PHOTO CREDITS

ABOUT
THE AUTHOR

Bastian Meiresonne is an expert in Asian cinema and the co-author of a dozen books, including *The Dictionary of Asian Cinema*. He serves as a programmer and artistic director for Asian films at various film festivals. He has been responsible for several retrospectives featuring Mongolia, Sri Lanka, Indonesia, Thailand, and Korea. Additionally, he is the director of *Garuda Power* (2014), a documentary dedicated to Indonesian (action) cinema.

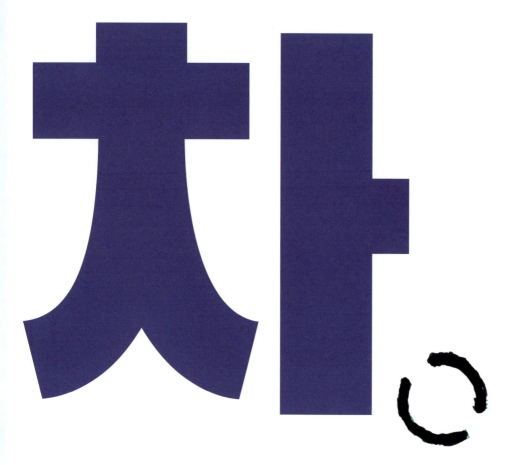

Translation by Caroline Higgitt and Paul Ratcliffe by arrangement
with Jackie Dobbyne of Jacaranda Publishing Services Limited

Original title: *Hallyuwood. Le Cinéma coréen*
Published by Éditions E/P/A—Hachette Livre, 2023

Black Dog & Leventhal Publishers
Hachette Book Group
1290 Avenue of the Americas, New York, NY 10104
www.blackdogandleventhal.com
 BlackDogandLeventhal   @BDLev

First English-language Edition: January 2025

Published by Black Dog & Leventhal Publishers, an imprint
of Hachette Book Group, Inc. The Black Dog & Leventhal
Publishers name and logo are trademarks of Hachette
Book Group, Inc.

The Hachette Speakers Bureau provides a wide
range of authors for speaking events. To find out more,
go to hachettespeakersbureau.com or email
HachetteSpeakers@hbgusa.com.

Black Dog & Leventhal books may be purchased in bulk
for business, educational, or promotional use. For more
information, please contact your local bookseller or the
Hachette Book Group Special Markets Department at
Special.Markets@hbgusa.com.

The publisher is not responsible for websites (or their content)
that are not owned by the publisher.

Additional copyright/credits information is on pages 339–340.

Print book cover design by Katie Benezra.
Production design by Anna B. Knighton.

LCCN: 2024930243

ISBNs: 978-0-7624-8901-5 (hardcover),
978-0-7624-8902-2 (ebook)

Printed in China

10 9 8 7 6 5 4 3 2 1